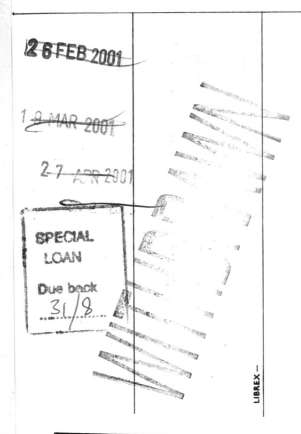

PRISM

D0995852

Published in Great Britain 1988 by:
Prism Press 1988
2, South Street
Bridport, Dorset.

in collaboration with Ultra Violet Enterprises
Series Editor: Gail Chester
© The Collection, Amanda Sebestyen, 1988

© Individual articles, the contributors, 1988

Distributed in the USA by
AVERY PUBLISHING GROUP INC
350 Thorens Ave
Garden City Park
New York 11040

ISBN 1 85327 022 9

Cover Design: Eleni Michael

Typeset by: Maggie Spooner Typesetting, London
Printed by: The Guernsey Press Ltd, Guernsey, Channel Islands

CONTENTS

Michelene Wandor

Asphodel

Mary Kay Mullan

Lucy Whitman

Rebecca Johnson

Jean Gittins

Janet Lesley is a pseudonym to protect those who did not have the opportunity to know any better.

Sue O'Sullivan

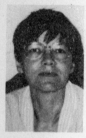

Lynne Harne

Sue Cooper

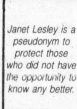

Alice Simpson

Lee Comer

Jane Wibberley

Linda Bellos

Sally Fraser

Marilyn Gayle

Griselda Pollock

Penny Holland

Christian McEwen

Alexis Hunter

Alyson Hunter

Birgit Voss

Maggie Nichols

Thelma Agnew

Zaidie Parr

Rachel Bodle

Aileen Christianson

Sally Collings

Rosanne Reeves

Jo Somerset

Gay Jones

Rosie Brennan

INTRODUCTION

"In 1968," Jane Fonda told an interviewer four years later, "people all over the world were standing up and fighting for their freedom. And what was I doing? I was flying through the air in falsies."

(Rolling Stone, 1972)

Snap.

In 1968 my friends from LSE and the Radical Students' Alliance were breaking through the thin blue line round the American Embassy, blood from baton blows pouring photogenically down their young boys' faces and making images usefully recycled in this year of anniversaries. While I, far in the rear of those 100,000 people marching on Grosvenor Square to protest against the war in Vietnam, tottered along in my red velvet coat and white eyeshadow, convinced I had come to the wrong party.

Just over a year later I had somehow become part of a movement. How did an everlasting spectator stay inside — learning, arguing and even taking action — for 15 years? That is as much a mystery to me now as which particular wave of the movement set me down later on an altered shoreline, leaving Women's Liberation an echo in my ear like the sound of a shell. There was no one moment of joining, and even less of leaving.

One thing I remember clearly, far beyond the turbulence of houses squatted and habits changed, placards painted and pamphlet-presses rolled, violence (male) threatened and friendships (female) made across class and country. I can find it sometimes still in the opening of a page, the reading of a poem, the outline of an image: the quality of feminist *conversation*. Conversation for possibility — unmistakable, instantly recognisable wherever you meet it again.

Adding to that historical conversation has been the aim of this book. The idea of '68, '78, '88 originated with Gail Chester, my commissioning editor, who helped me with suggestions for contributors and then left me to make my own mistakes. We agreed that this would be no showcase for London literati but a picture of women's liberation all around the UK, mixing first-time writers with professionals, and the well with the little known.

* * * * *

Liberation was once something for which a thousand different schools of thought contended. Women's liberation saw itself as one of those schools.* Liberation — for anybody — in Britain now seems low down on the political horizon. Feminism on the other hand is thriving.

Relationships between women of all kinds have been explored and validated, feminists of the past have been honoured, barriers of privilege within the present-day movement have been challenged.

At the same time the world has changed around us.

The early demands of Women's Liberation envisaged a background of decent money for shorter hours of work, making space for shared childcare (since no mother would pay another women to do that work for her). How long ago.

One of the first consciousness-raising groups grew out of a One O'Clock Club for housebound mothers in Peckham; now there are Nannies' Groups for young northern women stranded in London with the children of professional couples. Women's achievements in the professions and management — which the movement often disdained — fill half the news stands. Women's culture — which the movement fought to create — provides a steady selling corner in the book shops. But childcare remains a private matter, which the mothers in these pages have had to deal with as best they can.

Feminists who move away from day-to-day organising have usually said that the movement is dead, or gone, or doesn't exist any more. This especially annoys the generation which has fought for a place and transformed the groups — mainly white, often Anglo chauvinist and ignorantly able-bodied — it has entered during the ten years since the last national conference broke up in pieces.

The word 'liberation' had been dropped from conference publicity one year earlier, and a 'Backlash Issue' of *Women's Report* was already around in 1975! Signs of love, maybe: fearing the death of what you love, feeling your absence from it as a kind of death, even resenting its survival without you. But does there ever come a

---

* *The subtitle of this book took off from the title of a now antique US anthology: 'From Feminism to Liberation', edited by Edith Hoshino Altbach (Schenckman, 1971).*

point when outsiders see more of the game? The premise of the women's movement is No — only those with personal experience can get the focus right. By putting many *different* lives together, over a span of 20 years, I hope to get a perspective for us all.

* * * * *

In 1978 I had an ambition to become the movement's historian. I compiled a meticulous chart of its emerging political tendencies, and succeeded in infuriating most of them.* In 1988 other women have written a history for me. As I came to the end of the book, I found that in reading other women's histories I had learned my own. So the introductions to each section will include references to my life, where it connects with what follows.

The original idea behind relating personal experiences in women's groups was to get a history of the present, the clearest possible view without interference from the experts or punters. But this consciousness-raising confessional has now taken on an accepted marketable shape. Women are *expected* to talk in first person singular, only to say certain things. The writers here break a few of the rules of the feminist anthology game, getting us to something original — in both senses. They've come up with a mix that keeps on surprising me.

There are many more men inside these pages than you'd find in the usual feminist anthology, and many more children. Sometimes they go together, more often apart. Some of these children are growing up in the "pretended family relationships" that Clause 28 of the Local Government Act (now Section 28 in law) is seeking to obliterate, so descriptions from the inside are especially precious.

Facts have turned up through this collection of life stories that I never expected, and perhaps might never have noticed before these particular Thatcher years — a high rate of Christian childhoods among more often acknowledged feminist origins; a big proportion of women disliking the 60s and at home in the next, undervalued decade; a lot of clothes and fashion.

I don't think any British feminist book up till now has achieved such a geographical spread. And we were lucky in the number of working-class women who wrote, nearly a third of the book (not

---

* *The chart was preserved in a politer form by Anne Oakley in her book 'Subject Women' (Martin Robertson, 1981).*

many in comparison with the living population of women, not bad in terms of the publishing world).

But every book is haunted by ghosts of perfect books it might have been. There are gaps here that later historians will have to fill. Our friendship networks showed through, not in the range of writers who were invited (they would have made an encyclopedia) but in those who stayed the course. Some women had returned to their countries of origin, others were doing demanding work which left no space for writing, others found personal crises cut across the book's tight deadlines. I miss everyone who could not write but I am proud of everything that's here, and of the fact there are no tokens.

This is *a* history, not *the* history. No one here speaks as a representative, but as herself.

The book is not a history of 1968 — though it originated in an editor's accurate suspicion that women were going to get left out of '68 all over again, in the anniversary recounts.

It is not a history of 1978 — though that was a watershed year for the organised women's movement, with the last national conference, big actions against violence and pornography, and another anniversary 50 years on from the Vote.

This book is a picture of 1988. It was conceived on New Year's Day and brought to birth nine months later — a record delivery and a heavy labour. Women who said they never wrote and couldn't write, wrote wonderfully. Women who are quite famous enough already wrote for peanuts. Women under huge pressure of time made a bit more to write, and re-write. Women who couldn't contribute in writing had the best of personal and political reasons, and their discussions also made the book. Thank you all.

Amanda Sebestyen

A DIARY IN KEEPING

Michelene Wandor

At school and at university, when things were either going very well or very badly, I would try and write some sort of journal, usually in an exercise book. My eyes would start closing with boredom before I even reached the end of the first sentence. The excruciating pretentiousness of this first person 'I' who was trying to write the 'truth' made me want to disappear. Not surprisingly, the very few efforts I made soon dried up.

I do keep diaries, but of a simple, functional kind, and these diaries are my key back to past years. I keep them (the diaries and the years) in a plastic carrier bag in a cupboard in my upstairs hall, and they are a fascinating collection of motley volumes which hold my factual life. My emotional life is in the blank bits — if a name appears because it is someone I have to phone or meet, there is something in my handwriting that reminds me whether I loathed that person with fiery fervour, or lusted after them. The other keys to my emotional life of the past twenty years are in my books and my other writing — plays, poetry, occasional apparent notes for fiction. No-one but me can tell from those what experiences and what people I refer to, what I might really have felt as opposed to embroidered, and certainly not what I did. Nothing about times, places or names. Secretive, eh.

In these two kinds of writing lives a single fictional character — the me who has decided to look at three dates, 1968, 1978 and 1988 — and see who emerges. And for this I go back purely to my functional diaries, because the other stuff is either raw and unformed if it is jottings, or finished and available for all the world to read if it is published.

So here goes. Problem number one — I don't have a diary for 1968. That is in itself very telling indeed. While it was all happening in the alternative culture, while the political radicals were storming various barricades, where was I? Married, with sons of two and four; still trying to come to terms with being a housewife and mother, though of a highly educated kind, giving dinner parties, cooking elaborate meals, wearing mini-skirts. I must have been doing all those things, because that's how I remember it. But with no diary of my own, how did I know what I was doing? Did we have a house diary? Did my (then) husband have a diary in which he wrote what we did? How did I know when a child was due to go to the doctor, when I was due to go to the dentist? I have no idea.

The first year for which I have a diary in my plastic bag is 1971. In here the information is mixed; I was now separated, having to earn my full living and partially support the children. This diary has lots of entries of the 'Phone Margot' variety (which reminds me, I must phone Margot), lists of children coming to tea — plus two new things. Lots of entries about poetry readings; I was reading my own work, and running a poetry column for *Time Out* magazine (which I did until 1982), and I was also going to lots of Women's Liberation meetings. Life, art and politics, you see. What the diary doesn't record is how impossible it was to juggle and relate all those three. Baby-sitting was a constant problem and drove me spare with resentment, jealousy and rage (not at the children, though I'm sure they got some of the spin-offs); my political friends largely seemed to scorn the poetry, the poetry people seemed to be completely apolitical, although they were radicals on the aesthetic scene.

At the back are some pages headed 'Memoranda'; here there are three 'journal' jottings. One is an outburst at how impossible it is for mothers to go to events that start before 8 o'clock, because of putting children to bed (always something I loved doing, when they were clean and warm and tired and cuddly). There are two poems, one of which I thought I wouldn't reproduce, but that might be cowardice, so here they both are:

> He's bright but he can't write
> Got built-in itchy powder.
> He's white but he's not right.
> If you're a white, middle-class liberal heterosexual male, you've had it, baby.
> This is the voice of doom, baby.
> Mutate.
> That is the new order.
> You are at the bottom of the list, kid.
> Dregs, sediment — on your sedimental journey down the rapids.

The other poem is a little less violent (I think):

> If you never get married, you'll never be a widow
> We'll have our own nest

where marvellous things will be done
and wonderful things will be thought
and we'll call it Chez Guevara.

Both those pieces have been provoked by something or someone, but I haven't a clue what. There is one more entry, which jumped out at me when I read it. Where the two things I've just quoted feel rather dated — I can't empathise with those passions now, really — the following is still emotionally unfinished business:
'Women have only half the consonants of men because their voices are higher.'

(Stockhausen)

Why did I write that down? I don't know. But the fact that it is about music is what's important, and I'll come back to that when I get to 1988.

1978 seems to have more entries for theatre in it than for poetry. I was doing a lot of theatre reviewing, and was having meetings with theatre, radio and television producers. The latter came to nothing (so what else is new) but the former two paid off. My first radio play went out in October 1978. I see also that in January 1978 I finally had enough money to buy a washing machine — well after the kids had grown out of nappies. I remember being so freaked out by this piece of high-tech machinery in my house, that it took me two months to get the courage to put on a plug and work out how to use it.

1978 is generally a far more work-oriented diary. The kids are now old enough to make their own social arrangements (though not yet to keep their own diaries, I don't think). 1978 has quite a lot of union meetings (National Union of Journalists) and virtually no Women's Liberation meetings. I know from memory that I was doing a lot of work on theatre and sexual politics — editing anthologies of plays, writing a contemporary history of feminist and gay theatre — but of course none of that appears in the factual diary.

Both these diaries (and all the intervening ones) are heavy, hardcover desk diaries which I kept at home. By 1988 I have a filofax, first bought in about 1982 and invaluable ever since. In the 1988 diary, there is virtually no entry about the children (young men now), not a political meeting in sight; the occasional 'ring Tony', the odd theatre, but overwhelmingly the diary for 1988 is about music. Concerts, and my own playing — lessons and consort playing with other people, or music courses.

I don't know what an outsider would make of this person. Does it look on the surface as if she's travelled one of the following paths:

from wife and mother to professional writer; from politics to music; from hardcover to filofax? All those, I suppose. It is not that my politics have disappeared. My feminism and socialism are no less fierce than ever they were. They are weary, it is true, because our culture does not make it easy to enact radical politics in the world of art and the media. I am still passionately involved with my children, even though I see far far less of them now. Music has become the new force in my life — a strange, frustrating, rewarding thing that I am not yet prepared to write about in this seemingly 'truthful' way. It finds its way into my fiction, and it has always been there in the way I structure my writing — poetry and prose fiction. So while music is not new to me, it has begun to manifest itself in new ways in the structure of my life. The warning lights are flashing — this writing is beginning to move away from the fictional persona of someone looking back a twenty-year span, to the confessional.

I find myself, therefore, feeling strangely inconclusive; my life feels, if anything, busier than it ever has been — although as I write I am reminded of those heady early days of the Women's Liberation Movement where there was meeting after meeting to go to, exciting, earnest, intense, funny conversations about the lousy world we were going to transform into the new utopia where class and gender antagonisms would be thrown out of the window. Well, twenty years of living, getting older, beginning to go grey, watching the boys grow up — becoming even more cynical than I ever was (if that is possible) about people's abilities to really change — have made the utopia a little sepia-coloured, like a Victorian photograph that is quaint but fixed. The desire for utopia is to a degree a desire for a world in which things go well, in which collaboration and pleasure are part of living. That never happened often before, and it doesn't happen often now. But sometimes it does: playing a piece of music that goes well; watching my son iron his shirts on Sunday before his next week's work, having a haircut that makes me look good.

Perhaps the next twenty years will swing round and bring the politics back into explicit rather than implicit prominence. Perhaps the next twenty years will bring my art and politics into a real collaboration. Perhaps I have always been a utopian. Meanwhile I listen to the music of the early sixteenth century.

TURNING POINTS

There are moments when public history steps directly into private lives and rearranges them.

The first writer here was 45 in '68, the second was 19, the last was eight. All were born into a class that is not expected to write history. One is Jewish, one is from Northern Ireland, one is Black. To understand the last 20 years, the word "British" has to be read through eyes like these.

You wouldn't find anything like these three voices from 1968 in the whole orchestra of broadcast and print reminiscence that's been recording itself all year, not only for the present but for the future. People you want to know about are hardly ever in history books, or else put there to occupy a demeaning role (tyrannical queens, passive slaves, revolting peasants, dangerous perverts, sensual nudes). Radical history sometimes just relocates the blind spots.

The events in the next pages taught people things about themselves that they never imagined: Jean Gittins turned from scribbler into poet and travelled across the world, Lucy Whitman turned into Lucy Toothpaste and got a place in the pages of punk, Rebecca Johnson left a well laid-out plan for a career up an ivory tower for the life of a full-time campaigner for peace.

This book is full of glimpsed events that deeply changed individuals' lives. Start with the image of a tank on a screen ...

1968: PRAGUE WINTER, FEMINIST SPRING

Asphodel

When I remember 1968, what still hits me are the pictures on television of Russian tanks rolling through Prague. You could see those people in the streets, stopping the tanks, arguing, waving their arms about, trying to tell the soldiers that this was not a reactionary counter-revolution, it was true Socialism — "with a human face". The camera caught a close-up of one tank soldier looking upset behind his massive guns and arguing back, another with his head in his hands. It was no use. Very soon the Soviet leaders withdrew the "European", Russian-speaking, troops and sent in fighters from far-off Kazakhstan who would be less able to "fraternise with the enemy".

I remember the pictures of the Czech leader Dubcek, after he had been arrested and then released before the final show-down. He told us, with that wry sad smile of his, that when offered a cup of coffee before his interrogation he had scooped up all the sugar available — he knew he would soon need it.

While all this was happening, the student revolt in France, USA, Germany and Britain was a backdrop which did not interest me much. I was then 45, had brought up my son on my own, was working as a trade press journalist, and had been a left-winger ever since I was 20. I spent 15 years in the Communist Party, leaving in 1956.

Yes, the bell tolls for 1956, just as it does for 1968. Here now, in 1988, they are talking about "rehabilitating" Bukharin and some of the older Bolsheviks murdered on Stalin's orders. As far as I know they haven't yet got round to the so-called "suicide" of Jan Masaryk in 1948, felt by many Czechs to be no such thing, but political murder; nor have they faced the implications of the judicial killings of Slansky, the Jewish Czech leader and his comrades. The latter deaths open up the whole question of Soviet antisemitism, since Slansky always appeared to be a loyal Stalinist as well as a Jew. I am a Jew by birth, though not by observance since I became adult. Left-wing antisemitism, then as now, cut to the heart my idealism and devotion to the Socialist cause.

1968 was the final betrayal for me of all the ideals, the work, the dedication, indeed the obsession that had been the major part of my life and of the lives of so many like me. We had believed that Socialism was really here in the world — in the USSR and the "New Democracies", and in China — here to stay. It was the finest effort human beings could make to get rid of oppression, to become "new people". It was, we thought, worth living and dying for.

I wasn't interested in the students' revolution. I thought of them as privileged children, able to take part in all their exciting events because of the work my generation and those before me had put in to make their privileges possible. (I myself left school at 16, though marked down as "university material" — I eventually got there when I was 60.)

I was overcome with sadness when Rudi Dutschke was shot, and overwhelmed, in a way, with admiration for all the mad daring — except that it reminded me of the romantic heroic novels and films about Rupert of Hentzau or Richard Hannay. Poor Rudi didn't escape unharmed like Douglas Fairbanks or Ronald Coleman.

It came through to me pretty quickly that women were getting the worst part of the students' new deal. They were obviously being used by men, sexually and for all the other services of the usual kind. It was men, men, men who were the heroes. I remember looking for news of women, sometimes reported, but always in an understated denigratory sort of way, unless there was also a sexual titillation to be achieved.

When all the demagogy of "revolution tomorrow" came along, I dismissed it as nonsense . . . Look what was happening in Czecho-slovakia, what did these students know, or it seemed care, about what was really happening to the revolution?

The final defeat was fixed for me not in 1968 itself, but on January 1st 1969. A student (yes, a student) Jan Palach set himself on fire and burned to death in the main square of Prague as a protest against the betrayal of Socialism and of his country. We saw the flames.

Against that, pictures of London School of Economics students tearing down the college gates (because they didn't like the syllabus?) just didn't seem to matter.

I realise now that the anti-Vietnam War movement was colossally important. I realise too that something was happening to young people that I have never understood. I only came near to getting a glimpse of it in the late 70s — say 1978 — talking to younger feminists who felt they had been not only inspired but in some way moulded by the events of '68. At the time my work in the rag trade only showed me rather cynically that the young had become a new and substantial market for consumer goods — in one year alone I think, 7 million yards of denim were made into jeans in this country.

I did see in 1968 that the behaviour of the police — both in America where they shot down students, and in this country where they trampled them under horses' hoofs — had come out again into the open: brutal and oppressive, unchanged from the 1930s when the father of my elder son had been beaten up at the anti-fascist rally at Olympia, with the police looking on and clearing the way for the fascists.

But when the New Left talked about Marxism, Trotskyism, Maoism in tones of rigid dogma, it was, for me, all just a nonsense. In particular, I saw and heard no analysis of the Chinese Cultural Revolution, which first of all I had welcomed. I had thought, yes, once bureaucrats get into power they become tyrants: unsettling them is useful. But after a year or so I realised something of what actually was happening — the unthinking, uncaring destruction of people and of culture, and the setting up of an even more rigid bureaucracy. I rejected the Cultural Revolution entirely, and with it the Maoism of the New Left.

A bitter aftermath of that period for me is what happened to Chang Ching (Jiang Qing), widow of Mao and leader of the so-called "Gang of Four". She was used as a scapegoat for the Cultural Revolution and sent to prison, where as far as one knows, she still remains. Descriptions of her, after her arrest, as a "white-boned demon", a "perfidious serpent", a "Harridan" and a "trollop", are distinctly sexist in tone. It appears that the Chinese authorities had little difficulty in transferring massive blame on to this woman for much of their own guilt.

At that time, and earlier, one of my most important reasons for being a left-wing fighter was my belief that Socialism stood for the emancipation of women, and that only in Socialism was there the opportunity for us women to become part of the human race. If the 1968 events showed me anything, it was that this was just not true. Socialist men were just like men everywhere else, women being allowed token action and rhetoric, but only really required for cooking, laundry, sex — and as scapegoats.

Above all, in the US and the West generally, the advent of the birth control pill had given men the final opportunity to get rid of all sense of responsibility about sex. They had not had much until then, but somehow, somewhere, they had still recognised that sex with a woman usually meant the chance of a baby, and they would be called upon to do something about it (even if they sloped off somewhere and hoped never to be heard of again). Now, with the Pill, they could exploit women completely, with no comeback. If the woman became pregnant, it was her own "fault". And the pressure on women to provide constant sex was something new. Of course we had always been importuned, but against a background of the nuisance, shame, danger, trouble and financial expense of an unwanted pregnancy. We had some "excuse" for drawing back, if we wished. Not so any longer.

If indeed women in 1968 had been achieving real sexual partnership and mutual co-operation with men, that would truly have been a revolution. Of course no such thing was happening. But there was something else in the wind — something enormously important — based to a large extent on a conviction that no such real partnership was possible in the foreseeable future. In America the Women's Liberation Movement was under way, and in Britain the first meetings had begun, though I didn't know about them for another two or three years. Were these an offshoot of the 1968 students' revolts? I don't think so. The roots of the WLM were much older. I was introduced to the work of Simone de Beauvoir in the forties by a friend, now 80, who was my transformer into understanding the power of consciousness-raising for women (though we did not call it that). She was a feminist in a period when the word was hardly known.

By 1978, things for me had really changed. By then I had been working in the WLM for about eight years. That period was my "bliss to be alive" time. Those years really did break my shackles, release the chains — all those clichés — they really happened to me.

Of course there were dissensions, differing opinions, women got heated. But I had been in politics for over thirty years. It was all part of life for me. The basis of universal sisterhood, the struggle to raise our consciousness and free ourselves from the ultimate oppression — of believing that men had the *right* to oppress us — was the most important thing that ever happened to me. My identity was not only personal. I was a woman among women. Whatever our sexuality, class, religion, age, disability, or even (I believed) race, this overthrow of our inner put-down was the real revolution and would lead to the final egalitarian just society.

By 1978 we had found ourselves, our voice. We had, I believe, irrevocably, broken down major barriers that had confined the female spirit. The rage let out was, to some extent, to turn back against women themselves and lead to what I believe is a temporary fragmentation of the liberation movement. But the spirit had been released, and is released.

By 1978 I was working in a women's group which asked itself whether women had always been "the subordinate sex". We found, by research, that we had not. We also found ultimate sources for this Great Lie which has had such disastrous consequences for women (and indeed for the earth) in the male-centred religions which dominate the world. Their woman-hating, woman-obliterating thrust has shaped society and poisoned our view of our selves. I looked for and found evidence of other societies where the female way of life, its biology and its values were honoured and not degraded. Menstruation was not "unclean" or "the curse", it was a sacred time. Childbirth and motherhood were actually treated as important, not given mere lip service. Older women were respected for their experience and capabilities. The sense of the divine included female personages or aspects. Above all, women were not sexual slaves of one husband, but autonomous in their sexuality. Children did not have to be of one known father, so that women did not have to be herded into confinement to ensure paternity.

I approached this work in a purely political and intellectual manner at first; in fact, the reason I went to College was to find out more and to achieve some scholastic affirmation for what I was retrieving. But there was an added effect. As I read invocations to goddesses and looked at their pictures, and found out why, for example, George or Michael or Perseus killed the dragon (then as now an elderly powerful female) and was rewarded by having a young submissive damsel in bondage to him, there came some unfreezing of my spiritual sense. From being a confirmed atheist I moved to an awareness of a new dimension.

I cannot describe this in rational terms. It happened when we were studying an area we called "Goddess in the Landscape". We visited ancient sites that we had reason to believe were scenes of early goddess worship. Many of them are built in the shape of a huge women — you can see one at Arbor Low in Derbyshire, another at

Scara Brae in the Orkneys and several in Malta. These massive stone and earth sites were sacred not only to the earth goddess but also to the Queen of the Heavens and to the Mistress of the Underworld. It appears that they were not only temples but to some extent models of the moon's phases, and certainly indicated the equinox and the solar round.

It was in taking part in simple rituals on such an occasion as an equinox or solstice at such a site, that I was opened up to feelings that I had never before experienced. These goddesses had been murdered, wiped from the earth and from our knowledge. Just in the same way, women have been continually degraded, belittled, made to feel as if they were nothing and no-one. Yet their ancient monuments still remained and their enormous achievements in astrology and other sciences are only now being recovered.

In visiting these Goddess sites and marking the changing seasons regularly, I felt an enormous sense of one-ness with our foremothers. It went with a feeling of awareness of union with a universal force that contained a powerful female element, divine and cosmic, made out of heaven, earth, the oceans, rivers, trees, animals and all natural objects and all those that had gone before and were yet to come.

I felt that for us females to be raised from our oppression in the here and now we had to raise the *idea*, the concept of the Female. This led to the work I have been doing for the last decade.

I research the past and talk, give workshops, slide shows, classes and discussions on such subjects as Female Aspects of Deity, or Images of Women's Power in the Past. Never in an academic manner or to make some scholarly point; always because finding out about our history empowers us for the present and future struggle against our oppression, and for a just and rightful way of Living.

By 1988, the splits and dissensions in the Women's Liberation Movement have cast it into a thousand thousand pieces. We hurtled (rather like some star) towards a dream of universalism. The various differing energies inside the whole shot off in a mass of different directions, but I think each piece, each spark has the essence of the whole within it. We were torn apart too, by the energy of our own liberation and sadly we felt we had to turn on each other, rather than on the male domination system, when we could not achieve the whole as quickly as we wanted.

Each separate oppression — class, race, age, colour, sexuality, disability, or any other — needed its own separate care, space, exploration. The old rigorous linear "Movement", on the march, forging ahead (all those patriarchal images) has broken down into varying groups of women and even individuals or twos and threes, breaking out, demanding recognition, refusing put-down. In 1988 I see signs that women are coming together again in larger groups, but more aware of their different needs, more tolerant of diversity.

There is no space here to go into my own odyssey. All I can say is that I was woken from rapturous dreams of universal sisterhood. I see now that women do still exploit women, that all the particularities are important. Yet above all and including all is the need to understand that women *as women* are oppressed. They have need of each other's recognition and support in their universal struggle, no matter how different their situations may seem.

I need to say here that my own view of the next phase of the Women's Liberation Movement is that the personal struggle between women and men now has to be recognised and women given support. The Women's Movement will need to recognise women who are working with men and will need to take part in their lives and their struggles. If we are to get anywhere now, men too must change, must become aware of their oppressive powers, and the use they make of them, and must face egalitarianism with women. This may need a huge amount of work on their part — and that is their business. To the men who say "why should we?", women's answer is that it is time to do so.

As for politicians, union activists, freedom fighters, (who all include women, and at one time myself), we all have to see that no matter how much we rant about justice and freedom, unless we specifically recognise and struggle against the exploitation of women and the power base of men, we will achieve nothing. Male-oriented politics leads to nothing but pain, suffering, war, torture, and if we continue in the same manner will probably lead to the end of human life on earth.

Women as well as men have drunk the poison of patriarchy. We all have to sweat it out, vomit it up, to get rid of it. What does this mean? Simply, that women will have to be recognised and recognise themselves as normative, powerful members of the human race, not its under half. When this starts, the revolution will really have begun.

1988

I can't end, in 1988, without a reference to the disaster of AIDS. My grandchildren are now young men, I look around and see a new generation of women and men practically on the verge of being wiped out. There is only one point I can make. I hear a lot from men about how terrible it is to have to connect sex with death. I say: women have always connected sex with death, for generations until only this century it has been for many women a nine months' journey to death. Every time a woman underwent sexual intercourse she was put in danger of death through childbirth. In many places of the world this is still the case, and it can still be here.

I don't know what will happen about AIDS — no-one does. Women are now in danger from it as well as men. I only feel it is telling us something about man's continuous exploitation, rape and torture of Nature and of women, and his scorn for them. Perhaps "safe sex" will lead to care and responsibility and forethought and recognition of one's partners' needs, and tenderness instead of force. Perhaps the male urge for dominance and machine-like methods of prowess for "fun" will be mellowed by his greater understanding of what things have always been like for women. Emotions and caring may be esteemed instead of demeaned. If it needed an all-out plague to set us free, then let us take advantage of the lesson it teaches us.

1968: BURNTOLLET BRIDGE

Mary Kay Mullan

'68, '78, '88 have all been landmarks in my life. Personally and politically.

In 1968 I was 18 years old and had just left boarding school — "the sheltered life" — to go to University, the first member of my family to do so. During a summer spent working in canning factories in England and Scotland, I'd discovered the friendliness of local English people and their quaint customs (Yorkshire Pudding every Sunday, Sundays spent sitting fishing on the riverbank); but I'd been shocked at their racism and at the dreadful working and living conditions given to immigrant seasonal workers. I'd enjoyed my first chance to meet so many foreigners — Maltese, Yugoslavs, East Europeans — and it was especially exciting to meet women from different cultures and speaking different languages. In Scotland, I'd been amazed to meet entrenched "Green and Orange" bigots outside of Northern Ireland.

Now, on 9th October 1968 — my second day at Queens University, Belfast, — I was "marching for Civil Rights". Such simple demands, six in all:

One *Man* One Vote
One Family One House — Houses on need
Jobs on Merit
Fair Electoral Boundaries — an end to Gerrymandering
Free Speech
Repeal of the Special Powers Act

The world in Northern Ireland was going to change by non-violent means! I had grown up in a society with an armed police force, police stations barricaded with sandbags, with look-out posts and neighbours (Protestant) armed with guns and formed into the "B Specials", armed part-time militia. Each week we listened to them practising their shooting on the nearby hillside. We had always been second-class citizens. I grew up hearing tales of discrimination, killing, torture and bigotry against the Nationalist Community. Now people were rising up and taking to the streets in demanding a few basic rights.

Last week, in Derry, they had been brutally batoned by the Police and the "B Specials" and bombarded by water cannons. Banned from marching in their own towns, from having their voices heard. But they had discovered that they had a voice! The students formed 'The People's Democracy' (PD) within that week.

I wholeheartedly joined in the protests. With raincoat and book in hand I spent the autumn travelling to demonstrations. Taking my knitting, I sat through seemingly endless PD meetings. An introduction to political life! I enjoyed hearing Bernadette Devlin expressing my frustrations. I found Michael Farrell's well thought-out speeches an interesting introduction to socialist politics. I knitted furiously through many boring self-centred speeches from men who liked to hear themselves talking! Few women (apart from Bernadette) spoke up and although at times I longed to express my opinion, I was too scared and inarticulate to speak out.

I had come through an all girls' school, and had been successful academically (I was now studying Mathematics); I had worked on our farm and driven a tractor; I felt every bit as capable as men. However I discovered that men did not consider me nor my women friends capable and equal. What a shock! We were welcome to do all the hard and tedious tasks — distributing leaflets, helping out with organisation, collecting money, secretarial duties, etc. But we were just girls — huh! — we were there to be useful and for their enjoyment. I was furious at this treatment. I was a person with a mind and intelligence and was to be regarded as an equal human being! In this area I found support from other young women involved — we spent hours discussing our lives, our hopes, our ideas and our frustrations as women, but we had not heard of Women's Liberation. Although our natural instincts encouraged us to believe in ourselves we were still vulnerable and uncertain, especially in personal relationships with men. I still blamed myself for a lot of things wherein I had no fault. I remember being "mean", at any opportunity where I had "power", to any fellow who had annoyed me.

We were busy with marches, meetings, pickets, leafleting, sit-ins, traffic disruption and all types of non-violent public direct action, rushing home to see ourselves on the evening news and checking the front page of the *Belfast Telegraph*. I was very active but politically naive — believing in the power of reason and of the media to get the message across. We were, after all, asking for very little. On our first march, we had our first sit-down and I remember how impressed I was by the presence of the international camera teams.

For me, my first term at university was a crash course in political action and a great way to overcome my shyness and to get to know people. We had "important" issues to discuss. It was a period of confidence-building — learning to manage money, drinking, socialising, coping with unfamiliar situations, overcoming problems, often with the confidence of ignorance, and learning to work with others. I even did a stint as an Election Agent in the Northern Ireland elections to Stormont.

A 75-mile march from Belfast to Derry in December seemed exciting — certainly a noteworthy event, influential in making people see that our basic demands had not been met. A friend and I, sleeping bags on our backs, set off to join the trek on its second day. We were a bit perturbed to hear of the violent reaction by some Protestants to what had initially been a long walk by a small group of students. The march was turning into a *cause celebre*, a challenge to the traditional order. Fortunately we got a lift with a friendly lorry driver who decided to take us to join the march. The marchers had been diverted from the main road, and we turned back to meet them at the junction. In the growing dusk of that winter's evening we came upon a bizarre scene. Dark shadows "danced" around in the intermittent glare of headlights, brandishing sticks. As we slowly approached, we could hear the heart-stopping, gut-wrenching boom of the tribal Lambeg drum, the screaming of the milling crowd. They had gathered to stop the march reaching the next town. We had to drive through this throng. They banged on the lorry and questioned the driver. I was filled with horror and dread in case they would open the doors and discover our sleeping bags. It was with great relief that we were allowed to drive through and join the marchers in a wayside hall, where there were whispers that men with guns were guarding us. A riot was taking place in the local town. Next day the weather was fine as we climbed over the Glenshane Pass to my home town of Dungiven to be warmly greeted, fed and helped on our way by the local people. The march had become a populist show of defiance to the Unionist regime. The third day passed without incident.

On the last morning, after a lot of discussion which I did not follow, we set off under dull grey skies, flanked by armed RUC, who kept us close under a steeply rising slope on one side of the road. Seven miles from Derry, at Burntollet Bridge, we were suddenly ambushed by men throwing stones and wielding sticks. I received a blow on the head as I jumped through the hedge and raced down the field towards the river. Surrounded on all sides by angry men brandishing nail-studded cudgels, we were forced to jump into the river in front of us. As I stood knee-deep in freezing water I came face to face with the sectarian fear and hatred on the faces of our attackers. In their frenzy these men had lost their normal humanity. They had turned savage and demented. It was a horrifying sight and it has had a lasting effect on me. I felt a responsibility for having raised this spectre. I did not want to take away all that belonged to them, I was only asking for basic justice. These were the same people who gave me a lift home the next day, who were helpful neighbours. How could we cross that divide?

Shortly afterwards the PD decided to put up protest candidates in the elections to Stormont Parliament. I acted as Election Agent for Fergus Woods in South Down. We had no experience of electioneering, but were helped in our campaigning by local people. We were astounded when Fergus lost the election by only 220 votes. After hearing politicians mouthing the same old platitudes, I became rather cynical about standard "political" methods and diverted more of my energy into voluntary community action. I was tired of attending large meetings where I did not feel able to express my opinion — it was usually the same few who talked at length on each occasion.

My natural instincts were against violence, I had grown up surrounded by the violence of the state. I did not have a theory of non-violence but I felt energised by the power of people united, sharing similar views. There was such a great divide between the communities — entrenched by over 50 years of deliberate "divide and rule" policies from the Unionist government. I was learning that solutions are not straightforward or simple — just as in Mathematics there are many variations to a perceived truth.

1978

1978 was also a year of change for me — new directions, new confidence. A lot had changed in the decade since 1968. In 1972 I had finally graduated from University, after my first experience of academic failure. I chose to ignore this failure at the time but it was to have a strong influence on my actions later. I had taught in schools in Belfast and Lurgan, taken a course in teaching English as a Foreign Language, visited France, Spain, Italy and Greece on holidays, lived in the USA and Quebec, travelled in Mexico, been seriously ill twice. I returned to Northern Ireland in autumn 1975 and due to family commitments I came to live and work in Derry, teaching Mathematics at first.

Over the years I had discovered Feminism through reading magazines and books. But it wasn't until Siobhan Molloy from Belfast organised a course on Women in Irish Society that I became actively involved. The course led to a consciousness-raising group and many long hours of fervent discussions with like-minded women (now my friends). There was no time for knitting now, I was too excited and contributing to the discussions on the many problems facing women in Derry. One main concern was violence against women, especially in the home.

Previously a battered woman might have escaped for a few nights into Bed and Breakfast accommodation or into a local convent, but she would eventually have had to return home. We decided to set up a Woman's Aid Refuge in Derry. We had to find premises in a neutral area to be accessible to all women whatever their background. We did so in a most unconventional manner — by squatting, negotiating, publicising, fundraising, learning about Social Security, housing laws, and laws affecting women's status. This was the first refuge in the North-West.

We discovered that the laws in Northern Ireland were archaically backward. Under the Unionist rule at Stormont, British legal reforms on divorce, matrimonial protection, abortion and homosexuality did not apply in Northern Ireland. We had to learn to take advantage of the system of Direct Rule from Westminster to campaign for improvements in the laws affecting women — organising petitions, lobbying MPs and Ministers to have 'orders in Council' passed at Westminster for each individual case or injunction. We were fortunate to have a sympathetic Labour Minister at that time.

Working in Women's Aid was a great learning experience for me. I liked working in a non-hierarchical structure and taking collective responsibility. In this supportive atmosphere I pushed myself to speak out at larger meetings. I remember the first time — stumbling, stammering, blushing and hiding behind my hair but persevering and completing a sentence.

I admired the strength and resilience of the women who came through the Refuge. Not only had they to cope with violence in the home but also the problems of living in our war-torn divided society. Entrance to the city centre was restricted by security checkpoints which were guarded by soldiers levelling guns. Everybody was bodysearched, the searchers' hands following the contours of our bodies and then expecting our gratitude for permission to pass. The security gates in the 17th-century walls were closed at night, and entry into the Refuge was restricted. This was useful at times to protect women from violent husbands, but it also gave rise to some odd situations. There were no corner shops near the Refuge. One night the women ran out of bread and a volunteer, Eileen, brought a loaf from her own freezer. Rita from the Refuge went to meet her only to find the gate shut. So the two women stood on either side of the walls trying to negotiate with the British Army for delivery of the loaf of bread.

In Women's Aid we protested at violence against women from the Police, the British Army and the Republican movement.

1978 saw one of the most widespread and successful campaigns against violence against women, the Free Noreen Winchester Campaign. Noreen Winchester was a young woman who had for years been raped and abused by her father, whom she one day killed in defence of herself and her younger sister. She was given a long prison sentence. Outraged Women's Aid groups across the province spearheaded a campaign to have her released. We held public meetings, press conferences, performed street theatre and collected signatures in the streets. It was the first time people were publicly confronted with the issues of incest and child abuse. I discovered great solidarity among women over this issue. I remember one older woman willingly signing our petition and telling us that years before, she had had to take her daughters away from their father in order to protect them.

During this period I was struggling with my growing awareness of being a Lesbian. I was receiving support from friends in Derry and elsewhere but this did little to change the isolation of "coming out" in Derry. That spring I attended the first All Ireland Lesbian Conference in Dublin, the warmest, most supportive conference I have ever attended. Another step forward for me, declaring in public for the first time that I was a Lesbian.

At the same time, I was discontented with my work — I wanted to be involved in direct action for change. I also felt a personal need to prove to myself that I could push myself and succeed in a new field.

Over a few years, a group of like-minded individuals — mostly active in politics and community work — had been discussing setting up a radical bookshop/community centre/ meeting place/ cafe in Derry city centre, inspired by Centerprise in Hackney, East London. We came up against problems of funding and the scarcity of suitable premises. Local councils had less money and power than they did in England, and there were no grants available in Northern Ireland for setting up a shop. Derry's central shopping area is divided by the river and within the walled city many buildings were wrecked and derelict. There were few side/shopping streets outside the "ghetto" areas. Rents being asked for ordinary commercial premises were very high. We were inexperienced in business and also in fundraising.

The idea became for me a personal challenge — I wished to prove to myself that I could succeed, especially in the unknown field of the business sector. I was interested in feminism and non-violence as a way forward for me. I was also an avid reader and believed in the power of ideas for change; the local newsagents wouldn't even take personal orders for *Spare Rib*! I visited radical bookshops in England and Belfast, and our group discussed the viability of the venture. I pooled my savings, which together with donations from friends and well-wishers came to less than £1000 in all. We received a small grant of books (ancient tomes) on non-violence from the Peace News Trust, and with generous help from many unexpected sources we opened Bookworm Community Bookshop in November 1978.

The premises were tiny and off the beaten track, a two-up and two-down terrace house shared with an advice centre. The shop was a great success and received a lot of local support: one night our display of badges was stolen from the window, and the young people of the community recovered them for us the next day.

For me 1978 was an exciting year — personal achievement and a lot of work.

1988

Amazingly, a decade later I am still living in Derry and working in the bookshop. Bookworm has grown and changed beyond our original plans into a successful city centre bookshop. It operates as a workers' co-operative and still sells radical literature providing a focus for alternative information and ideas. Once again I am looking for a change — a new challenge, a new skill to learn. I would prefer to be more directly involved in working in the community, especially on women's issues. At this stage the day-to-day running of the shop has come to seem too much like a normal business venture, no longer a challenge.

Today I have more confidence in my ability to try new tasks — although writing this article is severely testing my ability! I have had to become a much more public person, because of the need to publicise the shop, and through organising events for women in the city. I am involved in the group running a central Women's Centre. I am also a member of Carafriend, an information and befriending service for lesbians and gay men.

After years of slow growth, there has recently been a great surge of interest in working on issues affecting women. Women have been setting up local groups in many districts, organising creche campaigns, playgroups, researching the viability of women's co-ops and daycare facilities. *Derry Women's Newssheet* is being published monthly. A women's health collective have produced a video on cervical cancer. There has been enthusiastic response to plans for an autonomous Well Women's Centre. There is a Rape and Incest Line; a Family Planning Association branch which gives a lot of advice, information and courses on women's health; A Women in Trade Unions group; a Sinn Fein Women's department; assertiveness classes; plans for second-chance education for women . . . Women's Aid, despite many set-backs, is still going strong. There was even a shortlived Lesbian Action group last summer.

Most of these individuals and groups have united to form a Women's Council to exchange information, share ideas, and campaign for more facilities and funding. At present the Council is spearheading a campaign for a creche in the city centre shopping complex. On March 8th this year, we had our first International Women's Day march through the centre of Derry.

Funding has always been a huge problem, as the local council is not interested in women's issues, and also has so much fewer resources and less responsibility than councils in the rest of the UK. I would like to work as a full-time organiser in our Women's Centre, but since we have not succeeded in raising the money I must look for new ways to fund such work. I am considering organic horticulture, personal development, or learning to use computers so as to put the technology to work for women's groups and also perhaps gain funding for women's retraining. We urgently need alternative employment in this deprived region.

There is still a strong feeling of solidarity among women and there have been some advances since 1978: improvements in legal status — divorce law, injunctions and exclusion orders, Domestic Proceedings, reform on rape law; assertiveness/health courses; women-only groups. For me, it has been really exciting to meet such numbers of newly-interested and active women. Many of them have been active for years within their local communities, in Prisoner's Relatives Action Committees, campaigns against strip searching and army harassment, protests at the treatment of men and boys by the 'security' forces. Now they are also deciding to make demands for themselves — a slow process. The war has been ongoing since 1968/9. A solution looks unlikely in the near future, but these women have decided to work for change at a community level, and are a force to be dealt with in any future state.

As a supporter of non-violent action, I have been ambivalent about the militarism of the IRA. I see it as a reaction to state violence — the state is the main source of violence in our community. I feel that without the IRA we would all be cowed by the British Government and the Unionist powers. But fear and hatred are embedded on both sides and I have no overall solution. Such differences can only be worn away by people working together in common cause, getting to know and trust each other. There will be no solution while the British Army remains in the six Counties, oppressing most obviously the 'nationalist' community and preventing all people working for self-determination. When the powers-that-be and the media talk of "peace", they mean the defeat or demise of the IRA — while we still suffer the violent repression of a police state.

For the moment, despite all the cutbacks, I feel personally optimistic. I have a supportive network of friends to guide and encourage me. This year, after the murder of the three IRA volunteers in Gibraltar, the ensuing media coverage, and the horrific attacks at the funerals, I have once again had to fight my feelings of powerlessness. As an individual I can only continue to make space for women to take control of their own lives, and to co-operate wherever possible with other communities across the country.

In 1988 I can still offer enthusiasm and commitment — I now also have organisational skills, knowledge and experience. My life has been enriched by exchanges of information and ideas from many people, especially women, worldwide. I need to keep that wider perspective on all our struggles to change the capitalist system.

I feel it is important to have a theory to guide our action, but not rigid doctrines reminiscent of fascism. The warmth and humanity of oppressed peoples working for change have always given me strength and encouragement.

1976: ROCK AGAINST RACISM

Lucy Whitman

1968

I was thirteen at the beginning of 1968. My family was reeling from the shock of my brother's death: killed in a car crash aged twenty-one in the summer of '67. That meant I learnt very early not to take anyone's continued existence for granted.

I was a glutton for study, guzzling lessons and homework like chocolates, but very ignorant about the world around me. Politics didn't interest me, though morality did. My information and my understanding were very patchy, so I didn't make connections which now seem obvious.

I watched the Paris uprisings on my TV screen, horrified at the sight of the riot police clubbing students to the ground with enormous truncheons; but I didn't have the faintest idea what the riots were about. Even when student unrest erupted on my own doorstep — Hornsey Art College was only five minutes walk away, and students from the college were living in our house — I still didn't have a clue why they were rebelling, and I don't even remember asking anyone.

But one thing I was clear about. I knew the US Army was committing atrocities in Vietnam, and I knew there was a big anti-war movement. I didn't know what the Americans were doing there in the first place, but I didn't need to. No war was ever justifiable. It could never be right to kill people. I remember arguing the case for pacifism vehemently with my friends at school. I was an ardent Christian, an intransigent idealist.

I had drunk pacifism in with my mother's milk. She had been a pacifist throughout the Second World War. She wasn't sophisticated politically, and I don't think she really grasped the threat of fascism. But then I don't suppose many of the English people who supported the war did either.

At this age I took it for granted that when I grew up I would marry and have about three children. All I knew about lesbianism was what I had gleaned from watching 'The Loudest Whisper' on TV, which was not encouraging. The message of the film was clear: love between women could only mean shame, misery and suicide.

If I had known that women were beginning to fight for their liberation, at this time, I would have thought it was ridiculous. Liberation from what? I would have asked smugly. It was obvious to me that women were equal to men, if not superior, so what was the problem?

1978

At the beginning of 1978 I was in the throes of my first lesbian relationship, which was fraught with conflict and pain. I was full of Anarchy In The UK, and wanted to blazon my new identity around with all the brashness of my new hard punk persona. But my lover, who looked like a much harder, tougher punk than me, was terrified of being a lesbian and insisted on keeping our relationship a secret. She also kept on calling the relationship off and then coming back to me, so that I began to feel distinctly seasick.

I was just working up the courage to talk to my mother about it all when the 'Dr Strangelove' furore hit the headlines in London: lesbians were using artificial insemination to get pregnant! This precipitated the worst quarrel I have ever had with my mother and set me back a long way in coming out to her. I had never discussed lesbianism with her before, and was appalled to hear her recite the whole catalogue of prejudice and stereotypes. I didn't dare broach the subject again for about four years. That summer I wrote my first short story, 'A Dangerous Influence', which is not directly autobiographical, but which I now realise explores my relationship with my mother in a roundabout way.

My hair stood up on end from 1976 onwards. I got into punk right from the beginning, fascinated and terrified at the same time. My friends couldn't understand how someone as gentle as me could be drawn to something so aggresive and horrible, but I enjoyed the energy and the boldness and the wit. And besides, it gave me the chance to have a belated adolescence. (I'd been such a conformist teenager!) So in 1977, instead of concentrating on the final year of my English degree, I dreamt up the name Lucy Toothpaste and launched my fanzine *JOLT*.

JOLT was a feminist, anti-racist, anti-fascist intervention into punk. It was also totally individualistic: I produced it virtually single-handed and it didn't arise out of involvement in any political group.

I had been a feminist ever since reading *The Second Sex* on the road to Damascus in 1974. I had been reading *Socialist Worker* avidly but sceptically each week for a couple of years. I was never tempted to join the party, but I certainly absorbed a lot of the SWP's ideas. I was more attracted to anarchism than to organised socialism. My heroines were Emma Goldman, Valerie Solanas and Patti Smith. I had studied virtually the complete works of Brecht, and I think that what I really liked about punk was the way it *made strange* everyday life:

I wanna be instamatic
I wanna be a frozen pea
I wanna be dehydrated
In a consumer society

Thus screamed Poly Styrene of X-Ray Spex. Vi Subversa of Poison Girls developed the same theme:

Have the shops run out of rubbish? Is it time to have a crisis? . . .
Is it normal? Is it normal? Is it JUST ANOTHER DAY?

Most punk women in the public eye, such as the Slits, ran a mile from the term 'feminist', but they projected a fierce, sarcastic, independent image which was far from 'feminine', and consistently mocked the stereotypes. Whether they liked it or not, these groups had definitely been influenced by the Women's Liberation Movement.

What I tried to do in *JOLT* (and later in *Temporary Hoarding* and *Drastic Measures*, the Rock Against Racism and Rock Against Sexism magazines) was to articulate the connections between what was being said by women punks and what was being said by feminists. I was quite consciously trying to popularise feminist ideas amongst angry but unpoliticised young women (and, dare I say it, men). On the other hand, when I started to write for *Spare Rib* in 1978, I often felt I had to defend and interpret punk to the sceptical, older feminist readership who were convinced punk was vicious and misogynist. Later on, punk styles invaded the women's movement, but in 1978 the 'typical feminist' could still be recognised not by her spikey haircut but by her dungarees!! No wonder there was such deep suspicion between the two camps of punks and feminists!

The relationship between punk, women and feminism fascinated me, but what was actually obsessing me, and all my friends, throughout this period was the threat of fascism.

The National Front had been steadily growing since 1974, and was well on the way to being seen as a legitimate political party. Things had taken a decided turn for the worse in the long hot summer of '76. A barrage of anti-Asian racism in the press was followed by the brutal murders of three Asian men in London. It was these murders, more than anything else, which spurred me into action.

In the summer of 1978 I was living on my own in Hoxton, the heartland of NF activity in East London; scared of skinheads, nervous that I would get beaten up for my punky appearance and my Rock Against Racism badges. Every boarded-up shop, every sheet of corrugated iron surrounding every derelict piece of land was daubed with racist graffiti. About half a mile away was Brick Lane, where each Sunday Asian shopkeepers and anti-fascist supporters would confront the Front. For the first time in my life, it was possible that fascist councillors or even MPs might be elected: 100,000 people voted for them in local elections in London that year. But the bigger the NF grew, the more determined and better organised the opposition became. For every fascist who reared his ugly head, a hundred anti-fascists sprang up out of the soil.

We knew it was a matter of life or death. "Only one thing could have stopped our movement," Hitler had said: "if our adversaries had understood its principles and from the first day had smashed with the utmost brutality, the nucleus of our new movement."

Some anti-fascists got into the 'smashing with the utmost brutality' side of things with a glee which disturbed me, although I acknowledge that physically preventing the Front from marching was essential. Wood Green, April 1977, was my initiation; from then until the '79 election, when the NF fielded more than 300 candidates, going on anti-NF demonstrations became a regular part of life. The highspot of 1978, for all of us involved in Rock Against Racism, was the Victoria Park Carnival Against the Nazis, which was huge beyond our wildest dreams: thousands upon thousands of people, celebrating life and love, defying the fascist threat of hatred and death.

Anti-fascist culture was flourishing. We had to educate ourselves and each other about what the National Front actually stood for, about the Nazis in Germany, about racism and fascism in general. I've still got stacks of leaflets and pamphlets from this period. Magazine articles, books, plays and films about fascism all began to appear: *The Men With the Pink Triangle*, Brecht's 'Fears and Miseries in the Third Reich', Gay Sweatshop's 'As Time Goes By', the

Newsreel Collective's 'Divide and Rule Never'... Although the threat of fascism was truly menacing, the fight against fascism liberated a surge of creativity.

I learned a lot from being involved in Rock Against Racism, and it was often really good fun, though in retrospect I've got quite a few criticisms. The organisation (in London at least) was male-dominated and not very democratic. I couldn't participate fully in meetings because I felt intimidated by everyone else's years of experience. But I had quite a lot of power as the resident feminist on the *Temporary Hoarding* editorial collective, and I got the chance to cut my teeth on some juicy interviews and articles. Some of the vocabulary I used then makes me wince a bit now — but I am still rather fond of my pioneering piece, 'No More Normals' which, although I didn't have a word for it at the time, was actually a critique of heterosexism.

The National Front were totally demolished in the 1979 election and have never recovered since. Of course, this was partly because the Tories attracted the racist vote: but I am still convinced that the anti-fascist movement — in all its manifestations — really did have an impact. Without that mass movement, we might have had National Front MPs in the House of Commons for the last nine years.

1988

As it is, of course, we have had nine years of Thatcherism, and I must say it's hard to imagine how it could have been any worse.

Lines from Macbeth keep floating into my head:

> I think our country sinks beneath the yoke,
> It weeps, it bleeds, and each new day a gash
> Is added to her wounds.

It's really hard to fight back at the moment because we've had so many defeats and we're being attacked on so many fronts. I haven't been fighting the Alton Bill because I've been too preoccupied with Clause 28. I can't do much about the NHS because the Inner London Education Authority, which I work for, is about to be abolished.

It wouldn't be quite so bad if the mass media weren't giving such a perverse account of what's going on. The government's crimes — such as the execution of the IRA members in Gibraltar — are applauded, while local councils which try to put limited equal opportunities policies into practice are presented as sinister extremists. The way the press responds to anti-racist and anti-sexist initiatives reminds me of the warped mirror in Hans Andersen's 'Snow Queen':

> The loveliest landscapes reflected in this mirror looked like boiled spinach, and the handsomest persons appeared odious, or as if standing on their heads, their features being so distorted that their friends could never have recognised them.

The lives of lesbians and gay men, and our demands for equal rights, have certainly been served up as a plate of boiled spinach in the press, and Clause 28 is a direct outcome of this sinister right-wing plot. I, personally, have never felt so oppressed as a lesbian as I do at the moment. The increase in harassment and hostility is quite dramatic.

At the same time, I'm probably in a better position to resist anti-lesbianism than ever before. In 1978 I was a feminist who hadn't had much contact with the women's liberation movement, and a lesbian who didn't have any lesbian friends. Nowadays, I have a solid circle of lesbian feminist friends and a much wider network of contacts, gained through ten years involvement in various women's groups. Recently, working as a teacher in Hackney, my politics has found expression mainly in my job, since I have precious little energy left over for outside activities. However, Clause 28 has galvanised me, and thousands like me, back into action. Lesbians and gay men made visible strides in the 80s, and we aren't about to let our hardwon gains slip through our fingers.

Mrs Thatcher certainly seems to think, like Macbeth, that she bears a charmed life, and that none of woman born can harm her. But Macbeth got his come-uppance, and we can only trust that the Tories will too. They are not invincible, though they are certainly giving a good impression of it. But one of these days they'll go too far — perhaps it will be the Poll Tax, or the Education Act, or something we don't know about yet. Something will snap, and the people will rise up and cut off the tyrant's head.

I'm thirty-three now, and there are still lots of things I haven't sorted out in my life. I have a permanent conflict between my desire to write and my need to earn my living. These days I hardly ever write the music reviews and interviews which I did so much of between 1978 and 1982; I have decided, since time is short, to concentrate on my own creative writing. I only wish I was more prolific! It probably wouldn't be so bad if I didn't feel so committed to my work as a teacher, which tends to dominate my life. This problem of juggling time, energy and money will not be made any easier if I realise my other desire, to have a child in the not too distant future.

The thirteen-year-old Lucy would have been astounded if she had known what was going to become of me. The Christian teenager grew up and committed herself to other causes. But I'm just as much of an idealist as ever.

1982: GREENHAM COMMON

Rebecca Johnson

Non-violence — a feminist journey

"Greenham, and the whole nuclear issue, is a diversion for women".
The year was 1983. I had just served my second prison sentence for
refusing to be bound over to 'keep the peace' after British justice had
ruled that 44 women dancing on Cruise missile silos were breaching
Her Majesty's peace.

I had never before felt so strong and powerful as when we danced
on those silos or when 100 women sitting in the road managed to
turn back twice the number of police and a convoy of military
trucks. So it seemed paradoxical that shortly after being vilified in
the Press for being fey Tinkerbells and burly Lesbians we should be
informed in a feminist pamphlet that actually we weren't any more
feminist than the Women's Institute.*

I was raised by Christian pacifists, but feminism was the first
conscious political choice I can remember making, and it seemed to
involve rejecting feminine stereotypes, of which passivity was a
characteristic. In a way my story of the last 20 years has been a quest
to reconcile my passion for justice with an abhorrence of violence
and coercion.

Greenham is part of many women's stories now. There isn't a
definitive 'truth about Greenham', but only thousands of different
experiences made up of the reasons why each of us got involved in
the first place, and our hours, days or years there.

A brief summary. The camp was started on September 5th, 1981,
after a ten day walk from Wales by 40 women, three men and
assorted children, to focus on the proposed deployment of Cruise
missiles at Greenham Common near Newbury, Berkshire. Early the
following year, for practical rather than overtly feminist reasons, the
camp decided to become women-only. At the end of 1982 35,000
women encircled Greenham to 'Embrace the Base'. 6,000 stayed to

* *Breaching The Peace: a collection of radical feminist papers* (Onlywomen
Press, 1983)

close it with blockades the next day. During the following years camps were set up at gates all round the perimeter, and more and more women came to Greenham to live or to visit.

Many took nonviolent direct action: entering the base, cutting the fence, blockading and painting military equipment with messages. Many extended their actions to other bases and targets, including Parliament and porn shops, South Africa House and warships. Many, many women were sent to prison for sentences ranging from a day to a year, usually for refusing to pay fines.

The authorities first tried to close the women's peace camp by evicting the caravans and dumping boulders. We built villages of tents and benders (igloos of plastic and wood). 600 police and 50 bailiffs were sent in, and the road was widened at the main gate (our Yellow Gate — we named the different gates by colours). We slept in the open in Goretex bags. Eventually laws were changed to enable the local council to send bailiffs and police in every day — and sometimes every hour. So we adapted by becoming very mobile.

The evictions became routine; costly for the Council, irritating for us: never effective. We didn't prevent the actual siting of Cruise. We did succeed in stripping away the veils of secrecy, exposing the military blunders, the dangerous irrationality and incompetence of the deployments. On December 8th 1987 the INF (Intermediate Nuclear Forces) Treaty was signed, agreeing that NATO Cruise and Pershing missiles and Soviet SS20s would be scrapped. Already there are signs of military sabotage, with plans for compensatory deployment, substitution, modernisation... the euphemisms for further war preparations are nauseating but unsurprising.

Volumes could be written, but here I just want to look at how living at Greenham helped me to negotiate a truth between pacifist beliefs (instilled in me before I could speak) and the feminism that burst on my consciousness in the early 1970s.

I was less than convinced by the pacifism of my upbringing. When I heard how Gandhi had tested his powers of sexual restraint with young women I was bemused by the hypocrisy of those who venerated him. Then as a student I rejected pacifism completely. Allende had just been murdered, and Chilean refugees began to arrive, speaking of the tortures, killing and repression. If only Allende had armed the people...

I wanted to do something about the overwhelming poverty and injustice in the world. But the greed and control of the wealthy elite was so determined that they would assuredly point their guns at us if we turned the world upside down. Minimal bloodshed to achieve their overthrow would be inevitable. That or defeat. So went the argument, and it seemed to make sense. Pacifism was for the privileged, with plenty of time, but if you were really up against the wall then you'd have to be prepared to use violence.

At this time I was also discovering what being a woman meant. My pervading feelings were of confusion, insecurity and repressed fury. I suspect these were common emotions among young women of the early 70s.

This is not the time to write about the journeys I took hitchhiking and wandering through Europe, Africa and Asia, trying to sort out a reality from the confusion books had left me with. My travels forced me to re-examine theories of liberation by armed struggle. A change of men at the top might bring about a few useful reforms, but the new regime would consolidate its own system of repressive power, backed up by arms and revolutionary rhetoric to conceal the price paid by the people . . . and especially the women.

I worked for a while, then studied some more. On 9th August 1982, I turned up at the Women's Peace Camp on my motor bike. I came for a week's holiday and stayed for five years.

I arrived in the middle of a blazing row between two women about the use of drugs. This peace camp wasn't the sweetness and light of mawkish reporters, nor the suppression of pain and anger that had characterised my early immersion in pacifism. This nonviolence women were talking about wasn't the virtue of suffering; it was about taking power, *our* power — empowerment of ourselves, not power for use over someone else. The nonviolence that inspired me to stay at Greenham was the daily attempt to share resources, deal with our anger and conflict, intervene effectively against military stupidity, and learn to live with more care and love and reason. Cruise missiles, though a focus, were not an exclusive reason for being there.

"It's not nonviolent to abuse your body and mind with drugs." "It's not nonviolent to make rules which restrict women's right to choose for themselves." "When people fuck up their brains they lose the ability to choose." I can't remember if these were actually spoken during that row on my first day, but over the years there were to be many similar arguments: "Cutting the fence and painting are violent." "The fence itself is a manifestation of violence, like chains and shackles." "Our cuts are doors and windows." "Painting is creative. We're transforming the base." "Don't shout, it's violent." "It's not shouting that's violent; what causes me such pain is what's violent." "What about Black people in South Africa — they have to fight back, and we must support them." "We can't cope with mad women here." "Madness is a response to this violent world ... and besides, who's to say who is mad?"

Denial of the conflicts would have been the worst betrayal. In some ways I think the gloss at times applied by well-meaning supporters to hide Greenham's flaws was more harmful than the outright vilification heaped on us. How many times, sitting round the fire or at a meeting in some draughty community centre, would I hear a woman say sadly: "I do admire you, but I could never do all that at Greenham. I'm sure I'd lose my temper and hit a policeman. You're so *good*. I'd get too angry."

Despair would well up in me. That's exactly how I felt growing up: crushed by inadequacy in my attempts to suppress my anger because I knew it was wrong to show it. Greenham was never about angels or martyrs, superwomen or saints. Putting some women on a pedestal leaves the rest feeling paralysed by failure, which stops all of us getting together to create a just and peaceful future.

We live in the shadow of nuclear annihilation in a world already poisoned and wasted. So very few girls and women have not at some time experienced rape and male violence, and even those who have escaped so far tread warily, trained in their vulnerability from an early age. We look around at the greed, poverty, racism and desolation, and are expected to smile like Barbie dolls or pad out our designer shoulders and join in. No wonder in every woman there is an inferno of rage bubbling just beneath the surface.

I don't use the term passive resistance, because effective nonviolence is not compatible with passiveness. We've learned from Rosa Parkes, Martin Luther King and the civil rights struggles in the Southern USA; from early anarchists, suffragettes and the women of the Chipko movement in India, defending their forests. Feminist nonviolence acknowledges a spiritual heritage which includes early socialists, wise healers and witches. Above all, I don't think Greenham would have happened without the Women's Liberation Movement of the 70s and its insistence that the personal is political.

Nonviolence is not easy and may not get immediate results; but I feel much stronger, less afraid, more effective when I try. We've been accused of naivety, as though when we smile at soldiers we expect flowers to bloom from the guns — instead of which we are smashed to the ground and hurt. I don't expect instant conversion, for conditioning in violence goes very deep. Yet anyone, seeing large policemen hacking away at delicate coloured strands of web woven to close military gates, would begin to understand the power of the contradictions. Nonviolence undermines the authority and justifications for state coercion.

The web became symbolic of Greenham, with many associations — spiders, weaving women of ancient myth, the indomitability of repeated endeavour . . . For me the web also came to represent the power associated with nonviolence, very different from the pyramid hierarchies of armies and society, with leaders and rulers at the top and the toiling masses below. The strands from the centre show ways we can work: different, equal and all necessary. People acting autonomously, but with collective responsibility, are the linking threads. Our power and the strength and stability of the web (community/society) come from our interdependence and the connections between us. There is an inherent strength and balance in this structure, made up of individually fragile strands.

No leaders send us to be cudgelled in successive waves. We each choose, and if there aren't enough to blockade a base or take the fence down then the action doesn't happen. A liberation struggle by nonviolence doesn't require a leadership to control and distribute the arms and therefore the means of exercising force. It is more difficult to take over or corrupt people who refuse to abdicate responsibility for their own actions, as has been discovered by organisations as diverse as the CIA, the SWP and Wages for Housework.

My time at Greenham was one of constant questioning, growth and change. There's nothing like coming face to face with nuclear war preparations to cut through the crap compromises most of us lived with. Greenham provided the stimulation and opportunity for us to take our lives seriously. By using nonviolence to undermine the nuclear deployments, military and police, we tried also to develop nonviolent ways of living. For this it was crucial to recognise our own needs and gain confidence to challenge our oppression *as women*, asserting our right to peace *for ourselves*. For many, that was most difficult of all. Early appeals by Greenham enabled women to take the initial step 'for the children' or 'for the human race'. We were criticised for this in feminist pamphlets, but I think it was necessary because of women's conditioned perception of our own interests as selfish. Many who got involved with Greenham spoke of having felt daunted by 'Women's Lib', and Greenham seemed to provide a less threatening way in. However, that didn't mean women who joined the camps were exempt from attacks for being bad mothers, abandoning homes. We also came under hostile pressure from 'right on' men who became defensive/aggressive at being excluded from the most successful of the peace actions. It was all very well for feminists to campaign about abortion, but not to organise autonomously on such a central issue as peace! Meanwhile women were increasingly making the connections between rape, pornography and globally threatening nuclear pricks, challenging male violence across the board.

Since everyone at the peace camp was subject to anti-Lesbian abuse, Greenham paradoxically became somewhere relatively safe for women to explore their sexuality. Since the military spied on us constantly we had to decide to live openly, without subterfuge though not without fear. So we came out as Lesbians, changed stultifying jobs or broke free from violent husbands or boring relationships, to take fresh paths in our lives. Not all women, of course, for some had already confronted their choices, and others felt reasonably content; but the possibilities were raised. For some women the oppressive constraints of poverty, class, racism and prejudice limited the degree to which choice could be exercised. To effect change, nonviolence cannot be just a personal philosophy but must aim to intervene and change coercive political conditions too.

Greenham tapped into a consciousness among women not previously involved in either the women's movement or CND. I had wanted to do something about the nuclear threat, but CND in the early 1980s reminded me of factions and frustrations in student politics and without Greenham I doubt if I'd have got so involved. I'd probably still be tucked away, doing research or teaching Japanese politics in some provincial university!

It's not my intention to argue that all feminists should be nonviolent. But for me the development of feminist nonviolence offered a synthesis of means and ends that I had not found in theories of passive resistance or violent overthrow. In my practical experience it has been remarkably effective in breaking out of sterile confrontation and creating constructive alternatives. We haven't always succeeded in being nonviolent in thought, word and deed. In this society where assertiveness by women is easily condemned as aggression, there is a persistent tension between challenging violence, being perceived as violent and becoming violent; between

acknowledging and expressing anger and using it destructively. We
don't always get it right.

Nonviolence develops in action, as women's philosophy develops
from our own experience. Though many may disagree with what
I've written, I hope I've been true to my own journey from 1968 and
the route I chose by living at Greenham Common.

1984: THE MINERS' STRIKE

Jean Gittins

Looking back over the past 20 years, I find it almost impossible to pin-point any areas of my life that would be of the remotest interest to anybody else.

True, I could tell you what my parents' daughter was doing at such and such a time. How my ex-husband's wife faced up to such and such a crisis. There would always be the bit about my children's mother. But me, I don't think I really began to exist in my own right, until 1984.

Brought up in the "You make your bed, you lie on it" school of thought, I 'played house' from the age of 18, and until my divorce 30 years later I was always 'somebody's something'.

If this sounds as though I was dissatisfied with my life, I am giving the wrong impression. Because, whatever else I would change in my life, I am eternally grateful for parents who loved me, and for sons of whom I am intensely proud. But looking back, I see myself not as a whole person. I was unfulfilled, and I didn't even know it. It took the Miners' Strike in 1984 to let *ME* be.

Everything seemed to come together at about that time.

My mother died. And, God forgive me, that set me free from her image of what I should be. My husband and I finally put an end to a miserable marriage, and a hysterectomy was a symbolic ending to the first chapter of my life.

Over the years I had filled dozens of exercise books with the products of my fertile imagination. My parents tolerated what they regarded as my peculiarity, as long as it didn't interfere with 'real life'. They worried that an over-absorption with this 'rubbish' might detract from my ability to cope with the world.

As I grew up, I became more and more interested in current affairs and politics, but with three children to bring up and little or no help from my partner, my crusading energy was somewhat depleted. It's hard to give one's attention to worthy causes when the foremost worry in one's mind is finding the money to pay the electricity bill, before the power is cut off.

But in March 1984 I found a role in life that I had never imagined in my wildest dreams. They say there are turning points in everybody's life, that determine the course of their lives from that moment on. Well, March 1984 was the turning point in mine.

I can honestly say, that, from the beginning of my involvement in the movement which was later given a structure and called Women Against Pit Closures, my life has certainly been . . . different. Had I been born a man, I suppose I could have finished up working at the coal face. My father, his brothers, and both of my grandfathers had been miners. My two youngest sons were working at the same pit as their father, so I could not help being deeply affected by the prospect of a lengthy dispute.

The official starting date of the strike was March 6th, and the Ledston Luck Family Support Group received its first donation of food and money on the 25th.

I had gone to a meeting of the Workers Revolutionary Party Young Socialists at Blackpool. Such was my political naivety that I only knew of the Labour Party Young Socialists, and thought that it was they who had invited me to speak about a letter I had sent to the women of the Nottingham Coal Field.

During the conference there was a 'fringe' meeting of delegates from coal mining areas, and I was astounded to realise there was a feeling throughout the whole industry that this strike would not be resolved in a few weeks, and that the whole tenor on both sides would be different from anything we had known before.

When I asked to address the local NUM meeting, I was unsure of the reception I would receive. I knew many of the men on a personal basis, I had grown up with most of them, and as having a woman addressing them at all was somewhat of a novelty, I had to cope with a certain amount of lighthearted silliness and banter.

But over the next couple of weeks the men took messages back to their wives, and by the middle of April one of the first and most successful Support Groups was already in action.

Hardly had we got ourselves organised when I had to go into hospital for major surgery, and when I was finally well enough to get back into circulation everybody was managing the day to day arrangements without me. So I put what energy I had into more of the political and money-raising sphere.

I began to 'put our case' at public meetings, found myself on the platform with nationally-known personalities, and had my opinions actually listened to.

Is it over then, the struggle, have they won, and have we lost?
Is the final outcome what we should expect?
Shall we 'wake up' in a year or so and realise the cost
When it's much too late to save our self respect?

Should we 'give the ghost up gracefully' and slowly fade away?
Should we disappear like out of date machines?
Well, I tell you, if you feel like I do, 'That'll be the day' —
You can't make Dodos out of Human Beings.

(written on the day Carton Wood colliery was closed)

My poetic scribblings were collected, and published. I saw parts of
the country that I had only ever heard about before. That year gave
me confidence in myself that almost 50 years of life had been unable
to do.

Of course, I wasn't the only woman in our community to
experience such a metamorphosis. I really believe that, due to their
experiences during the Miners' Strike 1984–85, and the confidence
gained from facing and coping with difficulties that had hitherto
been outside their experience, countless women will never be quite
the same persons again.

Up to that time, I had known only home and family, now I
realised that these things do not exist in a vacuum, they rely for their
stability on a great many other factors.

THI SAY
Mam says that when we've won
She'll go an' buy a joint o' meat
We'll all 'ave pocket money
An' new shoes upon us feet

An' then she'll 'ave 'er 'air done
An' she'll buy mi dad a 'jar'
An' we'll 'ave trips ter't seaside
When we've paid t'road tax on t'car

Mi dad won't go an' picket
'Cos theer won't be no more strike
An' when we've got all straightened up
They're buying me a bike

This year we'll 'ave an 'oliday
We'll 'appen go to Spain
An' they'll bring our telly back
When dad's in work again

But I can't talk to our Uncle Charlie any more
It seems 'is legs 'ave gone all black
An' 'ee 'as got a sore
Mi Gran sez Uncle Charlie 'as betrayed 'is kith an' kin
'Ee's not a son of 'ers no more
Since 'ees been goin' in

Mi Grandad wishes 'ee could go an' picket with the rest
But 'ee dun't gerrabout much
'Cos 'ees got dust on 'is chest
'Is 'ead looks like blue marble
An' 'is face is ashen grey
But Gran sez 'ee were quite a Labour Fighter in 'is day

She sez that it were men like 'im
As fought for't NUM
An' we'd be daft to let 'em
Get us on us knees agen.

I realised that I had begun to exist in my own right when, instead of being introduced as " David's mother", I heard someone refer to my eldest boy as "Jean's son".

Perhaps the limits of my old existence were, to some degree, of my own making. Because, once I started to 'do my own thing', I coudn't have wished for a more loyal fan club than my own family.

They were so proud when I was invited to go to Trinidad in June 1987. Here I was — a Grandma, four years on supplementary benefit, no passport, never been in an aeroplane — flying off to read my poetry as a guest of the Oil Workers' Trade Union at the First Caribbean Book Fair and Festival.

So, you see, just at an age when I should be looking forward serenely to my rocking-chair and shawl, I seem to be experiencing a sort of delayed adolescence.

ONE WOMANS LIBERATION
I'm a fifty year old adolescent,
I'm a Grandma who's never quite grown.
All the people I loved, and who knew who I was
Have passed over, and left me alone.

I was Daddie's girl when I was little
And, for thirty years, I was 'The Wife'.
I knew just who I was, when I was someone's Mum
But now, I'm in control of my life.

Now I know why a songbird still stays on its perch
When an open cage door sets it free
Because, freedom's a beautiful concept to hold
But, it's scaring the knickers off me.

So . . . where does all this leave Jean Gittins? Well, for a start, I am once again known by my maiden name. I always felt 'robbed' having to discard it anyway.

I live alone, and often I am lonely. Sometimes the inevitability of my old life seems comfortably 'safe'. But, knowing what I now know, there is no way that I could go back to what I was before.

Perhaps, once I have worked out what I want to be "when I grow up", I'll be half-way there.

Like Mr Micawber, I am waiting for something to turn up. I only hope that I recognise it when it does.

Jean Gittins is now writing her memories of a Wartime childhood for publication.

1968–88: RIVERS OF BLOOD

Sona Osman

1968: I remember that year well.

Imagine if you can a brown-skinned little girl of four foot plus,
with dark brown shoulder length hair and brown eyes. I was eight
years old, and used to wear red Alice bands and eat loads of
sweets — hence my present bad teeth.

My parents had been married for two years and I was their only
child. My father is Pakistani, a Muslim from Lahore who came to
the UK after the religious massacres following Partition. My
mother is Finnish. She had fallen in love with a man whom her
father would not let her marry, so she left home to come here.

My parents met at a YMCA dance, and very soon after she
became pregnant with me. The three of us lived in this two-
bedroomed flat in a tenement block in South Brixton. Imagine
that, living in Brixton before the yuppies moved in and took
over!

In lots of ways my parents were quite extraordinary. (I am sure
we all feel that way about our own parents.) Mine were acutely
aware of the important and historic times we live, and lived,
in.

My father was anti-British — he had an anti-imperialist
perspective. He had lost everything through Partition and
become a stranger in a foreign land. He put up with a load of
heavy stuff: racist attacks both in the street and in his car, bricks
thrown through our windows. Although he was intelligent my
father would always be shunted into low-grade jobs.

He realised the importance of education, and made sure I
joined the local library when I was about five. He would take me
round the London museums and art galleries and he was
particularly fond of the British Museum. In his favourite
Egyptian, Indian and Islamic rooms he would point out to me the
objects that the British had stolen from their colonies.

My mother also realised the importance of education —
particularly the importance for foreigners of speaking with a

'good' accent. She would hit me whenever I asked for "Bread and 'utter, please", in a South London voice.

Unfortunately neither of my parents were very good at nurturing. They had a lot on their plate. Money was very tight and both of them worked so hard.

We did not have many mod cons — a black and white television and an ancient vacuum cleaner. I don't think I realised then how hard my mother used to work. She would get up first, prepare breakfast for us all, get me ready for school and then go off to her job as a secretary at the National Coal Board. At 6pm she would collect me from a friend's house, cook a full evening meal, and then — after all that — start the housework, and wash our clothes in the bath tub.

Toward the end of 1968 my Auntie Sadia, a diagnosed schizophrenic, came to live with us. Auntie Sadia would wear wonderful coloured saris and sit in the same place in the flat all day. She was not capable of doing much so she became a new burden for my mother. I saw my parent's relationship begin to break down.

1968: I remember Enoch Powell's "Rivers of Blood" speech. I felt so scared. What was going to happen to us? Were we going to be repatriated? If so, where?

I remember my parents taking me to the Canadian High Commission. They were going to get me out to safety even if they had to stay behind themselves.

We used to read *The News of the World*, and I cut out a photograph of National Health Service workers, from doctors to cleaners. Every Monday morning at school you were meant to show the class something interesting you'd seen over the weekend. The others took in leaves and flowers — I took my photo. It was pinned up on the notice board in pride of place.

I wrote a piece about what Enoch Powell had said, and what that meant. All these Black people would be sent home, and who would look after the poor sick English people? My teacher must have thought I was crazy.

1968: I remember when Martin Luther King was assassinated. My father cried.

1968: I remember when there was the big anti-Vietnam War demonstration outside the American Embassy. My father was there. My mother and I watched the fights between police officers and demonstrators on the television.

Ten years seem to have passed by.

1978: My parents got divorced in 1976. They don't speak to each other any more.

In 1978, when I was 18, I thought I should make the effort and get in touch with my father. We met a few times, but it was hopeless.

I was miserable being a teenager, and he had always said I could go to him if I had a problem. So I did. His answer to my problems was an arranged marriage! I was to stop wearing Western clothes and being independent. My father even had someone in mind ...

I could not believe it. Here was someone who had taught me, brought me up to be independent — now he was expecting me to change radically into something, someone I was not. We parted company after that row.

1978: I passed two of my three 'A' Levels. I was very disappointed to fail in English, and slogged my guts out to get three passes the next January, waking at 6am to study before school, and revising afterwards from 4pm until late.

1978: The year I lost my virginity — in a very crass way. I had become aware of my sexuality, but if that was being heterosexual, forget it. I started to read *Spare Rib*, and become aware of feminism.

There's not much to add about 1978. It was not a good year for me. It was a year of crossroads — changing from a child into a woman.

1988: In the years since 1978 I have done so much. I took a degree in French and History at Keele University, lived in France for 18 months (1978–9), helped set up a women's refuge in Stoke-on-Trent; worked at *Spare Rib* magazine (1982–4), for a housing co-operative (1984), and as an outdoor clerk for a firm of solicitors (1984).

Then I was involved in a car accident, and incapacitated. I became suicidal during my time in bed, and it forced me to think. I realised I had not learned how to deal with the incredible anger I felt rising up in me.

Through therapy, I gained confidence to move from my casual

jobs to a law course and, with support from friends, to qualify as a barrister in 1986.

1988: Being a barrister. After doing pupillage and working in an advice centre in Brixton, I've realised it's no good being a barrister if you are not a "tenant", with a permanent place in chambers. I am at another crossroads in my life. Will I be taken as a barrister? Maybe I am too threatening? A colleague (male, white, middle-class) told me so . . .

I enjoy the job, I identify a lot with my clients. Most of them are working class, and I come from a working-class background so I have real-life experience of what they are up against.

Most of today I was in a magistrates' court, trying to get bail for two brothers. One was up on a charge of deception, and when police officers tried to arrest him his brothers had come to his aid. This man had been severely beaten up by the police — his left hand was swollen, and looked as if bones were broken. It felt so good to have got all the family unconditional bail.

1988: Another crossroads.

I suppose being a lawyer means that I am aware of what is going on in Britain today. The Housing Bill, which will be an Act by the time this is in print, will mean the end of Council housing. The Act is supposed to give tenants the right to vote between the Local Authority or a private landlord, but the thing is that if tenants do not fill in their ballot, they will effectively be taken to vote for the private owner. The original tenancy agreement's terms and conditions will mean nothing any more; the tenant will have to negotiate again with the new landlord, who of course will put the rent up and decrease the services provided.

I never thought I would advise people to buy their property if they have the means . . .

By the time this article is published, Clause 28 will be in power. God knows what that means as to what can be published? Said? Done?

By the time this article is published, we shall have seen how the Social Security changes have affected the poor.

By the time this article is published, the Immigration Bill will have become an Act, taking away even more rights from Black people wishing to come into this country. It's quite ironic when I think about Enoch Powell's "Rivers of Blood" speech ... He knew how the writing on the wall would be written.

OLD LAGS

What makes some people stay in a movement while others move on? When I was choosing writers for this book, that question was first in my mind.

What these life stories show is that there's *no answer*. The pattern here goes like a row of dominoes: optimist followed by pessimist, traveller by homelover, organiser turned writer by writer turned organiser.

Sue O'Sullivan has been in the Women's Liberation Movement for 19 years, Lynne Harne for 17. Both started as unaligned socialists, both have become lesbians within the movement — and their articles disagree on just about everything else.

Sue Cooper's moved from job to job, place to place and skill to skill since she started out as a teenage feminist in 1970; Alice Simpson helped found the Laurieston Hall commune in Kirkcudbrightshire in 1972 and has lived and worked there ever since.

Lee Comer was one of the founding mothers of British women's liberation. She put ideas in print when there was almost nothing for us to read. Now, when a paper mountain of publishing looks like the movement's most lasting monument, she works as a council women's officer. Like many of the old suffragettes she has taken her feminism to the town hall, and the note of questioning on which she ends is typical of the feminist conversation.

Today Sue O'Sullivan works in a feminist publishing collective. Click. The dominoes come full circle.

FROM 1969

Sue O'Sullivan

1968: The Year Before Year One

I had a baby in 1968, and was deeply shocked by the experience of giving birth. I was 27 years old, married since I was 22, a dancer (but I didn't aim for a career). Suddenly after something like 30 hours of labour, there I was with a damaged, bleeding, aching cunt, a flabby stretch marked stomach, hard milky breasts, and a shell shocked 9½lb baby boy beside me. Through the next few months I would suddenly be seized by unreality — who was I, who was the baby, or his father?

I first came to this country in 1961, and then came back to be with the young man I'd fallen in love with; a few months after my return we were married, like many of my friends, soon after college graduation. You finished with one institution and entered another.

We spent two years in New York City, where, through a series of serendipitous coincidences, John met up with Students for a Democratic Society (SDS) and was invited onto the editorial board of 'Studies on the Left'. Then we returned to London in 1967, me pregnant. (It seemed like a good idea, although my teenage ideal of five or six kids had waned over the years.)

Nationalities were not the only differences between John and me. His family took the *Daily Worker* and lived in debt, mine were Quaker pacifists and middle class. His parents sniped at each other across their Communist/Labour Party divide, my parents never fought with each other and belonged to the United World Federalists.

1968, a political marker in the history books and in many other people's lives, was for me a lead-up year — of demonstrations in Grosvenor Square where I stuck to the side because of my pregnancy, of Martin Luther King's assassination, of student uprisings which I was moved by, but outside of. I was sometimes on my own with the baby in a part of London where I knew no one, while my husband was off working and taking part in meetings and demonstrations.

(I'm alone with the baby asleep in his little room. I'm watching our rented black and white TV — a television film of Dracula is on and I'm terrified, convinced that by getting sucked into the story I've made it possible for a vampire to have access to me and the baby. I break open the garlic, making a circle of cloves around the cot. In the bedroom I place more garlic on my pillow and get out my grandmother's gold cross which I clutch. Hours later I drift into sleep.)

Our little family spent the summer of '68 in a sweaty, noisy New York tenement flat, seeing SDS friends; I heard about women's liberation but it didn't strike a chord.

Home in London, isolation struck again, bringing with it doubts and uncertainties. It was my husband who told me about a small group of women, mainly Americans, who were meeting in Tufnell Park. Perhaps I should go? Did I finally ring someone or did one of the women get in touch with me? I can't remember; but early in 1969 I found myself sitting somewhat self-consciously in a living room, talking with other women about isolation, feelings of inadequacy, ambivalences towards motherhood, and hearing sympathetic voices confirming, identifying and expanding. I know, even if I can no longer touch its electricity, that I left with a wonderful feeling, a spinning head and a churning stomach.

I didn't rush out into the night with the course of a new life shaking the old. I didn't fling open the door at home to announce changes to be made there. My relationship was a good one, I neither did all the housework, nor did my husband oppress me physically or emotionally. At that point it was a shaded shift in my perception of the world. I suddenly saw myself, my marriage and motherhood, in a critical light. I saw without fully articulating it that my (and many other women's) feelings of inadequacy, guilt, loneliness sprang in good part simply from being a woman. It was exhilarating and scary. Women's isolation from each other, their emotional and physical work on behalf of others, helped perpetuate the rotten society we lived in. These may seem like clichés now — they certainly didn't then.

But where did a good marriage fit into the oppressive nature of marriage as an institution? I sensed huge personal contradictions to come, and was anxious even as I lunged forward. Would women's liberation demand changes of me and my marriage which I didn't want or couldn't take on? The implications of the liberation movement were vast and yet for our particular, mainly white, western urban variety, so incredibly personalised. For many women involvement in the movement relatively quickly provided the courage to exit from miserable oppressive relationships with men or prolonged domestic battles. What took *me* literally years to get a grasp of was my own level of unease at the separate compartments I had to maintain in my life. My pleasure at being with women — talking, planning, eating, organising, writing, studying — a togetherness which was based initially on a deep loathing of the assumptions and abuses of male power and the framework of 'naturalness' it resided in — jarred with the individualised equality my husband and I enjoyed. The violence and 'otherness' of the dominant (and different) worlds of men which produced such rage in me insinuated itself into my privatised nuclear family, where I was the only woman.

1969–78: A Calendar of Action

From the few initial small, mainly localised, small groups, within a year there had grown a movement of thousands of women. In London the Women's Liberation Workshop brought together the mushrooming groups, primarily through the weekly newsletter which I took from the first copy in 1969 till the last in 1985.

Being part of one group threw up possibilities (or demands) for other projects. There was so much to do and everything appeared to be linked. I can no longer separate out the perfect chronology of events which I took part in, when I think of the me who lived through the last 20 years. But I was active on some level throughout that time.

Spring 1969: My first meeting at Tufnell Park; Women's Workshops at Essex University Festival of Revolution; Women's Liberation attend the big equal pay rally in Trafalgar square after leafletting the Underground from 5.30am; Sticker campaign against negative images of women, stickers huge and homemade and very difficult to slap on quickly; Tufnell Park group goes to Ideal Home Exhibition with questionnaire and statement about manipulation by advertisers; Group starts making a short film, 'Woman, Are You Happy With Your Life?'

Autumn 1969: First regular get-togethers of London women's liberation, discuss whether we can 'use' the media to get our message across. Dominant opinion is that the media will distort whatever we have to say and we should spurn them, developing alternative modes of communication. Some women disagree and do go on TV and radio. First Miss World protest: *Mis-Fit Refuses to Conform, Mis-Conception Demands Free Abortion for all Women, Mis-Placed demands a Chance to Get Out of the House.*

Early 1970: Meetings to work out a statement of aims and purpose for the Women's Liberation Workshop, the umbrella organisation for small groups and individual women in London; First Women's Liberation conference at Ruskin College — Men attend, are involved in making a film of the event and run the creche. I go with John and Tom who is almost two years old. I'm very pregnant and give birth to second son about ten days later.

Summer 1970: Write article on my post-natal depression for *Shrew*, the magazine rotated between groups in the Workshop. This issue produced by women centred in a communal house in Grosvenor Avenue, Islington, some of whom go on to produce the short-lived, libertarian and lively *Women's Newspaper*; Dialectics of Revolution at the Round House — Women take to stage to protest men totally dominating the event.

1969/70: A group in North London leaflets against the Vietnam War every week, plays volley ball on Hampstead Heath with the Vietcong flag flying on the net pole, sets up Hole in the Wall community centre in a few rooms above a shop near where I live. We have mixed meetings (men and women) to discuss childcare. Rudi and Gretchen Dutschke are living in London and join meetings, we read translations of German SDS' papers, particularly one by Helke Sanders on men, childcare and women.

Autumn 1970: Second Miss World protest — five women arrested, four go on to stand trial, lots of media coverage, full page in the *Observer*. **Winter:** London open meetings to formulate Demands of the WLM in time for the first big International Women's Day march in London. Arguments about nature of transitional demands, histories of left groups etc, but four demands decided on — Equal Pay Now, Equal Education and Opportunities, Free Contraception and Abortion on Demand, Free 24-hour Nurseries.

March 8th 1971: Large march, snowing, hundreds of placards with the demands, women's street theatre, leaflets, big media impact. Women's Liberation Workshop shoots up to over 80 groups in a year.

From 1971: Talks to secondary school girls and boys, and all sorts of groups both sympathetic and antagonistic.

Autumn 1971: National women's liberation conference at Skegness. International Socialists and miners holding conferences at the same time and holiday camp puts on strip show. The WL conference is primarily organised by two Maoist sectarian groups but it backfires for them — women chase men off the stage, lesbians hitherto more or less invisible raise hell and demand a voice.

1972: Study groups for women — psychoanalytic Family Study group, then a number of Marxist study groups; I join Women in Ireland group, *Red Rag* starts up, and *Spare Rib* the following year. I join *Red Rag* after the first issue which was produced by Communist Party women; Community organising. I know women setting up Essex Road Women's Centre in shop front underneath a feminist's flat (now Cheer's Wine Bar).

A number of us in Camden and Islington decide to set up different, grass roots women's centre on site in Maiden Lane with tenants' association, old age pensioners, free school, and first incarnation of Greek Theatro Technis. Leaflet local estates, set up pregnancy testing service, run jumble sales. Good links with the tenants but limited success in drawing other local women in to rather depressing collection of old, run down railway buildings. Free school kids hate us and destroy our tiny room repeatedly.

Still, from about 1972 until 1974/5 all sorts of things appeared possible. Study and the beginnings of analysis felt utterly connected to the 'doing' of women's liberation, necessary to what seemed more and more likely to be a long hard slog. Community-based organising around birth control, childcare and consciousness-raising meant that the personal was still political, that women's subjective experiences were still central to the action.

Somewhere along the line, "small groups" became "consciousness-raising groups", and still later "women's liberation" became "feminism". Feminism has outlasted women's liberation, perhaps because it is the easiest label to apply individually. Feminists can fit, even if uncomfortably, into board rooms and academia. Feminism doesn't suggest a political movement.

Sisterhood was powerful — for some. Those who defined it, felt it while caught in their own movements of struggle with men and society. It's hard for me to grab hold of the 'we' in this. I don't want to deny or disown my part. But for me and others, there was a recognition that all was not right in the women's liberation movement which led us in the early 70s to Marxist study groups in an effort to understand class divides.

I was profoundly affected by Mao's notion of contradicton. It spoke to me on a gut level, explaining not only the differences so painfully surfacing between women, but also those submerged in individuals. It seemed to me that if women's liberation could speak to the contradictions which existed in society between class, race and gender as well as those that tussled in our own psyches and heads, then we just might be able to develop a politics which would hew out paths of radical resolution. Ideological struggle came to the forefront of my political vision in the 70s and I still see it, undoubtedly differently, as a key to political change.

But there's no doubt that for all the talk, many of us white, middle-class women just didn't grab hold of the most basic bit of the conversation and taste it. We could explain difference, acknowledge it, but continuously round the corner was the need to move out of the centre of our self-defined circle, to question the circle's parameters. Even the idea that room should be made in it for others missed the point: other women needed to set their own agendas, had their own specific, complex histories.

But I am glad that I was part of that particular historical moment almost twenty years ago. I think of other white middle-class women when I say that, who avoided or rejected feminism, *not* because of its very real problems in relation to the complexities of race, class, sexuality and age, but because of its radical challenge to men. The inadequacies of the early movement may ironically have been part of its life spring as well. The anger of women who were excluded or absent may eventually be seen as part of a longer process of definition and political agency. Nothing is inevitable — neither success or failure.

1974: I go to China on a Society for Anglo–Chinese Understanding tour and come back full of excitement for the Cultural Revolution. Become active in SACU, working with men for the first time in five years. Particularly keen on enabling more working-class people to go to China, and one workers' tour includes members of Camden Tenants' Association. For a year I am part of a Marxist study group with four older local working-class people, and two middle-class women. A spin-off from my Chinese experience is the name I use now, inspired by 'liberation names' to replace my husband's surname.

1974: Start teaching in Holloway Prison — first dance, then women's health and women's studies. From then on, I remain focussed on women's health issues in one way or another, and teach at Holloway for the next ten years.

1972–1978: Attend every national and London Women's Liberation conference, always riveted, sometimes confused, adrenalin flowing. Conferences seem like vast yearly consciousness-raising exercises around specific issues — wages for housework, lesbianism, internationalism and imperialism, racism, battered women, rape, abortion — and increasingly around the different tendencies defining themselves within feminism. There is no concept of different *feminisms* yet and it is as if we are all struggling over a patch of contested ground.

1976: Women's liberation movement spins off a subsidiary women's health movement, starting early 70s with small groups learning vaginal self-examination. Now conferences to share information, devise alternative health projects, organise campaigns to fight within the NHS, and increasingly to defend it against hospital closures. **Summer:** Join Women Against Racism and Fascism.

1978: Take a Health Education Diploma at South Bank Poly.

1979: I begin a five-year stint on the *Spare Rib* collective, the first time I've been involved in a journal since leaving *Red Rag* in 1976. Some of the most stressful, chaotic, painful times I've ever been through, but I fall in love with the process of putting a magazine together. Wake up in the morning with *SR* and go to bed at night with it. All the issues and projects I've been part of in one way or another show up in the magazine. And I feel driven, sometimes against my will, sometimes late in the day, to say what I see even if my heart sinks and my stomach heaves as I say it.

1978–88: Growing Up Backwards

By 1978 the first batches of my friends were dropping away from the women's liberation movement but not from feminism, either worn out with the bickering, fed up with meetings, explaining things again and again, alienated by one or another groupings of different women who were appearing all over the place, or perhaps wanting to move on to other time-consuming work. Or simply to fall away and live a quiet life. A significant number of women were getting jobs in which they could be, or fight to be, feminists — in education, trade unions, women's centres. Some, having gained new confidence through feminism were deciding to train for new careers or entering previously male-dominated areas of work.

I don't understand the generation gap. I maintain peer group friends but get to know much younger women. Throughout the 70s I feel more and more able: more energy, skills, ideas. More confidence. It's the WLM which enables me — why should I want to leave that?

Growing up backwards. I can try things out — teaching in Holloway Prison, going for a diploma in health education. I never had a career to be thwarted in, so everything I learn and discover through feminism is an awakening, a new possibility, a plus in life.

By 1979 there were a lot more visible lesbians around, and a not insignificant number of heterosexual women, particularly those who had been inside the movement for a while, felt silenced and criticised. Classic manifestations occurred when I was working on *Spare Rib* at that time. The magazine was accused of excluding heterosexual women's lives and experiences, yet even a casual adding up of 'lesbian' material in the magazine revealed how little space it was actually allotted. It was lesbianism in itself which created an uncomfortable challenge.

Myself, I'd been fantasising about lesbianism for a long time, but was convinced that it wouldn't happen to me. I had seen some friends come out, and read all the lesbian pamphlets and newspapers from the States I could get my hands on. I was angered and attracted by a lot of it. Any woman can? Sure. As far as I could see a lot of the American literature featured pictures or drawings of young white, slim, free women, who seemed to spend a lot of time with their long straight, clean hair blowing romantically in the wind. Where were the images of women as objects of lesbian desire who had stretch marks, flabby tummies, little kids demanding crisps, or even male partners they loved and hadn't simply been enduring until their repressed lesbianism was allowed to flower?

Being with women was always a pleasure to me, but any discussion about making a political choice to be a lesbian left me cold. I supported lesbian demands within the women's liberation movement but not because I saw myself there. Now it's not surprising to me that I fell madly in love with a woman completely outside of feminism who had been a lesbian since she was thirteen and was part of a much older lesbian subculture. Making love with a woman was a revelation to me; my fantasies had been all about being swept off my feet and being made love to. What I discovered were the acute and breathtaking pleasures of making love to a woman.

> I fall madly in love with younger women. I play 'mother' when I've refused to 'mother' my own children in traditional terms. I want passionate sex, fun and intensity. I fall for the girls who I think offer that and find out they need to be looked after. I walk around dreaming of my object of desire, I suffer through violence and dramas, acting 'grown up' but not getting out — I get something from it. I return regularly each week to the ongoing domestic life of my family — a refuge which drives me nuts. My kids make me mad. I'm the screaming witch bitch there. Back to my lover who manipulates and demands, and I service.

All along my ambivalence about motherhood continued. I rarely found another woman who shared the frightening rages and frustrations which I felt with my little boys. I identified more with non-feminist women who went to pieces over nothing than my sisters who had children in the movement, who always seemed more together about things than I did. I knew that even if the 'problem' was social, it expressed itself through something deeply disturbing and unresolved in myself.

Into the 80s — two more relationships, still living with husband and kids. When my third relationship founders, on the surface because of her infidelity, I go to pieces, sobbing in the toilet at *Spare Rib*, curled up in a ball on the floor at home.
"What's the matter, Mummy?"
I'm propelled into moving out of my domestic set up. The disjunction between the parts of my life, the constraints of playing out relationships only on my lovers' home ground, are impossible. I'm out into a temporary, short-life flat, on my own for the first time in my life, still howling in agony over my relationship. But there's a silver lining. I'm in love with my tiny place. I luxuriate in being alone. I talk to myself. I eat in bed.
And continue regular visits to my kids and husband.

My husband never joined a men's group or knew anything about them. His political and personal integrity, and a kind of stoic attitude to life, meant that he had the ability to empathise with my changes while expressing his own sorrow. He chose to be the mainstay in the children's lives. He scrubbed and cooked and cleaned and took them to the One O'Clock Club, the zoo, cinema and plays; he liaised with the schools, spoke to the teachers, took them juice in the night. Only a mother's role — as many women know full well — but one I didn't want, couldn't do with any grace. One which filled me with resentment. He isn't a saint, but if he hadn't been who he is, could I have left my young children, with pain but little guilt? And would I still be welcomed back, the lesbian who lives alone, to visit and do their washing and mine in their machine?

*

(I'm standing in a single changing room in a lingerie shop in Manhattan, 18 years old, trying on bras, flat-chested and cornered. The sales woman whips open the curtain and seeing me in a 36AA bra which still crumples, tells me she has the answer. Leaves and reappears with a padded construction, stays for the trying on and crows with approval once it's hooked into place. I'm caught, buy it and wear it back to college, sweating and near tears. I recount my shopping trial to my three room mates. I don't want a bra. I wish I had bigger breasts but this is no solution. It's not me. If a boy thinks I have bigger tits with my clothes on, how will he react when he sees (or feels) the truth. My roommates commiserate and one suggests we get rid of it then and there. She gets out the scissors and with increasing

wildness and laughter we proceed to snip it into strips, bits, ripping
out the foam rubber. Finally we burn the remains in a waste paper
basket. A stink but satisfying. It's 1959. Who's heard of a bra
burner?)

I can't remember when I stopped wearing a bra of any kind, but
I'm sure it was post women's liberation. I'd always been interested in
clothes and fashion since about age 14, but nothing that took a lot of
time and effort — a mild bohemianism. After having a second baby
I felt overcome with personal sluttishness. A lot of the time I wore an
old army jacket, jeans or trousers, and big sweaters because it was
easier to breast feed. I pulled my long hair back with a rubber band
because it was so often in need of washing. I didn't have the time or
the wish to 'look good' and it was a relief that within the women's
liberation movement no one expected you to be trying.

The overwhelmingly heterosexual movement also incorporated a
critique of fashion. Women wanted to be accepted as they were, they
wanted to dress for themselves, not to attract men. The fashion
business was there to feed upon women's insecurities, declaring last
season's fashions obsolete and making a fortune in the process. Well
fuck that. We would wear what we wanted, which for many women
then was loose, trousered, functional, recycled or cheap. To talk
about clothing or make-up as creative expressions, as some
feminists continued to do, struck most of us as a poor justification. I
remember one friend in a fury when another feminist appeared at a
mixed party with a low cut dress on. I don't believe she was envious
or puritanical in her reaction — she saw it as a betrayal of all we'd
said.

My interest in clothes resurfaced at about the time my children
were both in school, but it wasn't until I started having sexual
relationships with women that reformism really hit. Dressing up in a
way that you knew another woman found attractive didn't feel the
same as within the confines of heterosexuality. All the clothing and
style signals I now experienced as if in an unidentical twin world, a
subculture of opposition. Dressing up before could have been
interpreted as for me, which spoiled the pleasure. Dressing up for
myself and for other women's eyes was delightful, sometimes wicked
and always pleasurable.

In 1985 I joined the newly opened London Lesbian and Gay
Centre, and soon found myself in the midst of an almighty row
about whether gay and lesbian sado-masochist groups could meet

in the centre. After much discussion, the small group of lesbians came down in favour. Thinking through the storm that followed brought me to a place of relative certainty which I don't think I'd ever felt about any decision before.

Between feminists it's still horrible to think of women hating each other, not speaking. Hating me, me hating them. It's hard to acknowledge my own anger. But my lesbianism has been the thing that's finally given me the courage I wasn't sure I had. I can still tremble, but I'm much more able to speak out troubling and unpopular things if I believe they should be heard. My lesbianism has made me less fearful of being disliked by others, including other lesbians.

My Quaker background has sometimes led me into a mediator position. That way I'm in less danger of personal rejection, of course. But I'm also enabled to see the changes in the women's liberation movement without feeling pushed outside.

In 1984 I left the *Spare Rib* collective, wanting to stay forever but tired out. Two years later I came back, not as part of the collective, to co-ordinate a monthly health page which I packed in this spring, tired out again. In the meanwhile I took up an invitation from the quarterly *Feminist Review* collective in 1985, amazed and secretly flattered to be asked, as I don't see myself as an academic. In 1986 I started work at Sheba Feminist Publishers, and am still there now.

A small racially-mixed collective — prioritising writing by Black, working-class or lesbian women, and first-time writers — we manage to sort out most of our personal problems in a way which doesn't totally take over our publishing work. After all the mixed-up bitterness between women on *Spare Rib*, after its well-intentioned but ultimately flawed attempts at creating a racially-mixed collective, I was still left with the knowledge that I found working in all-white collectives limited. I do work in other groups with all white women, but see it as a defeat, if only a temporary one.

The women I've worked with, been friends or lovers with, cut across the decades from '68 to '88. I find it amusing and beyond my experience when I hear women of my age, dedicated feminists, declare themselves outside of the movement or excluded from it. I don't see myself as some sort of wiser elder mother. I see myself as learning, swimming with more resilience and fewer illusions. I work with younger women often — I don't deny our age differences but frankly they're not that important. I work primarily with lesbians —

that, whatever our age, does seem to give us something in common. We're all intrigued and in love with the possibility of passion between women and, in the present climate of Section 28 of the Local Government Act which seeks to silence homosexuality and make it more unacceptable than ever, with maintaining our courage and will to fight.

I identify with the oppression of all women; for me lesbianism is not necessarily political. But living in this society as a lesbian, while it has shot me up to the stars, has grounded my sensibilities firmly. I'm unwilling to waste time by keeping my mouth shut when I know what I think. And as long as I have something I'm eager to say, then I'll stick around with other women in feminist collectives and projects and hopefully live to see a popular resurgence of resistance to the conservatism of the 80s.

Nothing stays the same. The specific historical moment which gave rise to the WLM has passed, but the time for feminism continues. The underlying causes remain, although they may be subject to shifts and changes. I've chosen to ride with subsequent waves, because this movement is where I still want to be, where I experience extremes of pleasure, passion, possibility and a collective identity with women. Sometimes it comes apart and seems lost, but I don't much fancy any other alternative.

The WLM was the beginning of something I'd lived without before. I developed myself in it, found my place in a foreign country through it, became a lesbian through it, separated from my roles as wife and mother, understood and was part of a politics which spoke to me, of me, about others, to others, about others and me. I feel lucky to have been where I was, who I was in the late 60s. I can see its flaws, but I could never wish the movement had passed me by.

FROM 1971: REINVENTING THE WHEEL

Lynne Harne

In 1968 I had not heard of the Women's Liberation Movement. Like many women from a lower-middle-class small town background I was looking for some kind of identity which seemed elusive. I had dropped out after 'A' levels for two years and defined myself as a hippy, taking soft drugs and LSD, and trying to get some kicks out of the sexual revolution. I had no idea who I was, where I was going or what I wanted to do. All I knew was that I rejected my mother's values and what she wanted me to be, *ie* educated but married to an educated man and bringing up his children.

Life seemed very meaningless, I spent a lot of my time with men, either sleeping with them or hanging around them, for the most part silently. I was very much taken in by the ideology of sexual liberation and spent a lot of time pursuing this goal. I constantly felt humiliated by my sexual encounters and never got any pleasure from them, but I believed that *there was something wrong with me*, and if only I could get it right I would find 'fulfilment'. I soon discovered that the equality that women were supposed to get from the sexual revolution was a myth. Men still regarded women who slept around as whores or an easy lay, although for a long time I thought this was just my own paranoia. All women were just chicks or birds to them, there to be screwed.

By summer '68 I was finishing my first year of college and enjoyed studying, but my main aim was still to have a boyfriend and be 'way out'. I had just about heard of the Vietnam War and the civil rights movement in the States, largely through rock music, and had attended a few political demonstrations. I had also heard of the French student uprisings and got involved in the college action of liberating student files, and refusing to take our first year exams. None of this however felt much to do with me. I was just following the tide of male youth, who were rejecting things that women had never had anyway. Life continued to feel meaningless and my few encounters with male lefties, (I never met any women on the left) did not convince me that political action was the way forward. The most political books I ever read were by RD Laing and Timothy Leary; I attended a lot of rock concerts starring people like Jimmy Hendrix and Bob Dylan singing blatant messages of objectification of women. The few female rock heroes, like Janice Joplin, mainly sang about being rejected by men. I had no means accessible to me of analysing these messages, and looking back it seems that I internalised them.

In 1970 I only got a second class degree, mainly from being stoned out of my head when taking the final exams. I was incredibly disappointed and felt even more of a failure. Buddhist enlightenment (*ie* self-obliteration) seemed the only way forward. I had made no plans for what to do on leaving college, the options for a woman social science graduate being mainly teaching or social work. I didn't feel able to do either, and anyway within the hippy counterculture to pursue any career was an anathema. I set off with my live-in boyfriend to India, to find enlightenment on £40. On arriving in India, however, I experienced my first encounters since a small child with real poverty, and a class and caste system that controlled people through religion. Overnight I became an instinctive Marxist, and felt incredible ashamed of the counterculture of which I had been a part, and of the hippies in India who represented an imperialist decadent West. I also found after being in India a few weeks that I was pregnant. The birth control pill, which had been heralded as the means by which women were to achieve the fruits of the sexual revolution, had failed me. I had no means of getting back to England quickly and by the time I managed to leave I was over four months pregnant and had already decided I might as well have the child — what else was there for women?

After a job working for the DHSS, where I was sacked for being pregnant, I sat in my one-room bedsit on Social Security and saw the first women's liberation march on the telly. The demonstration seemed to be pointing out how women's bodies were exploited by men and used as sex objects, how women were assumed to exist only for men and their sexual gratification. The song 'Stay young and beautiful if you want to be loved' was being played ironically on a loud speaker as the march progressed. I identified.

The programme gave information about the London Women's Liberation Workshop, and I made contact and found I could join a local consciousness-raising group. When my daughter was born I joined this group and felt that my life had been saved. By the time my daughter was six months old, and after several months of consciousness-raising, I was a committed feminist and a lesbian. I belonged to women's liberation, which was the first movement which had said I had a right to exist and a right to control my own life and sexuality.

I have gone into some detail about this period of the late 60s and the early 70s, because I feel it is still important to counter one of the many myths of the movement's early history, that its impetus came mainly from women out of left groups, or women fighting for equal pay. Though there were many women who had been and still were politically on the left, there were also many others coming from the hippy counterculture, from being bored housewives, mothers going off their heads at home with their children, from being women with no reason for existence except to service men.

Looking back, the early 70s were years of incredible optimism in Women's Liberation; we believed we could change the world, and had not yet understood or analysed the extent of the forces ranged against us. For me the time was characterised by periods of collective direct action, and an emphasis on changing our lives now.

In 1971 I was particularly influenced by the Miss World action, when a hundred women demonstrated inside the contest hall, throwing flour and stink bombs, and shouting slogans like: "We're not Beautiful. We're not Ugly. We're Angry". This action received widespread media coverage and doubled the membership of the Women's Liberation Workshop in a month. It had obviously captured the minds of many women at the time. I was desperate to get to know the women who had taken this action, and to get involved in direct action myself.

A year later I was to be part of a small group planning the occupation of Trafalgar Square post office at the end of the national women's liberation march, in protest against government plans to stop paying family allowance to women. In those days this sort of action seemed incredibly easy. A small group of women would meet in someone's flat and we would work out our strategy. The keynote was secrecy and never discussing it on the phone beyond the small group involved. Someone would be delegated to phone the media just before the action took place to ensure maximum coverage. For the Trafalgar Square post office action, two women got up on the platform during the rally at the end of the march and announced the occupation; in the meantime others had been passing messages round in the crowd. Huge numbers of women took part, and the action contributed to the government withdrawing their proposals.

Another year the national women's liberation demonstration marched through large stores in Oxford Street, giving out leaflets to women shoppers about how they were being exploited by the fashion industry, and the ideology of dressing to please men. I was also involved in smaller local actions: as single mothers (then called unsupported mothers) we occupied social security offices to get payments for ourselves and our children, and squatted houses so that large groups of us could live together.

One of the key principles of women's liberation at this time (now accepted as a truism) was that the personal is political, that areas which had been previously disregarded by other political movements — such as sexuality, relationships and the nuclear family — were at the centre of our oppression and needed to be changed now, not in some long-distant future revolution. So about a year and a half after joining the movement I moved into a lesbian collective in Hackney where everything in our lives was collectivised from childcare to clothes. We were actually living the revolution, and taking control of our lives now.

Political lesbianism was very much a theme of the time. In 1971 many lesbians had left gay liberation, which had been dominated by gay male interests, and joined the women's liberation movement. Writings by Jill Johnston (*Lesbian Nation*), and by other political lesbians in the States, saying that any woman can be a lesbian, were soon to become popular in the movement over here. These writings were the beginnings of an analysis on the construction of heterosexuality; before this there was still a very strong belief that you were born one way or the other, or that you were a lesbian as the result of some early childhood experience viewed through Freudian ideology. Many women including myself were to make the connections between women being *for women*, and being sexually, emotionally and as far as possible economically independent of men in order for women's liberation to succeed. But of many who embraced political lesbianism at this time a number were later to go back to men, when unrealistic expectations of lesbian relationships were not met (women are not always nice to women) or when the extent of the lesbian oppression was fully experienced. The political lesbian position was only to get formal expression as a women's liberation demand as late as 1978, with the rise of revolutionary feminism.

As the movement grew it was inevitable that factions would occur. By the mid-70s there were two main tendencies, radical feminism and socialist feminism, although there were many smaller factions within these.

I went with the socialist feminist tendency as a non-aligned libertarian feminist, mainly because libertarian feminist groups seemed better organised and were involved in local action. For a short time I even joined a mixed libertarian socialist group, Big Flame, but left in disgust when it proved just as male-dominated as more orthodox organisations, and insistent on putting male class interests before the struggle for women's liberation.

During this period, I also went to work at Lesney's, the Matchbox Toy factory on Hackney Marshes. In those days Lesney's was one of the largest employers of women's labour in the East End, with a Queen's Award for Industry. Now it no longer exists. As a group of mainly college-educated white feminists wanting to "bring women's liberation to the shop floor", we felt the only way was to work there ourselves and experience the same conditions. Our way of organising was in direct contrast to the old Left and its 'armchair socialism' — we even advertised in *Spare Rib* for women to come and join the Lesney's group. I feel now that we ourselves also had a romantic view of factory work and felt that women "at the point of production" were the *real* working class.

We all went to work in different sections of the factory, and would meet two or three times a week to discuss our experiences and produce a monthly *Lesney's Women's Bulletin*, based on conscious-ness-raising and given out anonymously before we went in to work. Though we rejected any idea of ourselves as a vanguard, we still saw ourselves as catalysts, working under cover (if we had been found out we would all have been sacked).

For at least six months Lesney's took up the whole of our lives. We went through a high point of wildcat strikes, and finally an all-out strike. But when the management conceded and we went back to work, we found our bonus rates had been switched around so that the advantage we'd been fighting for had been wiped out. After that it became clear that we weren't going to stick it — no one would choose to work in such a place unless there were no alternatives. We did have alternatives. And it was clear that most of the women who were forced to work at Lesney's knew very well how they were exploited, but there was very little they could do about it. We were there under false pretences.

By 1978 I was feeling depressed by the direction my politics had taken. I had taken a road where my political activity was getting more and more cut off from my personal life. I spent years in women's health groups and later teaching women health classes (persuading heterosexual women by indirect means that hetero-sexuality was bad for their health). But I was living in the lesbian feminist community and regarded myself as a social separatist, spending as much of my private life as possible with lesbian feminists and going to lesbian feminist events. Although I didn't attend the Birmingham Women's Liberation conference in 1978 the debates which emerged — putting the oppression of lesbians and the centrality of male sexual violence back on the agenda — had a profound effect on me. Over the years I had felt drained by having to suppress the fact that being a lesbian was a central part of my politics, and had felt betrayed and let down by heterosexual women whose loyalties were in the end to men.

Later, I was particularly to identify with the Leeds Revolutionary Feminist paper called 'Love your enemy?' which stated explicitly that all men were the enemy, since they all benefited from male supremacy, particularly where male sexuality was used to control women through heterosexual relations and sexual violence.

By the early eighties I was defining myself as a revolutionary feminist, active in Women Against Violence Against Women, and lesbian mothers' struggles for child custody. In 1983 I worked for a GLC-funded lesbian custody project, and in 1985 I joined the GLC Equal Opportunities Unit. The radical Labour left had taken power at County Hall in 1981, and municipal feminism was taking off in London. For the first time many women's liberation groups were able to pay workers and get permanent premises. Individual feminists started getting jobs with the GLC itself, and within other left Labour councils' women's units, equal opportunities units, and latterly lesbian and gay units.

The effects of municipal funding have been contradictory and the implications are still being worked out today. On the one hand there seemed to be a watering-down of autonomous and radical women's liberation politics in order to meet grant conditions set by a male-dominated bureaucracy. On the other hand, local government funding gave groups a stability they could not have while they depended solely on the political commitment of volunteer women who could get "burnt out".

But one problem with having a core of paid workers was that it tended to reduce the involvement of a wider group of women who had been active precisely *because they were* politically committed.

The movement was also having to struggle against encroaching co-option. I can remember one year when International Women's Day in London appeared to be organised totally by officers from the GLC Women's Committee Support Unit, and had, in fact, been turned into Save The GLC Day.

In 1988, at the age of 40, I would still describe myself as a revolutionary feminist, even though the autonomous women's liberation movement seems at an all-time low (in London at any rate). The strength and optimism of the early 70s and 80s have gone and it is now extremely unfashionable to call oneself a feminist, let alone a revolutionary feminist. Municipal feminism has risen and then fallen. The demise of the London Women's Liberation Newsletter three years ago has meant there is now little focus for reporting of London women's liberation activities or published discussion of the current issues, and for me this has been important in contributing to a pessimism about the state and fragmentation of the movement. The London movement, like its newsletter, has been shaken apart by the need to take on board the issues of class, race and disability, and in the process it seems almost to have destroyed itself.

The local government equal opportunities ethos has tended to lump lesbians and gay men together and perceive them as having the same interests and experiencing the same oppression. The more powerful gay male lobby has rendered invisible a more radical lesbian feminist politics.

In many ways, lesbian feminism seems to be going backwards and feminism is getting lost in lesbian politics. I find it disturbing that some women who call themselves lesbian feminists have joined up with gay men in London, particularly after the experiences of lesbians in the Gay Liberation Front who had to recognise in 1972 that gay male interests were as oppressive to lesbians as those of heterosexual men. But now lesbian feminists are working in the mixed Stop Clause 28 Campaign, the recently launched *Pink Paper*, and the London Lesbian and Gay Centre. The LLGC was initiated by the GLC's Gay Working Party, mainly consisting of representatives from white male gay groups; lesbians argued early on for a separate lesbian centre — the eventual mixed centre has its women-only space allocated next to the men's loos! Immediately problems began to emerge over the use of the Centre by S & M groups. The majority of gay men voted in favour while the majority of lesbian feminists voted against and, like myself, no longer use the

Centre. Some lesbian socialist-feminists have also supported or condoned the growth of lesbian sado-masochism, and sexual objectification of lesbians (dressing for sex as it is euphemistically called). It seems to me that this is just the con of the sexual revolution all over again in another form, where women internalise and glorify their own powerlessness and degradation through sex.

Of course Thatcher's regime has in many ways made it much harder for lesbian feminism to survive in a strong, visible and organised way. We are constantly fighting to retain some small gains we have made. Section 28 of the Local Government Act has launched a direct attack on even acknowledging the existence of lesbian mothers and our children within the education system. (At least this means that we are perceived as a threat to male control within the heterosexual family.) I am still politically active with other radical and revolutionary feminists in London in fighting such changes, but now I feel much more demoralised and drained. So little political activity seems to be effective.

20 years of women's liberation have changed and determined my whole life, and will continue to do so. I don't see this changing for myself. I do find it difficult to estimate, though, how it has affected life for women in general.

At 40, however, I take a much more long-term view about the time it will take to overthrow male supremacy, since it has been going for thousands of years. Our current failures have been due not only to underestimating the enemy but refusing to learn from history. As we learn more about the first wave of feminism in this country we seem to be repeating many of their mistakes as well as our own, particularly by allowing the autonomous Women's Liberation Movement to be co-opted into other struggles (such as the peace movement, the gay movement and the Labour Party). Therapy and couple-ism seem to have replaced consciousness-raising and the solidarity of the small group.

Even within 20 years we are reinventing the wheel. "The personal is political" to my mind never meant that each person should not be able to learn from other women's experiences, and we shouldn't have to expect each wave to go on relearning from the start, although obviously new conditions will inform the movement. I also feel that the current wave of feminism has confused organisation and structure with elitism. Political power has been confused with male power. Once the movement became so big, we were unable or unwilling to develop forms of organisation which could have sustained it as a powerful political force. The women's movement has always thought that power could be abolished altogether. The reality has been a 'tyranny of structurelessness'* allowing more powerful individuals and groups to reign supreme. I believe that we have to think seriously about how we get political power as a *movement*, not just as individuals or small groups, if we are ever going to overthrow male supremacy.

I don't believe the autonomous Women's Liberation Movement is dead, as a women's studies lecturer was recently heard to state. It does need to regroup, perhaps on a new basis; when or how this will happen, I have no idea.

---

* This was the title of a much-discussed article written by Jo Freeman in the US, and first circulated in Britain in 1970.

FROM 1970:

Sue Cooper

Writing about 20 years of my life is a challenge. A lot happens between 15 and 35 and I've led an active life. Feminism has been a constant influence since 1971 and this continues — in my work, motherhood, lifestyle and relationships. My family are Jewish, my parents run an independent film distribution company and are members of the Communist Party. We do not always agree politically but do support each other against the conventions and conditioning of a sexist and oppressive society.

In 1968 I was 15, at a girl's grammar school in North London, concerned with doing well at school and having a regular boyfriend (but worried about how to say no to sex). My identical twin sister was at the same school but in different classes, we did a lot together but had different friends. We were hippies in our spare time — beads, bells and barefoot. I went along to the Arts Lab and Middle Earth, read *International Times* but wasn't interested in drugs (though friends experimented with pills and hash). I'd never heard of feminism: the suffragettes had won the vote a long time ago and women in modern society could do as I intended, and combine careers and motherhood.

I was a pacifist, went on the CND Aldermarston marches every year and became involved in protests against the Vietnam War, going to meetings of the local Ad Hoc group and encouraging friends to get involved. I went to meetings and conferences of the Revolutionary Socialist Students' Federation, and when the Schools Action Union started the following year I was active, organising meetings and a demonstration. I kept a diary: one comment on an RSSF meeting reads "only 3 girls so I had to make tea twice".

A Christmas present in 1970 from our older sister, *The Female Eunuch* by Germaine Greer, had a dramatic and instant effect. I can vividly remember thinking that the book put into words something that I had always known. My dissatisfaction with the pressures and concerns of female adolescence suddenly made sense; romantic ideals were one big con trick, the obsession with boys a diversion, our political involvement trivialised to making tea . . . Overnight we were transformed and filled with enormous enthusiasm and energy. We started to go to the Notting Hill Gate Women's Liberation Workshop group, and others — the movement was growing at such an astonishing rate that at each meeting membership doubled and new groups formed. A few of us at school planned and presented a lunchtime meeting on Women's Liberation for the Sixth Form Literary Society, managing to invite other years too, and some of the teachers. A school group started meeting after classes in each other's houses and was a huge success — we talked and talked, turned boys away at the door, there was hugging in the corridors at school and a tremendous feeling of freedom and discovery. We planned and executed a 'political action' — setting off stink bombs in Kensington High Street boutiques and ringing the press, an expression of our anger at the exploitation of women as consumers of fashion.

Women's Liberation seemed an immediate and practical possibility, women would achieve equality through the demands of the women's movement: equal pay, opportunities and education; free contraception and abortion on demand; free 24-hour community controlled childcare; legal and financial independence. (Further demands were added later: women's right to define our own sexuality and an end to discrimination against lesbians; freedom for women from intimidation by the threat or use of violence or sexual coercion regardless of marital status.)

In my own life non-monogamy was an immediate issue — I expressed my freedom through the right to be involved with young men on my own terms. Looking back I can see that my understanding was constrained by my background, my class, my age and the development of feminism at the time. There were contradictions too. At home we had a housekeeper/nanny who enabled my step-mother to work full time. The dilemma for working mothers continues. I resolve it by living with another single working mother and my daughter attends nursery but I do not regard this as the best solution. A real change requires a transformation of society which addresses the position of young people as well as women.

On leaving school I worked in odd jobs, travelled to India, went to York University for one year, worked and travelled some more and then completed a degree in Social Anthropology at Sussex University. Whenever I was in England I joined Women's Liberation groups, consciousness-raising groups and campaigns, attended national conferences and local workshops. In my academic work I studied women's issues when I could, and in turn the concepts of social anthropology — that cultures and social organisations are "man made" rather than natural — developed my political understanding. I was interested in the arts: I ran the student's Arts Federation, helped set up a Community Resources Centre in Brighton, joined two theatre groups — one women only and one which was mixed but with radical and non-sexist politics.

Women's music was developing. The Northern Women's Rock band played at conferences and a series of women's music workshops were held in Liverpool. Inspired and encouraged by these, and by support from both women and men in a Brighton band, I took up electric bass. Meanwhile it was 1977 and friends in Manchester were also forming a band. I went to their first gig, supporting the Sex Pistols, and came into direct contact with punk. Punk was exciting and anarchic, encouraging anyone to have a go, and although it was predominantly male there were some exciting women musicians involved too. Our band in Brighton became the Poison Girls, we played our own style of rock and our lyrics expressed our politics, which included feminism.

I left the Poison Girls at the end of 1977 to go to India and visit my twin who was researching the 'te bhaga' movement of the 1940s there. The movement had been a direct result of Communist Party of India policy. For the first time in our lives our communist family background was validated and I gained a sense of a history of political commitment and action. India broadened my understanding of different cultures and of how political movements, including feminism, must change in different contexts — I realised that my feminism was 'culture-bound'.

Coming back in 1978, I moved to Manchester to help a friend manage a punk band — the Buzzcocks. I found the name, as well as some of the imagery of punk (I cannot separate swastikas and antisemitism) difficult but learned to live with it. My job was to keep track of the band's finances and administration whilst their popularity came and went. We also set up an independent record label and ran a weekly nightclub session. The work was both exciting and mundane as I was stuck in an office a lot of the time but also toured in England and abroad. It was an insight into the music industry, not a welcome place for women. There was isolation (for a long time I was the only woman in the organisation) and overt sexism (the road crew refused to let me help out even though they were desperately short of drivers) and a gulf which had as much to do with class as sexism. However, I did get some support from the manager and from the band's gay lead singer. In Manchester I joined a consciousness-raising group and a women's re-evaluation counselling class, found women to play music with and we formed a band, 'No Fit State'. I wrote songs with the guitarist, we played at both women-only and mixed events and recorded and sold a tape of our music. Eventually I became fed up with the job and moved away to a new one in York.

I was the first woman to join the team at York Arts Centre and used arguments of positive discrimination to recruit another as a technician. We organised a season called Women Live in May 1982, and developed women's arts in the regular programme. A thriving women's music scene was developing in York. I played in a women's rock band, 'Rassh', and in a women's big band, 'Contraband', set up with the aim of encouraging women to play music and sing. I acquired a double bass and learnt to play it both for the big band and to go busking with the York (women's) Street band. I also taught re-evaluation counselling classes for women.

Meanwhile the Israeli involvement in the Lebanon started me thinking about being Jewish. I had grown up in a Jewish–political environment but experienced antisemitism at school, in social relationships and at work, with the result that I tried to ignore and sometimes deny being Jewish. My feelings about Israel were ambivalent; I'd avoided having an opinion myself and seen my parents trying to reconcile the Communist Party line with their own experiences as European Jews this century. Antisemitism became an issue in the women's movement — both on and off the pages of *Spare Rib* and the London Newsletter — details reaching me through my twin and other friends. I started to talk to other Jewish feminists in York and we began to meet as a group. The first meetings were reminiscent of my first women's liberation groups, exciting and stimulating as we realised how important being Jewish was for us and how living in a gentile culture had affected our lives. I realised that I could define my own Jewish identity and choose how I wished to express it. I developed a perspective on Israel which supports its existence but not all the policies and actions of its government or people. It was a great help to hear about the Israeli peace movement and Arab–Israeli projects. I also support the Palestinians' right to a state but not necessarily their policies and actions for achieving it. It is interesting and supportive that by different routes other members of my family share a similar viewpoint. The York Jewish Feminist Group met for a few years, ceasing as women moved away. We spoke at a couple of meetings and held a fund-raising felafel party for the Women's Centre, but never really tackled communicating the issue of antisemitism with non-Jewish feminists.

What being Jewish means to me has taken shape now I am a mother. I was relieved to have a daughter and not to have to make a stand on circumcision (I had decided I would not have a son circumcised). I have continued a pattern, started in the Jewish feminist group, of celebrating certain festivals, in particular Passover with its theme of liberation. It is hard to know how else to communicate 'jewishness' to my daughter, especially in a town with no Jewish community, but I try to be 'visible' as a Jew to other parents, teachers and friends.

I thought about having a child for a number of years. I was approaching 30, which seemed a deadline of sorts, and I worked to set up a situation which felt right. I got a mortgage whilst I still had a reasonable salary, and another woman with her two sons came to live with me. I chose for a father someone who was a good friend, lover and shared basic assumptions and politics. The local midwife supported me in persuading my doctor to allow a home birth, which meant that I was able to do as I liked (walk round the allotments in labour) and be with the people I wanted (the father, my twin, my housemate). As births go, my daughter's, in September 1984, was easy and uncomplicated.

I found single motherhood hard going and was exhausted and depressed for the first months. I continued some of my activities (teaching, re-evaluation counselling but giving up playing music) and returned to work part-time when Emma was six months old. This gave me a sense of myself, but I did not find it easy to juggle work and childcare or fit in much of a social life. Her father eventually moved up from London to live near us and I developed a support network of other mothers.

I think that motherhood is still a difficult area for feminists. Much of the writing in existence focuses on the relationship between mother and child rather than the situation for mothers with children. Our original demand for free 24-hour childcare has not got very far; provision for under-fives is actually on the decrease as the current government attempts to dismantle state welfare and education systems. I think that there are two factors — one is rejection of the sexist line that women are only good for/fulfilled by having babies, the other is a lack of clarity about children and their needs. Both the traditional "children need their mothers 100% of the time" or, alternatively, "children don't need their mothers" points of view fail to tackle the real position of young people in this society and the role of parents, particularly mothers, as agents of the oppression of young people. (I am reminded of the *Little Red Book* of my Schools Action Union days.) In addition, for parents who challenge the conventions or fail to provide sufficient 'control' over their children, there is the threat of having the children taken away.

The women's movement's failure to tackle issues around motherhood has resulted in mothers continuing to work in isolation in the home, finding individual solutions to the stresses and problems. I wonder if feminists haven't also taken on the sexist devaluation of women's work in the home and with young people. This is an area which requires large-scale action and social transformation — of work patterns, family structures, living situations, lifestyles and culture — not an easy task. What I personally experienced most strongly was the isolation, with single women friends unable to understand my position, expecting me to behave as before and ignore the baby. My new friends are mothers of young children and I regret the divide which this sexist and oppressive society places between mothers and single women.

1988 finds me going in a new direction, starting a new job as a trainee accountant and hoping eventually to work with co-operatives, collectives and other non-standard organisations. Returning to work at the Arts Centre I'd realised I needed a change, and this career choice was in part precipitated by the difficulty of finding a woman accountant for the York Women's Centre. The household has remained remarkably stable for five years, despite ups and downs in our relationships. My daughter has two 'big brothers' now almost teenagers and has learnt, in part from them, to be very physically courageous and active and to enjoy making things (cakes and wooden aeroplanes for example). As the children have grown, the house has shrunk, and the household will change this year with the other family moving out. My relationship with Emma's father has survived and changed and he has a separate and thriving relationship with her. My family continue to be a source of support and challenges — my twin is a lesbian mother with a daughter a few months younger than Emma, my younger sister is a lesbian Labour councillor.

Feminism has been a constant thread through my life over these years, as circumstances and issues change, and continues to be so. I still want a different world for women, for me and for the next generation. 20 years of the women's movement have had a considerable effect in some areas, for example equal opportunities, but other issues like the right to abortion have to be continually reasserted and fought for. Awareness of feminism has spread worldwide but sexism is still deep rooted. The original demands of the Women's Liberation Movement continue to be relevant though the ways of truly attaining them have become more complex. I continue to be active as a feminist — a current campaign to shut down the sex shops in our locality has been successful — and my politics influence my childrearing and choice of career. I do not intend to give up trying to change things nor ever losing the feminist perspective I've held for so long.

FROM 1970:

Alice Simpson

In my childhood I was no stranger to muesli, second-hand clothes, self-build housing, or financial insecurity. Maybe because of the latter I sought out a straight marriage while still a teenager. I soon felt trapped. One evening, returning from one of the Grosvenor Square demos against the war in Vietnam, I was invited to join the Tufnell Park women's group and it started me off on yet another road.

The surge of energy in the Women's Movement was tremendous — the office collective were locked out one evening and fifteen of us managed to meet in the Ladies' on Waterloo Station. Revolutionary politics and actions were everywhere; in our women's meetings we discussed our personal oppression and the directions we could take. Soon a split occurred. Tina and I wanted a living situation where there was no distinction between money-earning work and support work; where all income and expenses were shared and everyone was expected to cook, clean, and collect fuel. We wanted to enjoy childcare, mealtimes, and living space with more people and less isolation.

The rest of the group wanted to delay individual changes until the revolution had changed everyone's lives for the better. It seemed as though real change was just around the corner, the struggle would take place in the cities and everyone was needed at the barricades. It saddened me to have conflict with newly found women friends, who accepted me in a way that was new and safe. But when I went home after the meetings I wondered what life would be like after the revolution, and I thought maybe it was no bad thing if a few of us tried out some of our ideas in practice. Tina and her husband, Mike, were for making the move; we put up notices, had meetings, and soon we had a core of people wanting to live communally in the country. We moved to Laurieston Hall in 1972.

For a few months the men continued to 'commute' from Scotland to London and Leeds to complete their job commitments. The women were able to work in the garden, milk the goats and later the cow, fix the vehicles, dig the drains, and saw the wood. Communal child-care was sometimes structured, but more frequently shared by arrangement, say with a new lover. Several children had four 'parents', or more, for most of their childhood. Since the mealtimes and living spaces were shared by up to twelve adults plus visitors this inevitably diluted the importance of parents. The children had a freedom to develop a world of their own, relating to each other and to people of their choice, and learning how to avoid the discipline of the ever-present adults who were not often as indulgent as parents can be. Children walked to and from school together, sometimes arriving home hours late, but adults were confident they'd come to no harm while they had each other and their adventures. As a parent I was freed from the treadmill of daily meal-getting, and able to develop new skills such as gardening and event-organising. I never once had the responsibility of producing a Christmas dinner, and, although we never abolished the traditional commercialised festivals, the necessity of poverty meant that indulgence was minimal. Over the years the Solstice festivals gained in importance, alongside wassailing and halloween.

When I arrived at Laurieston Hall I was in a couple relationship that had lasted ten years. I soon discovered the delights of independence. I had a room of my own and time to spend with other consenting adults who lived only down the corridor, without baby-sitting problems. During my fifteen years of communal life, I spent six months as a single person, the rest of it shared with four main lovers and a sprinkling of other shorter lasting affairs. Life was complicated and upsetting at times. In pre-Aids days, I had only to worry about curable venereal disease; nevertheless the nearest clinic to treat me with respect and care was eighty miles away in Glasgow. I wavered between the excitement and challenge of new lovers, and the dread of disease and expense of travel.

The local people were puzzled by the arrival, in 1972, of long-haired professional city folk with their oddly dressed children. The area still had vestiges of feudalism, and because we'd bought the "big hoose", which had once owned most of the land around, people maintained a respectful silence towards what at best seemed eccentric behaviour. Their children were not encouraged to play with ours, and since we were obsessed with our internal politics we were mostly happy to leave it that way.

They had their nitrogen fertilizers, pesticides, and the pub; we had organic vegetables, hand-milked goats, and home-grown. They had new cars and tractors; we had old bicycles and an even older Land Rover. We joined the Soil Association and tried to involve local mothers in setting up a play-group; they preferred the Rotary club, the Women's Rural, and keeping their children at home. The distance was maintained for many years, maybe for fear of meeting a naked body weeding the onions, or because the drugs squad raided us although no drugs were found.

The revolutionary politics of the late 60s gave the spark to kindle the commune, the income-sharing, and the adoption of feminist ideals. As individuals we had varying degrees of dedication to left-wing politics. Within the first weeks splits occurred that were reminiscent of the split in my women's group; a personal life-style politics against a striving to change the world, albeit by example. Some of us were happy to buy in food, paraffin and whisky to fuel us through the long hours of policy-making and the assault on class barriers and elitism; others, myself included, wanted to put energy into the garden, the animals, wood gathering and wine-making.

We tried to compromise by running a project for children from the inner city, liaising with social workers we'd known from London days who were keen to bring children to an environment free from the stresses of violence and authority. We soon discovered that for the new children to enjoy the countryside they needed almost one-to-one attention from a resident. Without this, the lack of shops, discos and chips became too much for them to bear and they stayed in bed, getting drunk. They experienced undreamt-of freedoms, but the risks were too high: we nearly drowned a boatload one summer, and a skater on the loch one winter. Our own children seemed to acclimatise to the dangers — it was naive to think it could be achieved in a few hours by children in a group. The project needed more dedication than we could collectively give, and after two years it ceased.

People left, others joined, we took our children out of the local school and taught them at home. They were with us all the time and their needs were discussed in meetings and became part of the daily schedule. The local education chief put every obstacle in our way, and against the threat of court action we lasted only eighteen months before most of the children returned to state schools. Two children stayed outside the system quietly for longer, and then voluntarily attended a local independent school. The low fees were raised by begging and borrowing.

By the late 70s our Women's Weeks had themes such as Manual

Trades or Compulsive Eating, and therapy was becoming more of an influence than radical politics. I was encouraged by women to express my opinions instead of remaining silent and avoiding conflict. This coincided with a discussion on whether or not to extend the principles that we held at Laurieston Hall to a wider network, pooling our properties. As I saw it, we had enough problems in our own commune working a policy of financial support for members who were less able to work or participate. If we extended the principle of "to each according to their need, from each according to their ability" to other communities, we were at risk of adding to our own problems without solving other people's.

It reminded me of the time in London when the earlier split occurred. I took a difficult decision — I used my personal power as a title deed holder to delay the transfer of property to the newly-forming group. Soon after, along with the three other owners, I did sign documents for us to become a housing co-op, but the matter was never raised again.

Now, in the later 80s, we no longer income-share. We work-share to produce our food, collect fuel, and maintain the property; we still meet as a group once a week. It feels as though politics has come home, and what was theory in the late 60s has become practice. It's more satisfying to eat communally when we are catering for our visitors in the summer, and to cook on the woodstove that heats my caravan and water in the winter. The more self-sufficient we are the less we need take from the poor of the world.

I'm still, after seven years, in a type of couple relationship with a man. At the moment he also has another woman lover and I do not. At times I'm upset, but mostly I get what I need from our relationship, and it leaves me time for my three regular women's groups. The massage group is intimate, with only three women, the CR group is fascinating as each woman takes a turn of meeting space, and my lover's lover is in the Tai Chi group. These groups all involve women who don't live at Laurieston Hall and reflect our improved relations with local people, who now understand our fears about the damage to the environment from modern farming methods and nuclear power.

Some of the community children have left home. One daughter, Sonya, is planning a white wedding, and yet she based her final year college project on a management study of Laurieston Hall; the other, Polly, is an *au pair* in Paris and taking an art course. Billy is in Sri Lanka helping with a hydro-electric scheme during a break in his three year appropriate technology course. Hannah is married and a well-paid medical secretary, Joe is as yet unlaunched as a theatrical star, and Joel is studying Modern Greek and drama. Ali, who grew up in London with his mother, now lives here with his father. They both milk the cows; however, it's Ali who has the car and his dad who has the motorbike!

Most of the adults are in the 30–40 age bracket, and as the children grow up and move on the thought of us all growing old together excites me. Twenty years ago the potential of women was grossly undervalued, and I see the same situation for old people in cities who have retired, often early, from conventional jobs. My politics led me to set up a situation where I could live, work, and raise children without feeling the immediate boundaries imposed by capitalism and authority. Very few jobs in Laurieston Hall require expert skills or strength for any length of time, and when the need arises we can call on people who are willing to help. The green politics of our community will lead to a revaluation of nurturing where old people can share in child-care, self-sufficiency and social skills — all areas that benefit from experience, patience, and devotion.

FROM 1969

Lee Comer

I was 25 years old in 1968, and engaged not in 'student politics' but in untying the loose ends of a disastrous marriage. Indeed, I was somewhat contemptuous of the excitement surrounding 'les évênements' because I'd lived in Paris in the early 60s when worker and student demonstrations had been an everyday matter. I did not even bother to write home about them. Police brutality and political instability in Paris had long made it an uncomfortable place to live if you didn't have your 'papiers', if you were a foreigner, or if you were white and mixed with Arabs and black people. 'Suspect' people in Paris who broke the curfew might well find themselves among the unnumbered unidentified bodies fished up out of the Seine each week. But these events were domestic and were not beamed around the world, or reported by breathless journalists. So there was nothing especially new for me in 1968. I was, in any case, too old and too blasé for all this nonsense. For me, political activity had meant wearing a duffle coat and trudging the Aldermarston March every year, singing "Ban the Bomb for evermore", and arguing over Cuba in a Left Bank cafe.

But the Prague spring was a different thing altogether. My mother was a Czech and a Jew, who had arrived in Britain in 1938, 16 years old, alone and penniless together with thousands of other Jewish refugees from Nazi Europe. When the Germans invaded Czechoslovakia her family packed a small overnight bag for her and put her on a train to meet a relative at the border. She was, as the eldest child, the first to escape and the rest were going to follow, one by one. But they never made it and all but her younger sister perished in the concentration camps — Auschwitz and Buchenwald. Her younger sister survived and returned to Prague, and to this day is my only surviving relative. (My father's entire family also perished in the camps.) The two sisters could only meet with difficulty — once on the beach in Bulgaria where no-one could overhear them whispering together, and once in London. Letters were strained and difficult things and I felt horribly confused, for my aunt had been so secretive that we didn't really know where her sympathies lay. My mother had boasted in the early 60s about my CND activities to her and had been shocked by her distaste. As a member of the Communist Party and a survivor of the concentration camps, she had certain privileges which were denied to other Czechs — a decent flat in the centre of Prague, permission to travel abroad occasionally. All this might have been affected by our existence in the West. We were never too sure; our uncertainty was well founded, for neither my mother nor I could ever get security clearance when we needed it. I stayed away from demonstrations against the Soviet invasion, fearing the outcome if I had been arrested. So I was not free to think too clearly about Dubceck and the events in Prague.

The year 1968 marked for me not a political upheaval but a personal one. I was living alone in London, writing furious poetry and trying as best I could to sidestep the swinging 60s. The sex, drugs and rock and roll thing just seemed as shallow and ephemerally juvenile as the politics. I caved in, instead, to romantic love and moved to Leeds. With 20 years of hindsight, and a smashing grown up daughter to show for it, I know that it was exactly the right thing to do at the right time, despite the fact that the romantic love ended in tears after all of three years.

I was in the right place at the right time. Although the women's movement combusted spontaneously throughout Britain, there was in Leeds already a core of women who were meeting as a group in 1969. We were all veterans of something or other — the alternative press, motherhood, rejected novels, infamous partners, low paid menial jobs. We didn't at all fit the neat sociological explanations of the beginnings of feminism in this country, which would have us all to have been spoon-fed girl children of the 50s and 60s, enjoying the fruits of the 1944 Education Act, educated at University to expect success and equality only to be disappointed in love and work. We were, instead, of all ages and classes, grandmothers and teenagers, with more children between us than degrees, drawn together as women, by our commonality, our energy and our will to share in each other's strengths.

We met every week in Jan Wallis' back-to-back house but there were soon too many of us to fit into her tiny front room. We fixed the time and place of the next meeting at the end of the one before, and though we didn't advertise and only one of us had a telephone, still more new women found us each week. I had to move from my small bed-sitter as I was six months pregnant, so I scoured Leeds looking for a cheap flat or house to rent with a room large enough to accommodate the women's group. I struck lucky just a month before my daughter was born and moved into a one-bedroomed flat in a converted mansion. The sitting room was the size of a tennis court. The group could at last take root and announce its existence. We put ourselves on the map in Leeds and to the world at large, for my address was to appear in the first home-grown anthology of women's liberation writings — *The Body Politic*, edited by Michelene Wandor in London. Visiting American feminists, thinking Leeds was in the home counties, came in droves. We began to organise public meetings, addressed countless organisations, orchestrated demonstrations, leafletted on everything from Family Allowances to Milk Snatcher Thatcher (yes). I never sat still long enough to breastfeed my baby, and though she howled all night I'd be out at dawn, hitching to London for conferences and meetings, running off leaflets, typing and copying articles or rehearsing talks and media interviews. Somehow, in all this, I held down a fairly arduous job, teaching children with learning difficulties.

The energy seemed not to be my own. I was drawing on a common bottomless well of reserves which each of us contributed to and which we drew on as we needed. Truly, the highest state of feminism, so it seemed. When I wrote, it was for the group. When I sat up late into the night, reading as much as I could lay my hands on — most of it from America — it was for the group. I wrote a discussion paper for the group on the myth of motherhood, what I perceived to be a patriarchal trick played on women in the 50s and swallowed whole by our generation — that babies needed the undivided attention of their mothers, and that many of the evils of the world and juvenile delinquency in particular could be laid at the door of working mothers. Working mothers then occupied the same territory as unmarried mothers (the term 'single parents' had not yet been coined) — social pariahs. I read avidly everything which came out of the women's movement in America and the UK and found nothing on these subjects, which seemed to me to be so much more relevant to the everyday experience of the women I knew than the more academic writings of the pioneers of British women's liberation.

The group received my paper very well and suggested that I try to get it published. I knew nothing beyond the world of the small poetry magazine about getting into print. Apart from *The Body Politic* the only homegrown publication in 1971 was Sheila Rowbotham's pamphlet 'Women's Liberation and the New Politics', so I sent 'The

Myth of Motherhood' to the publisher, Spokesman. I had wanted it to come out in the form of a cheap pamphlet but Spokesman published it in their journal, which was relatively expensive to buy, and not a publication with which women in the movement could readily identify. I remember having to scratch together quite a lot of money to pay the publisher to supply me with offprints which I then sold off at cost at the Women's Liberation Conference in Skegness in 1971. It was this experience which taught me how hungry women were for feminist publishing — I remember one woman buying 100 copies to circulate in Shropshire. It was some time before Spokesman realised they had a winner. Eventually, they spared me the cost of paying for more reprints by publishing and distributing 'The Myth of Motherhood' under their own imprint, as a pamphlet in a proper cover. It looked oddly conspicuous in their list, sitting alongside the great and the good of peace, socialism, workers' control and Bertrand Russell.

I knew I had more to say about women's lives, as mothers and housewives, and an audience to hear me. Hannah Gavron's *The Captive Wife* and Betty Friedan's *The Feminine Mystique* were the only books I knew of which talked about women's experience of being a housewife. Both seemed to me to be dated and neither had come from within the women's movement. Initially, I intended to work on a second pamphlet but as the theme developed, I realised that it would need to be a book. If the book turned out to be publishable I wanted the Movement to publish it in a cheap, accessible form, but there was no possibility of that yet. I finished in under a year, working evenings and weekends, and submitted the manuscript, *Wedlocked Women*, to two 'radical' publishers, both of whom, to my surprise, wanted to publish it. The left-wing publisher wanted to make it more palatable to their usual readership by "putting in the smell of the factory" and the radical but less political publisher wouldn't change a word but insisted on a hardback with no guarantee of paperback sale rights. I declined both offers and put the manuscript in a drawer for two years.

Meanwhile, three of us in the Leeds group, Jan Wallis, Sandra Allen and myself, had been working on compiling a second anthology of British feminist writing, to be called *Conditions of Illusion*. In 1974 we met with a benefactor from the women's movement in London and with her backing we set up 'Feminist Books' in Leeds, the UK's first women's liberation publishing house and distribution service. The word 'feminist' itself was something of

88

'68, '78, '88

a departure because the Movement was still termed Women's Liberation. Though we were an all-women company, we felt we would be taken more seriously in the mainstream world of selling to WH Smiths and the like with our new name. This was a time when Libraries and bookshops still didn't have catalogue or shelf space for 'Women's Studies'. They usually shelved our literature with books on pregnancy.

I dusted off the manuscript of *Wedlocked Women* and Feminist Books published it in paperback for £1 per copy. We brought out *Conditions of Illusion* soon afterwards. Because our motivations were feminist and not commercial we sold at break-even point rather than to build up a business, and we never again had sufficient funds to publish another book. Most of the effort went on buying in pamphlets and books which were unavailable in the UK and distributing them on to bookshops. We wanted to stay small and in credit so when Virago took off, and the rest of the industry woke up to women's writing, we wound up Feminist Books. There was no further need for our little outfit and we were tired of spending our days on the road, or in my front room packing books.

In 1978, when I was working as a part-time abortion counsellor and teaching women's studies in the evenings, I was out on the street for the umpteenth time, defending women's right to safe, legal abortion. I can't remember now whether it was the Benyon, Corrie or White Bill. Ten years later I am out against the Alton Bill, seeing the same women carrying the same placards. I have no sense now of being part of the same movement which first nurtured me, though I feel no less committed than I was then. But the sacrifices do not bring the same rewards. I draw, instead, on the dependable history of our small group. We have all known each other for 20 years. There have been three untimely funerals already and we will continue to watch over each other until the last one of us goes.

By the late 70s, when the movement had grown and fragmented and burst its seams so often that I would no longer recognise it if I saw it walking down the road, my friendships were made and the course of my life determined. I learnt some terrible things in those early days. Things which, 20 years on, I still hold as true and which still drive me. At 17, I believed I had everything to learn and that truth, beauty, art, learning, wisdom and politics were of men's making. Their doings, their writings, their actions. At 27, I saw that lie, writ large, across history, art, literature, politics, famine, war, the bomb, the planet. Men got everything wrong and they continued to make it wrong. And when women found them out, they derided them. They mocked the women's movement and competed even harder with each other to demonstrate their supremacy. But privately they were worried. They would have liked to give us a little more freedom, but they didn't like us taking it for ourselves and, even worse, showing them the door. Nothing much has happened since to make me see any of this differently. Except that they have tightened their grip on the machinery of power, let a few women in, and let the rest of us go hang on Page Three.

When people say "It changed my life", do they know how their lives might have been? The Women's Movement changed my life in the same way that unplanned motherhood did. Neither event was reversible. And they are inextricably woven. I had my first and only child in September 1970, just as the women's movement began to take recognisable shape. I felt equally responsible to both, and happily relinquished any inner needs I might have had (but could not readily name) to serve their every whim. They exercised complete control of me for ten years. I wrote about feminism, acted out feminism, scraped a living through feminism, and conducted my private life through feminism.

Now, in 1988, my daughter is grown up and no longer dependent on me. I live alone. I am paid to be a feminist, working in local government promoting women's equality. My parents are dead and all my choices and loyalties are of my own making. So I could, in theory, turn back the clock to resurrect what my life might have meant without feminism and motherhood, since neither of them want or need me any more. But 20 cumulative years of feminism are printed right through me. It is the distinguishing mark by which everything I do, feel and think must be measured. It is the stuff of every choice I have made, every job I have done and every friendship I have.

But I lose sleep, unable to accept that I have come full circle to find myself living in the tenth year of regressive conservatism. If 'it' hadn't changed my life, I might have found all this easier to bear. And I am no nearer to naming the inner needs I so readily relinquished 20 years ago. They might have come in useful now.

INNER BREAK

Some time in the 80s I felt what I can only call an inner break from
the movement. It will probably take another two decades for me to
tell if this was a lovers' tiff or a divorce.

In the course of 20 years, Women's Liberation has thrown up its
waves of opposition. First lesbian women, then working-class
women, then Black women, then women with disabilities have
changed the movement that they joined. You could call these groups
the official opposition, the political conscience.

There has also been an *unofficial* opposition, eventually voting
with their feet. It seemed to me that we could learn something by
bringing different oppositions together in one place.

Each of the writers in this section has experienced an inner break
in her own way. Most are not ex-feminists, even less post-feminists,
more what I once wrote about as *graduate feminists*: "that moment
when a woman shifts from being feminist-as-*noun* (radical feminist/
socialist feminist/lesbian feminist...) to feminist-as-*adjective*:
feminist academic, feminist writer, feminist therapist".

(New Socialist, December 1986)

PROGRESSIVE WARDROBES

Jane Wibberley

Clothes tell the story of my last 20 years, so I have described my essential outfits of 1968, 1978, 1988 as well as the events of those years.

January 1st 1968:

I lay in bed at my cousin's trying to make my big toe burn like the Yoga book said. Having finished at Cambridge a few months earlier, I faced a void. My ambition was not to have a career and especially not to be a secretary, teacher or nurse and not to get engaged or married. As a child, whenever I declared 'When I'm grown-up I'm going to —' my mother would say bitterly 'Nonsense, you'll get married'. So now I had fulfilled my anti-ambitions but had no useful plans of my own.

My mother had died not long before. In the new family home I was failing in my daughter role as housekeeper and interior designer. My father and I devised bizarre schemes such as dyeing all the unmatching carpets black, thus to create (unwittingly) a memorial to my mother. He informed my grandmother and me 'I'm a normal man' and forced me to admit that no, I was not a normal daughter.

"Who wants to be normal?" I would cry, producing my copy of Laing and the notion that men like my father were the walking dead, while family scapegoats such as I contained all truth locked within our bosoms. A dip into Genet reinforced my childhood concern for the underdog, later the cornerstone of my politics.

The hippy movement I championed for its emphasis on the 'inner world' as opposed to the rationality, the ratrace of the academic world. Unfortunately most hippies I met did not want to boycott exams, but bowed their heads to the yoke as meekly as anyone else in 1967. The discovery that university was like school, being all about careers and not about truth, had hit me hard. In 1968 I hunted down the remains of the hippy movement at weekends in clubs; years later I was annoyed to find that several other political

movements had passed me by. My finger had not been on the pulse. But what I had heard (I did not read newspapers) had not quite struck the note of my protest.

Hippy treatment of women was a bitter disappointment, though at least no-one talked about marrying a virgin. But my analysing, theorising, mistrust of men contrasted with the desired female behaviour of posing beautifully in silence and giving up the will to the male. The hippy experience convinced me further of my basic deficiency as a female.

Yet I continued to carry out protests through men. In our black-carpeted sitting room, over tea, my father and I discussed art with the boyfriend who was twice my age and a pavement artist. His furcoat ponged powerfully. We were unable to restrain our smugness when he referred to artists running amuck. 'Don't you mean amok?' 'No, amuck.' My father and I smiled knowingly at each other. We had never heard of running amuck. Later this boyfriend took a regular job on a hotdog stand opposite my hippy haunt, hoping to save up enough money to marry me and set up house. That was when I graduated to the alcoholic boyfriend who disapproved of drugs and my hippy connections. He didn't talk of marrying me. He pointed to my housekeeping instead.

I desultorily pursued artistic activities at home and abroad: classes in mime and dance, writing children's stories for adults, a travel diary in the style of *I, Jan Cremer*. Influenced by the theatre of Prague and the mime of Decroux, I dreamt of putting adult fairy stories on stage in a new theatrical style.

Homemade needlecord trousersuits in sea blue and emerald green took me everywhere from hippy clubs to dinner parties (not many of those). Thus I conquered society's divisions and reconciled the irreconcilable. After the advent of the alcoholic boyfriend, the trousersuits were replaced with ready-made smocked mini-dresses of dull-coloured corduroy which he found more feminine. (His only clothes were one frayed suit.)

January 1st 1978:

I woke to ponder the current impasses of work and relationships and set off alone next day to the women's hostel at Glasbury. Being fit from my work as a theatre performer I got up mountains easily, climbing in wellingtons or army boots painted silver with spikes that clattered loudly on rocks, on my head a balaclava made out of a pair of black tights. My lover joined me in Glasbury: *de facto* we continued. On returning to London I took up an offer of collaboration enabling me to fulfil my Arts Council quota of performances.

My first women's liberation group in 1971 got rapidly taken over by the International Socialists so I left it for a small consciousness-raising group. After experience of a women's action group, I decided I was an artist and unfitted to be either politician or terrorist as I could never be quite sure I was right. My first play was put on as part of the first women's theatre season at the Almost Free Theatre in 1973. I started performing with other women at women's conferences, community events, took my first one-woman show to the Edinburgh Festival in 1976, later toured it and other shows round London.

After living in several all-women houses I ended up in an ex-women's centre in North London, once run by separatists, now shortlife housing but still bearing the sign 'Kingsgate Women's Centre'. The remnants of a generation of women activists mouldered in the basement. Two of us constituted a cosy weird last outpost of something-or-other. Under the slogan in the kitchen, left over from the vibrant summer of 1975 and carefully painted round by us — *Whose approval do we need any more? Who?* — we sat over the remains of custard and sponge cake gossiping, dissecting the women's movement, idly developing our fantasy of the New Woman and outlining the elements of the Great Love Affair between women which to our eternal regret we had not succeeded in having with each other. At times we defined our subculture: "It isn't them and us, Jane," she said, "It's them and me."

By 1978 she lived round the corner studying for a degree in film and photography while I and the cat awaited rehousing in the centre. She no longer did my sound and lights but she still took publicity photographs and we continued to discuss our subculture over baked potatoes.

Meanwhile, thanks to my new lover, my social horizons had expanded from feminist discos to the more traditional lesbian club. The shirt opened to the cleavage, heeled boots, glittering waistcoat joined my huge men's jacket, the favourite battered trilby from Cefn Foellat women's commune (my essential wear of 1978).

Clothes were a frequent theme in my plays. In my first one-woman show, a surreal streetseller offers clothes for the soul as ". . . the baggage you will need for your wedding to the world. Every woman, every man is a bride. Clothed you must go to the altar. A naked bride is torn alive . . ." The clothes seller weaves her wedding garments out of souls. Then we realise she herself is both seller and sold/soul.

The 1978 show developed the theme of transformation through the metaphor of alchemy. Out of women's unacknowledged and invisible culture, their secrets, would come the 'gold' of a new world. Women, by playing 'happy families' betrayed both the gold and the companion and lover of youth, later their husband's mistress. She, discarded in middle age, returns to a christening and upbraids them:

"Ladies, I have watched you through the window, puppets in the nursery. I bayed like the wolf, I cried like the lamb and you threw me sweet charity, sweet charity . . . The little king laughed when he saw [the gold], muttered 'Pooh, paste jewels' . . . You held his train, puppets." Betrayed and alone, without bitterness she passes on the secret to the women who come to execute her.

We did a performance for an invited audience in a lovely restored barn in the Home Counties. Afterwards our hostess asked us to wash the pebbles on the drive which we'd dirtied. This could have been my life, I thought.

When the run was over, two of us began making puppets. "Whose head are you baking today, Jane?" my lover would ask. A comic puppet play about the adventures of a small she-loving female species called the Whoshees developed the theme of obsession with Romantic Love, which usually caused the Whoshees' downfall but was also their glory.

In July I was 33. Shortly afterwards neighbours came to tell me about my friend round the corner going mad. She was taken into hospital and the doctor asked me if she had ever shown signs of manic depression.

The relationship I was in took a long time dying: I went away to help the process. At St David's Bay I threw pebbles into the sea, marked with my lover's initials to get her out of my head, and wrote her name in the sand for the tide to erase. When I got back, she was sitting on the doorstep, smoking, and it began all over again. My friend was out of hospital by now and she said "Not again" when she saw us together.

By Christmas my friend had fallen into a depression and my relationship with my lover had come to a head. I formed a new theatrical association with a feminist friend, who would do the sound and lights for the puppet show I was to put on in a month. In the New Year my friend committed suicide. Shortly afterwards, I moved out of the centre and a heterosexual couple with child moved in, painted out the women's sign and renamed it 'The Cottage'.

January 1st 1988

I wake up and go for a run. To return, puffing, to the darling little flat which I own.

Was there a day in the early 80s when I realised I had a survival problem? The television going on about Cruise missiles, unemployment, the Falklands and Arts Council cuts.

I laboured under the political (religious?) notion that I should share the fate of the most unfortunate. However, I decided this was masochism: not the principles, but the spirit in which I pursued them. I contemplated training as an electrician but the prospect of life between then and retirement utterly depressed me. Is that how electricians feel, I thought; is that class oppression of which you had no idea until you thought of doing it? And where, too, was the Jane who wanted to be a bricklayer in the early 70s? I now knew women who laid bricks. Had my previous desire been a fantasy?

I went to a Careers Advisory Service. Options: teacher, secretary, social worker... This sounds familiar, I thought. Having done teaching before, I trained to be a secretary. Digging out a skirt from my theatrical hamper I trotted off happily to play a new part. But when I saw them all in the typing pool of a solicitor's office, with wires coming out of their heads as if on a battery farm, I thought I would rather be a solicitor. I worried if I could do it. "Most lawyers don't have brains," was the comment from relatives, "If Gummer can do it, you can."

"It was easier when Gummer did it," said I. The day I started my training, the sun fell upon the Public Record Office, full of ancient seals and charters, and I felt very happy. Someone suggested there are two kinds of lawyers: the sort who want to impose order on their chaos and the sort who are naturally orderly. Obviously I am the former kind.

Unsure of my social instincts. Was I, after all I'd been through, to play the part of the spinster in this world of weddings and christenings? Getting the clothes right must be the key. One recruitment agency told me I looked like a ballet dancer when I thought I looked a model executive. For a long time I didn't talk about writing in case employers thought my soul was in the wrong place. One day I realised they didn't want my soul.

In the early 70s, involvement in the professions, possibly all jobs (even doing theatre in actual theatres), amounted to collusion with a corrupt system. The discovery of the political implications of everything was a liberating revelation. I remember being glad I was not working as a lawyer, doctor, teacher, social worker, because I should have felt called upon to sacrifice my career in a public gesture of solidarity with my clients, pupils or patients. Getting older, I realised that dirty hands were the inevitable alternative to paralysis. Years ago I thought I could fight on all fronts. Now I had to decide on priorities. I took comfort from the large numbers of leftwing and feminist solicitors, and at the same time my writer's curiosity triumphed over the mental cul-de-sac of my political purity; I set out to explore all sorts of sections of society of whom I had no previous experience.

I still put the truth of the underdog above that of the top dog, but in the course of the 70s, a few underdogs of the mad and other sorts pushed me about and threatened me. So I toppled them rather from their spiritual pinnacle. Living on the edge was a must for me in the 70s, there was no question but that the deviants and outcasts of any setup (including the women's movement) were always infinitely to be preferred to the mainstream. By the early 80s being a black sheep no longer pleased me, though I still got a gloomy thrill out of charting the iniquities of the pack in action, and undertaking crusades. (Standing up to the crowd still seems to me quite as crucial as uniting with it.) More prepared now to be part of the crowd — the conformers strike me as being as worthy of study as the rebels and freaks — nonetheless I still give scapegoats enormous credibility, no doubt as a kind of insurance, lest one day their misfortune befalls me too.

After I got harassed in a wood in 1985, I joined a walking club, so now I wear boots like everyone else and puff up big foreign mountains. But one day I shall go back to walking alone all day in the hills.

My friend's suicide was followed by a period of great self-doubt and reassessment. Close relationships with women acted as reminders and I avoided them. I stopped performing and began to write a novel about women and creativity. Bogged down by structural problems, I began a massive reading programme of all the patriarchal literature

I had previously dismissed. My favourite topics of conversation were 'realism' and 'naturalism'.

Props from my puppet shows were cleared out. Little trickles of sawdust ran from the holes in the papier mache cheeks of the rouged lace-ruffed bride; from the schoolmaster's red beak: book worms. Not fired enough.

In the last year notices from a local women's group about Clause 28, restricting the 'promotion' of homosexuality, and the Alton Bill, restricting abortion, prompted me to turn out after a long period of political inactivity. The last meeting was quite dominated by us oldies. So much less strain than meetings used to be. Is that because it isn't new or is it me? Deference. The old campaigner. But in the 60s and 70s fear of the crowd kept me away from marches: chanting still reminds me of school and Nazism. But now there's a warmer feeling of belonging and perhaps, too, a detachment. Just as well, in view of the way women's gains are getting whittled away. If I weren't detached, I'd get too depressed to turn out at all.

I work part-time as a solicitor so I can write. The novel continues and I have nearly finished a satire with a circus of intermittently naturalistic characters. One day I should like to write a lesbian tragedy with lots of big bad women rather than small nice happy ones: an inspiration for glorious intense relationships.

In the next few years I shall travel to expand my horizons. Enclose photo of self in sunhat from Lesbos: the hat of 1988. As someone said "You could go anywhere in that hat, Jane: Ascot, a beach party . . ."

THINGS MOVE ON

Linda Bellos

In 1968 I was 17 and going on 18, politically active, zealous and youthful. That Easter I went on my first Aldermaston march, and I think it was later that year I was on the March from Trafalgar Square to Grosvenor Square, protesting at American involvement in Vietnam.

It seemed in that summer that every progressive protest, march or rally saw me on it. I didn't belong to any political party during that year, having left the Socialist Labour League (now the WRP) after a nine-month stint.

1968 was the Beatles, Jimi Hendrix, Bob Dylan, Tamla Motown; it was Afro and flowing skirts, it was desert boots and jeans, it was espresso coffee in Soho and frankfurters in Schmidts of Charlotte Street, alas long since gone. It was 'A' levels and classical concerts and above all it was hope.

It did seem then that there were endless possibilities. I didn't know what I was planning to do with my life, I wanted to be a professional clarinetist but wasn't quite good enough. Living at home with my parents I was secure, active and happy in the unhappy way teenagers are at that age. Looking back I didn't feel adult but I didn't feel like a child either.

I wasn't a feminist in the sense of being actively involved in women's groups, but my actions were always of independence and self reliance. I had always argued with my father, protesting at his insistence that housework was solely a female domain and that I should cook and sew. Whilst I did cook and sew, I protested that I shouldn't have to do it; my mother and I shared the tasks and as she worked full-time in a factory I saw it as my responsibility to ease the strain for her by shopping and cooking before she got home. In a way I was a feminist but without that body of politics to support me.

The most significant political movement to affect me was Black Power, which for the first time gave me a positive image of blackness, unlike what I had grown up with from the surrounding society. My family provided me with support and understanding. My father, who is Nigerian, and my mother, who is white and Jewish, both experienced racism and made me aware that it was not simply my problem or something which was my fault.

In looking back I shrink with embarrassment at my naivety in thinking that fundamental change was just around the corner, but I have such fondness for that year, a year of awakening in which I also lost my virginity.

1978

Married for eight years, two young children and still hearing the emotional message against abortion. But in late 1977 I had decided to have an abortion myself. I also decided to do something with my life, so I applied for my driving test and to go to university. 1978 saw me a qualified driver and entering Sussex aged 27. That year had seen me more independent than I had been since marriage in 1970; organising a women's group within my community, active in community politics, mobile and reasonably well read.

University was an exciting experience, but in a wholly individual way. I couldn't relate to most of my student colleagues (who were 18 and fresh out of public school) but after initial self-doubt about my academic ability I learned to love the discipline of structured self-learning, essays on political topics with one week to prepare them. Between getting my children to nursery class and playgroup, shopping and cleaning I managed to attend tutorials, research and write essays and begin to find myself.

I came across feminism but wasn't particularly interested at that stage. Reading academic socialist feminists writing in patronising terms about working-class women had no appeal to me. It was only later, when I read a book by Susan Brownmiller called *Against Our Will*, that I suddenly made a connection between my experience as a woman and women as a group. It was a revelation, and was my first contact with Radical/Revolutionary feminism. However, back in 1978 I didn't identify myself as a feminist, just as a mature unqualified student with two young children and a house to keep. That first year was a struggle but it was also exciting, with doors opening in a way I couldn't have anticipated. I worked hard and retained a vision of myself 'making it' by the time I was 35. That was what I had promised my daughter two years earlier, as I fed her and looked into her eyes: I'd make something of my life. I didn't at that stage know what, but studying politics at university would at least give me the tools I needed.

1988

Leader of Lambeth Council, full-time politician and taking abuse from all sides. I've made it in the unspecified way I'd meant to back in 1976. The intervening ten years have seen major changes in my life, too many to describe in this short piece, but the most significant was becoming a lesbian. It resulted in the loss of my children and home amongst other things, and on the positive side the rebuilding of my life. After years of tending other people I was now reliant solely upon myself. I worked, bought a flat and later sold it to buy a house with my partner.

Becoming active in the Labour Party was a logical step from the frustration I had experienced in the lesbian feminist ghetto. I would not have joined the Labour Party had it not been for its Black Sections, which at least offered something relevant to me. I had always voted Labour, as had my family. I felt that it was self-indulgent merely to criticise the Labour Party from the outside for not taking on board feminism and black consciousness. If I wanted to change it I had to be on the inside, so that's what I did. As an active lesbian feminist I had become increasingly angry at those who sought to ignore the fact that the Tory government was doing things that affected women's lives; and that we couldn't retain our political parity by just not looking at the wider world. When I joined (rejoined) the Labour Party in 1984 I was appalled at the workerist approach that most activists took. Indeed it appeared to me no different from the white middle-class socialist feminists I read, writing in patronising terms about working-class women. The working class was seen as a monolithic whole without a gender dynamic, without a race dynamic and without individuality; in other words many activists and intellectuals wanted to lead what they considered to be the 'working class', without understanding what it was.

I had no romantic notions about the dignity of poverty, or that it was progressive to wear grubby clothes or squat a flat, indeed I was sickened by the 'downwardly mobile' who seemed to populate whole sections of the Labour Party, over-anxious to speak for working-class people. Having experienced poverty in many phases of my life, I became more and more convinced that socialism was about increasing choices for working people not reducing them.

As Leader of the local authority I have the opportunity to introduce my own style to the Administration of socialism — doing it, not merely talking about it. I want to see change occur despite the fact that the Tories have won their third electoral victory and imposed further cuts on councils such as Lambeth which represent large numbers of working-class people. I still believe it is possible to deliver what we *are* able to deliver in a socialist way. Whenever there are resources, there are politics, because politics is about the distribution of resources. As a councillor I conceded rate-capping because I see it as my job to ensure that all those who have a right to receive services receive the most appropriate and sensitive services possible. I still loathe the prejudice and discrimination of this society and will continue to do all in my power to confront and overcome them, whatever the press and the Tory party may say or do.

Postscript

This article was drafted in May 1988. Since its completion I and six other councillors have withdrawn from the Leadership elections for Lambeth, because we have not received full support from our local Labour parties for our strategy on rate-capping and maintenance of services to the Borough. Whilst I am convinced that alternative strategies do not have either sufficient support or credibility, our withdrawal will assist future discussion better than our remaining with only negative support. For my own part, I am not prepared to be a 'token', and consider my principles more important than holding onto power at any price.

We are all remaining as Councillors, spending more time working within our parties, and most significantly, encouraging more working-class people to join the Labour Party so that it reflects the community that the Council serves. And now I'm looking for a job with about four million other . . .

GOING ORANGE

Sally Fraser

Sally Fraser was 18 when she joined the Women's Liberation Movement in 1968. In 1976 she became a follower of Bhagwan Shree Rajneesh and took the name of Chandan. She has lived in communities of one kind or another for 16 years, emerging in July 1987, and she now lives in Devon. Chandan spoke to Amanda Sebestyen in London in February 1988.

The question I would ask is: why would someone in the women's movement turn spiritual? And to answer, I would have to say that there was no contradiction, because the essence of the women's movement and the essence of being spiritual were the same thing.

The great thing about the women's movement was that it was about us, it wasn't to fight somebody else's cause. I seem to remember that it didn't actually last very long — we ended up fighting other people's causes in the end. The group of people that I was with were middle-class — or were, say, born working-class and had been educated — and we all went and lived in Hackney, and it was important to be amongst the working classes. We were involved in alternative living; in squatting; in crêches and setting up nurseries.

My biggest switch from being political to being spiritual, to put it very, very simplistically, was that before I thought that I couldn't be happy unless the whole world was happy. The switch into the spiritual is that you actually turn that on its head — unless I'm happy, what can I give to the world that can make any difference, that can produce happiness? So, for happiness to spread, to grow and encompass the whole world, it has to start here.

The women's movement also said, it has to start here: the politics of experience. But that wasn't what was actually happening when we were living in Hackney. After a few years I felt like an unpaid social worker. Not only that, but if you go round patching up other people's lives, you're actually not doing them any good at all. I realised that we were damaging other people's lives, and I was horrified by this realisation.

I spent a couple of years where I didn't have anything to replace that with, so I had a sort of gap. And towards the second year of that gap, I labelled what was going on with me as a political/spiritual split. A close friend of mine called Penelope ended up taking Sannyas and going to Poona, so I was being directly challenged by that. And I was studying acupuncture at the time, which was again a big shift in me because earlier I had given up Tai Chi, which I really loved, when I moved into this political commune where it was frowned upon as self-indulgent. When I met Penelope in 1973, I started doing Tai Chi again.

I have a memory of you having some kind of physical illness.

Yes, hepatitis. We were all living in squats and not eating properly and not cleaning properly, and the doctor didn't diagnose the first person who caught it, so she basically spent a month infecting everybody else.

Eventually I started studying acupuncture, because I was very uncomfortable in my body, but really it came out of my fascination for China. I would read any book I could lay my hands on about the experience of just one village throughout the whole revolution. But at a certain stage I realised that I personally wouldn't be happy there.

And then I met Dinah again, who I hadn't seen for years, since the Belsize Park group, and she gave me a book of Bhagwan's; and it was just bells ringing all over the place, you know. Here was somebody who was expressing exactly what I was.

All my friends were feminists and socialists, and I didn't want to leave them, but I knew if I followed this direction, which was absolutely overwhelming me, I would lose my friends. So it took me a long time to go and visit Poona, because there were two things there which were absolutely dead against the women's movement — one was to have a leader, a guru. And second, he was a man.

Didn't you feel anything inside yourself abour wearing this man's picture round your neck?

Oh, when it came to the point I was terrified of coming back to Hackney.

But what about yourself? No problem there?

No.

No feeling of compromise or anything?

None whatsoever.

Quite happy to wear this person's picture round your neck?

Absolutely! That wasn't a problem for me, to allow him to show me the way, because he'd been on it. It was as simple as somebody who's been from London to Birmingham before — you let them drive the car because they know the way. No problem. But I'd always been somebody who was very influenced by other people's judgement, so it was very hard for me to come back, in orange, and with a *mala* round my neck.

I remember you as young and enthusiastic in 1969, very bubbly and a bit of a pet to everybody in Belsize Park . . .

Well, I was younger, yeah.

And then I remember you in Hackney, still very enthusiastic and popular.

Except that all the time that I was there I didn't feel right about this business of going out there on the streets and trying to persuade people to see things a certain way.

The move from the North London, middle-class women's movement scene, to Gloucester Avenue in Islington was in a way a movement towards inside the self, because the people in that commune were doing all kinds of very daring things — at one point they didn't even have their own rooms, everybody slept in any empty bed and they shared each other's clothes. I used to hear about these things and envy them like mad, because I was moving in this rather straight left world.

It *was* exciting. But when I actually moved there it was dead as a door-nail. It wasn't for real. The visual image I got immediately on moving in was that everybody was walking round naked with barrels around them to make sure they never met. The barrel was the ideology, and the people who were most articulate dominated.

Nobody would look at themselves — although there was all this talk, talk, talk, until 6 o'clock in the morning, endlessly. They were dealing with the outside: the structure of this household is that everything's shared, we have no possessions, we don't possess each other, we don't possess our own clothes, we don't possess anything. But what was actually happening was all hidden — all suppressed. They were trying to jump from here to there by going *there*, instead of starting from *here*. And I would try and get that across, but I didn't have the language that they'd developed at Cambridge and Essex, and if you didn't say something in a proper language you got torn apart.

They were against hierarchies, but there was a very strong one?

— You know the pamphlet of that time, 'The Tyranny of Structurelessness'?*
When I first got there people admired me because I'd come out in meetings and say things terribly simply. I still don't know what reify means. But I soon got pretty smashed, because I was hopelessly outclassed intellectually.

Was there no such experience with joining a religious movement? No experience of saying what you really felt and not being understood?

Oh god, there it was just like we all felt the same. But there is a difference between Bhagwan and the organisation. The organisation might use the words of Bhagwan to make people feel bad about themselves — that's the nature of organisations. But Bhagwan himself is continuously contradicting himself anyway. (And it's his organisation, obviously . . .) But in the early days I was nothing to do with the organisation anyway. All there was, was reading this man's words or hearing him just talk, and there would be no argument in me. He was just talking about natural laws.

We were against natural laws, weren't we, in the women's movement?

Oh I see, in terms of biology, male and female. When I say natural laws, I just mean the way life works, the way existence works. When

---

* *Pamphlet by Jo Freeman, also known as Joreen; see Lynne Harne's article for details.*

we were living in communes in Islington or Hackney, there was an ideology about how the commune should be. Whereas when we were Sannyasins living in the communes in India, or in England when we came back, it wasn't ideological, it actually started from where we were at.

You mean some people had money, some people didn't — that always used to shock us when we heard about your ashram.

If you lived in a commune you were completely taken care of anyway, down to your clothes, your toothpaste, your tobacco, your food — and you didn't need money.

So is that not true, that some people were living on earth floors and others in a comfortable ashram, where you had to pay?

There was a point when the ashram tried to make money by getting people to pay for rooms. Some people would wait two years to move in, because they had no money and they had to just prove themselves to be terribly good workers. But then, somebody else would turn up without any money and be moved in the next day. There was never any logicality about it. In fact, my mother had given me some money to make a contribution, and I never got allowed in anyway! There was no way you could buy your way in.

The women's movement would talk about how we were conditioned and try to recondition us — the whole point of what Bhagwan was trying to do was actually to de-condition us. You don't replace one belief system with another. You remove all belief systems, so that what's left is your individuality.

But if becoming yourself meant that you were against him, what would happen if you would try to challenge things?

Bhagwan would lecture every morning on rebellion and being individual, and then all during the day the organisation would basically try and mould you into a worker that was easy to manage. You were in this continual friction between the two, and in fact I got very sick when I first started work, because I couldn't contain those two things. But he's the master of contradictions . . .

The danger is that you can replace your capitalist belief system with your socialist or feminist belief system, and then you can replace it with a spiritual belief system, and it's just the same as any of the previous ones you had. You can live as a Sannyasin for years and years, and you've got absolutely nowhere. I think it's only in the last year or so that I could ever have admitted to the fact that when I took Sannyas I didn't drop belief systems, I picked up another one. Now, because I can see it, there's à slight separation. And then Bhagwan is always taking the carpet from under our feet, and we're always madly running after it and trying to keep it still.

Some of what you say reminds me of the transference relationship between an analyst and a patient; they say that the analysis really begins when the patient leaves.

Exactly. Yeah. And Bhagwan's always saying that too.

Although you're dropping the belief, you haven't stopped loving him or admiring him?

Not at all. I pursue my own . . . love . . . In fact the less I need to be around his physical presence, the more I'm relying on myself, the more I love him, actually. Because I *don't* need him, because he's given me so much because he's — you're making a face!

If you have't met Bhagwan it's hard to explain. When you sit with him, when he's talking, he's — oh dear — he's separate from his mind, he's in total silence. So when you sit with him, you experience your own silence, your own being. That's why there's such a tremendous attachment to being in his presence, because if you sit there you experience yourself, and it's such a beautiful experience. It's not like having a very, very, very good therapist take you through something, because that very, very, very good therapist has a skill but he's a blind leading the blind, or she's a blind leading the blind. Bhagwan's not blind.

He would answer people's questions endlessly, endlessly. And only now do I know what he was talking about. Before I would accept everything he said because it fitted, it made sense to me intellectually, but there's a huge gap between knowing that he's right and actually having experienced it yourself. There's no bridge between the two. You have to experience it.

Was it 12 years you were in those communities?

Yes, I've been nearly 12 years a Sannyasin, in Poona, Suffolk, Oregon . . .

How much did the world outside come in?

Not much. I never read the papers. The world outside came in, in the sense that we were very much harassed; also that we were running businesses so we were dealing with the outside all the time. For the first few years I was in the commune in Suffolk I ran the transport . . .

Were you one of those people who did motor maintenance when you were a feminist?

Yes. But I didn't actually hold a spanner when I was in the commune — I would direct the spanner, so to speak — but it helped me that I knew what I was talking about.

What about political issues, like racism, heterosexual attitudes, things like that; did they come up?

Racism came up from the outside, when our design department was asked by a mobile home company to make an advertising video. We produced, out of our lot, a family to put into this mobile home — and the company turned it down because the man we'd used as the grandfather was black. They said, he's got a West Indian accent, and in fact he had a Scottish accent. We went through a big thing about what to do about their racism. There was no doubt about the community being anti-racist or anti any form of discrimination. A homosexual relationship was just as much respected as any other relationship in the commune.

Except that you went to these talks in the morning and sometimes Bhagwan would say —

He'd say — homosexuality's an immature form of sexuality, it's an avoidance, and the true challenge comes out of the polarity of opposites. Two people of the same sex being together are avoiding something, and for you to get anywhere spiritually, you can't avoid. Once you've realised yourself, you can take all the contradictions and the opposites — you're not male or female, you're not old or young — you're you, you don't belong to any of those definitions any more. But unless you experience those opposites, you don't know what beyond is.

But he would say these things and people would still continue being exactly as they were, and not get any stick from anybody.

Did he say anything about race?

He says there are just beings, there's no race, there shouldn't be passports, it's all ridiculous. But you can't *say* what he says, because it's all contradictory. If anybody who had any -ism to them wanted to find something in him to criticise politically, they couldn't find a thing: also if they wanted to say he was racist, antisemitic, they could very easily, because he makes all sorts of outrageous statements — and one of his things is telling jokes, and all jokes are racist or sexist or something.

The biggest problem for me, I think, when I started working in the organisation, was not sexual politics but finding that I was afraid of authority. Because the person out there had the power to tell me what job I was doing, or whether I could move in or not move in to the ashram — because they had that power over me, it affected my ability just to be me.

What was it like when you were much younger, at school, or with your parents?

I was always cowed by authority. Always.

What, a good girl at school?

Yes always.

I can't believe it. It doesn't tally with what I see.

I used to not be able to understand any of the rebels at school because they were always getting into trouble.

But how interesting that you were so very much part of the '68 mood.

Although to the outside I might have seemed totally rebellious, within my peer group I was conforming. When I moved into

Sannyas, I moved into a different kind of peer group, and I'm not a
conformist, but at the same time I didn't have the inner strength to
be a rebel either, so I just got into trouble. I really got on the wrong
side of all sorts of people, because I would speak my mind, but I'd be
so scared of the consequences that it would come out heavily.

The authority thing is, I think, what I went into the deepest,
especially as I also ended up *being* the authority. When I went to the
Ranch in Oregon, at the end of the year where I'd been running the
commune in England, I was given one of the top jobs there, a
department of 300 people which was responsible for the whole of the
land — the land and the landscaping and the vegetables and the
milk. And on my first visit, after two weeks I was put in charge of
building bridges on the road, as well as the garage and transport.

*An incredible number of skills you had to acquire. Can you see ways that
our own movement could have used people's talents better?*

I think the very first thing that jumps out is that there was too much
judgement in the women's movement. Too much separating people
into goodies and baddies. And too much fighting. If you want to
reach people you have to respect them, and if you treat a person as
an enemy they're going to respond as an enemy. It's absolute.
There's no way, unless they're a highly intelligent person, that they
can actually deflect attack and still be themselves and come back
with warmth. It's impossible.

*Sometimes, inside an organisation, people start being treated as enemies.
You had that experience with the Sannyasin as well, you saw this happen
in Oregon when people started trying to poison each other.*

As far as I can understand — retrospectively, because one still
doesn't know the facts, only what was in the papers and what people
said in rumours — there was one woman who was trying to preserve
her power. She saw a group of people who she felt threatened it, she
wanted to get rid of them, and maybe she tried to poison them — I
have no idea. I personally did experience her as somebody who was
into power. I had also had experience of her at times before as
somebody very warm, so I've seen both sides of her.

After everything came out, lots of people were very angry and felt
very ripped-off, and other people were not angry because they saw
how they'd supported what had happened. Not consciously —

nobody knew there were poisonings going on — just the power trip.
To me it was very important to see how you'd supported that
yourself, by just letting things pass; hearing little voices in your head
saying, Hey I don't really like the feel of this, and then finding some
sort of convincing reasons to keep quiet, because you didn't want to
get into trouble. What happened on the Ranch was a really
important experience for people.

I was there for the last six months before the Ranch closed down,
and suddenly it was a totally different place. Suddenly it was like —
Oh wow, now we can run it how we want it to be run — now *we're* in
power. And it doesn't work like that. The next lot of people get in
power and boom, same thing. Not poisonings, but the same kinds of
trips.

The way I saw the communes being run was one of the reasons I
wanted to run one. I wanted to try running it without judging people.
What I discovered was that I *did* run it non-judgementally, as far as I
was capable at the time, but that it was very tempting sometimes to
use my power to squash somebody I felt was doing something that I
really didn't like. I never actually did it. But there's so much temptation. It's really interesting to know about power from a position of
power, because everybody around you gives it to you on a plate.

*I've noticed that the people at the top of spiritual organisations always do
seem to have personal privileges, even to the point of having full-time body
servants.*

A lot of it makes sense, actually. It frees you to get on with what you
really need to focus on — and on the other hand, I think it denies
you ordinary experiences. Some of the things I've really appreciated
since I left the commune are doing my cleaning, washing my
clothes, cooking.

You didn't take it in turns to do that in the commune?

No, we had a cleaning department and a laundry department and a
cook and a kitchen. But everyone's job would change a lot.

You know, if you've got a demanding job, it is really helpful not to
have to take care of personal tasks. On the other hand, while you're
doing these things, you're being ordinary, you're having a period of
time when you can just be rather than doing. It's really good to have
that balance in the day.

When does Bhagwan have the experience of being ordinary?

I would say never, in the sense he never cleans or cooks. He talks four or five hours a day, and it's exhausting. He's very fragile. He's got asthma and he's diabetic and he's got a bad back and he's allergic to everything under the sun.

What does he eat?

He eats a very pure diet, and when we were on the Ranch we used to grow his food separately. We had special greenhouses just to make sure that when his vegetables reached him they were completely uncontaminated and pure. They were guarded, that was another thing; there was always a threat to his life, and one easy way to kill him would be to contaminate his food or his milk. So he had special cows.

Why would people want to murder him?

Because he's totally outrageous and he says things that upset a lot of people. I've been there when somebody's tried to kill him, a Hindu. Bhagwan has attacked every religion.

I always think that in absolutist and totalitarian organisations the leader's constantly scared, and that's part of why the organisation gets that way.

I don't know if he's scared. I think it's the people around him.

Spiritual leaders have a sort of court, don't they? It's dreadful.

It is obnoxious, but the dreadful thing is that when you're in the organisation you want to be one of the closest people. I got very caught up in that, I would say that in some way I still am. It's always nice to sit up front because Bhagwan can see you and you've still got that kind of longing somehow to be noticed and for him to come along and say you're doing terribly well. Actually a lot of my last visit to Poona, six months ago, was to do with dealing with that part of me that wanted to be noticed and be close to him. I finally ended up not minding at all whether he knew who I was or not. I realised that another reason I had wanted to be in charge of things was to bring me closer to the core, and bring his attention to me.

All these things I'm saying now I would not have dared to admit before. I've always been a very purist sort of person, quite ideological in a way, and always wanted to be above my own judgement as well as anybody else's. Now the less I care about my own judgement, the less I care about anybody else's, and that is what gives me my freedom.

SEX DOESN'T FIT, RACE DOESN'T FIT

Marilyn Gayle

I was born at St James' Hospital, Balham, on 5th August 1953 at 6.20 pm. As my mother and I struggled through our agonising 23 hour labour, her screams were heard by everyone on Ward 12. I've been told I was distressed at birth.

My mother had come over to England from Eire at 17 in 1949, to be a student nurse. My father first came to England from Jamaica — where he'd joined the RAF — in 1944. After the War he went home to Jamaica for a year, and my two elder sisters were born within three months of each other. He then returned to work in England, where my parents were married in 1951. I, my mother's first child, was named in honour of Marilyn Monroe — she was worshipped by my father.

I was a bright child. At seven, thinking that it was a primer, I read *The ABC Of Anarchism* by Alexander Berkman. I can clearly remember thinking at the time that my life would never be the same again. It's probably about time I re-read it.

In 1968 I was in my fifteenth year. I now had three younger sisters and a baby brother — my parents' son, heir, pride and joy. Having earlier passed the 11+ exam (due entirely, I thought, to God's divine intervention), I was now the token Black girl (but politely labelled "coloured") in the 'A' stream of the fourth year at Garratt Green Girls' Comprehensive. This establishment contained over 2,000 girls, just under half of whom were Black. The regulation school uniform was grey; in their wisdom the school governors had decided that this colour would complement all skin shades (it didn't).

To date I had spent almost my entire career at this school feeling alienated and isolated. My mother had warned me against developing "a chip on my shoulder", however it was difficult to work with individuals and groups who revelled in their racist attitudes (which they, with Enoch Powell's blessing, deemed respectable and normal), and who felt totally at liberty to stereotype Black people as inferior subhumans. Occasionally attempts were made to include me in their racist clubs — comments such as "We hate Black people

Marilyn, but you're all right because you're half white", were commonplace. All Afro-Caribbean pupils were, regardless of origin, labelled as Jamaicans and in the twisted minds of these racists Jamaicans were scapegoated as the root of all evil in British society. Many teachers, including the headmistress, perpetuated these ugly myths. Although I have blocked out a lot of incidents, I can clearly remember one occasion when my maths teacher confidently announced to the whole group (all white except me) that Marilyn could never be a mathematician — science had proved that "coloured" people had a biological defect which made them less intelligent than whites.

At home, things were as bad if not worse. I was a well developed, overweight, rebellious 14-year-old who read *Jackie*, as well as the underground *Oz* and *IT* magazines. My interests were fashion, pop music, boys (no contact allowed), make-up (not allowed) and, amongst other things, politics. I had recently become involved with the WRP (Young Socialists) and was trying desperately hard to grasp the concept of dialectical materialism. I belonged to the local branch of the Schools' Action Union and had once taken a day off school (without permission) to march in solidarity with several of my more enlightened teachers who were campaigning for better pay and conditions. My political activities were tolerated — both my parents were Labour voters and my mother comes from an old IRA family — but in their eyes I was still a small child. I desperately wanted to be part of "swinging London", but my parents considered that as a girl I was at risk and needed to be protected from the outside world. They worried that if I was let out of their sight for an evening at a Rock concert, I might come home pregnant or, still worse, a pregnant junkie. They needn't have worried, I was very sensible.

At that time, my parents believed that their children belonged to them, body and soul, until the age of legal majority — 18 years. They tried to control my every thought, word and deed: my wayward thoughts and words (which were almost continuous in their opinion) were punished by beatings with a leather strap. My thoughts were more difficult to police, so they resorted to a method which left me feeling confused and miserable. I was told that my case had been discussed by several psychiatrists, all of whom had agreed with my parents that I was crazy. Various forms of treatment had been recommended and were, in fact, in operation. As I couldn't remember ever having met a psychiatrist, I asked my mother (I was even more afraid of my remote, untouchable father) for more specific details of my illness and its treatment. She mysteriously replied that I did not need to know. All that mattered was that I was undergoing treatment. I was desperately worried by this and I often wondered why none of my teachers had ever said anything. I thought that they must know! I, of course, never mentioned a word about it at school. In fact, I was so ashamed and embarrassed that I never told anyone, not even my best friend.

At home I washed, cooked, cleaned and looked after the little ones as I had been taught to, tried to respect my elders and betters and helped to run the family businesses, a driving school and a car hire company. I tried hard to please but was mostly unsuccessful. Homework was not a priority for me — there was too much housework to do. My parents considered that I was badly behaved and did not set a good enough example. They constantly threatened to withdraw their financial support and make me leave school. Their other threat was to place me in a Children's Home as "beyond parental care and control". I often wished they would.

Now I can see that, undoubtedly, my parents were making the best of a difficult time. They not only faced both anti-Irish and anti-Black racism; in addition intermarriage was frowned upon by most of society and many wanted to see them, and their children, fail. Both of them worked extremely hard to build up their business so they could maintain five children and improve the material quality of our lives. They believed that they had a responsibility to bring up their daughters to be excellent housewives. As regards discipline and punishments, well, we were often told that we were lucky not to have our grandparents as parents! Most of my parents' energies were taken up with survival in a hostile environment — they just didn't have the time or energy for the luxury of a political analysis of their situation.

As time went by I began to hear reports of the actions of women's groups up and down the country. I was particularly impressed when in 1970 four women disrupted the Miss World contest at the Albert Hall, in full view of the television cameras. Shortly afterwards I left school for 'A' Level college, but moved on before I took the exams, as my sister and I had successfully auditioned to become vocalists in a Soul/Reggae band.

I left the band after six months; I now wanted to be a writer, but I couldn't type.

On my 13-week long BBC secretarial course, I was rather shocked to find we were expected to learn not only shorthand and typing but also flower arranging, make-up and good grooming, how to serve drinks in their correct glasses, and menu and seating planning for dinner parties. During a talk by the Controller of Radio Four, he asked us our BBC ambitions and then smugly informed us "girls" that none of us could ever be Director General — that job was open only to male candidates. I also noticed that those few women who had achieved any kind of power positions within the BBC were sitting targets for ugly rumours and malicious innuendoes. For those of us who were going into humbler positions, however, all was not lost. Another lecturer told us excitedly that one of the perks of our employment was that the BBC was the largest marriage bureau in the world! My impression that there were hardly any Black people working for the Corporation was partially rectified when we were taken to visit Bush House, home of External Broadcasting. There, I saw more people of different nationalities eating lunch together in a confined space (the canteen) than I could ever have imagined.

When the course ended I was sent to Bush House (what a surprise!) to work in the Arabic Audience Research department, transferring to English by Radio and Television. By now I not only thoroughly disliked secretarial work but also the fact that I was just a tiny cog, made servile along with thousands of other women, in this vast bureaucratic structure. I still had much of my two year contract left to serve, but I couldn't stand to be expected to defer to white men in white suits, so I became a subversive and joined a consciousness-raising group formed with other BBC women. It was at about this time that I started writing as a feminist. Eventually, to my parents' disappointment (they had hoped I would eventually become a newscaster), I managed to leave.

I was living with friends in Battersea, actively involved in women's politics and working for *Rolling Stone* magazine, by the middle of 1972. Nearly all my friends were liberal whites — within the Black community I was regarded as something of a weirdo. Many Black women I knew were following a traditional path and were intent on settling down with the men of their dreams to have children; several schoolfriends had gone, not unwillingly, into arranged marriages. Embarrassed and frightened by my militant feminist stance, my family did all they could to bring me to my sense... My father opinioned that women's liberation was the worst thing that had ever happened to women (surely he meant men) and everyone present, including my mother, agreed with him. When my sister got married (to a man I considered was, in the parlance of the time, a male chauvinist pig), I rebelliously wore black to her wedding.

I was enjoying the social whirl around *Rolling Stone*, mixing with film and pop stars at parties, gigs, film previews, restaurants and nightclubs. I was also very heavily involved in many women's groups and campaigns, dealing with the issues of sexuality, psychiatry, Irish women prisoners held in English prisons, sexism in the music industry and abortion. Eventually I found that working for *Rolling Stone* and being an active feminist became mutually exclusive. I left the magazine and decided to get a job with an organisation which was working for women. I'd been involved with the National Abortion Campaign since its inception and, as I had also recently undergone the pain and distress of an unwanted pregnancy and its subsequent termination (on the NHS), I felt very strongly about women's rights to control over their own bodies. I became an administrative assistant with the Pregnancy Advisory Service. During this time I also campaigned with the Abortion Law Reform Association which, faced with the threat of James White's Abortion Amendment Bill, had become more militant.

At the beginning of 1978 I was three months pregnant. I was living in Leamington Spa (both LIFE — the anti-abortion pressure group — and the British Movement were based there), and I was working day and night to finish writing a book aptly called *The All Colour World Of Baby Animals*. In 1975, I had become infatuated with Andrew, who presented himself as an anti-sexist, anti-racist politically aware male but, as time passed, inevitably proved to be the opposite (he now works for the *Daily Star* as a production editor). If I had taken any notice of my friends, or of the glaringly obvious bad omens (Leo + Taurus = Natural Enemies), then the relationship would have fizzled out after two weeks (or better still, two days). In the event, it dragged on for five tortuous, painful years.

Unfortunately, Andrew and I were not only lovers/enemies we were also business partners who wrote, edited and designed books together and shared a large joint overdraft. I had planned the pregnancy well in advance, having decided in my youth that I would have a child, preferably a girl, by the time I was 25. Andrew had never wanted a child, and was often too angry and upset to work, while I was driving myself to exhaustion to get it finished. I had to carry on — commissions weren't easy to come by and I needed money to provide for myself and my unborn child. I asked Andrew several times to leave the flat we were renting. He could have gone home to his parents in Bolton, who were already scandalised by our relationship. I felt I could not leave, I needed a home for myself and the baby and I had nowhere else. When I had begun the affair, I had alienated myself from nearly all my friends. I was now far too embarrassed and proud to ask for their help. I could not expect anything from my own parents who adored and supported Andrew.

Although I had no emotional support during this uncomfortable, stressful pregnancy, I didn't care. I wanted the baby, was convinced that I was following the right path for me, and that ultimately, sooner rather than later, I could provide my daughter with a secure, happy environment in which to grow and flourish. I went to National Childbirth Trust classes and was trained, along with eight white, middle-class, respectably married "ladies", in techniques of breathing and pain control. During labour, I was surprised to find that these techniques actually worked. Our teacher was a LIFE supporter, and also a racist, and I had several heated arguments with her in her car as she ferried me to and from Coventry each week.

Eventually, I went into induced labour at 10.00 am on 24th June 1978, nearly one month early. After three excruciatingly painful hours during which I stoically kept quiet, I gave birth to a 5lb 2oz boy! Now it was my turn to be shocked. Although I knew that there was every possibility that I would have a son, I had convinced myself that I would be meeting a little girl. I decided, finally, that my son was sent as a test and a life task from the Goddess. I would do my best to help him become a non-sexist, caring, balanced human being who would never see any advantage in abusing his male power and who would always challenge woman-hating male attitudes. When I left the hospital, I continued to work non-stop on our commissions, in between breast-feeding on demand and violent arguments with the now ecstatically proud, possessive father. We argued over the baby's last name: My mother supported me when I insisted that Alex must have my surname. My father, on the other hand, declared that "a man is not a man unless his son bears his name".

As time passed, I became involved once again in the local National Abortion Campaign group and also went to meetings of the Leamington Spa Anti-Racist, Anti-Fascist Committee. I was too sceptical of Bhagwan Shree Rajneesh to have anything much to do with the Sannyasins living in the Centre next door (many of them had been Premies — followers of Guru Maharaj Ji — six months earlier). By the end of 1978, although I hadn't managed to extricate myself from the relationship/partnership, it was on the cards and I knew (or thought I knew) that everything would finally work out in favour of me and the baby.

In 1986 I again became involved with women's politics on a daily basis. I had managed to end the relationship with Andrew, buy our flat, and then fall straight into another heterosexual relationship with a man called ... Andrew. I wasn't learning my lessons very well. I was now living with the second Andrew in a house which we had bought together in Manchester, and was the mother of two sons — the baby, Damien, also had my last name. Living with the second Andrew was just as repressive as living with the first. I was writing occasional articles for *Chic*, a glossy magazine for Black women, attending the odd Greenham umbrella group meeting and also infrequent meetings of the Black Women's Network.

In September 1986, as part of a fainthearted commitment to equal opportunities, I was employed along with two other Black women at a large radical bookshop run at that time by a white feminist collective. Initially the new Black workers were bewildered by the hostility encountered from some of the collective members, not realising that we had inherited past problems from the collective's history. We endured a year of being ignored, and sometimes yelled at, until we came to believe that our presence was highly unwelcome and had caused dissension even before our appointments. We were given no real training, but after a few months were blamed for the dire state of the shop's finances. Our inexperience was constantly cited, after over a year, as the reason why we couldn't be involved in long-term planning. Four of us — half the working collective, two Black women and two white working-class lesbians — could take no more. We placed our resignations in the agenda book as a protest, mine to take effect from the following month, October 1987, and the others' in January 1988 after the Christmas rush. None of the other women showed much interest.

Feeling frustrated, hurt and angry, we prepared a press release and documentary evidence to explain the grievances which had led to our resignation: that three white, middle-class heterosexual women had monopolised management functions to such an extent that the collective was no longer working "in a non-hierarchical way with as much job rotation as possible" (*Statement of Aims — 10.1.83*) but was now polarised into a hierarchy. An accompanying document gave written instances of non-cooperative working.

The documents were distributed at the weekly collective meeting on 22nd September 1987. Unfortunately one of our four signatories was away on holiday — whilst all five of the remaining collective were present including, strangely, a member on maternity leave who didn't usually attend weekly meetings, and another who was also officially on holiday. We knew that detailed proposals for the reorganisation of the shop had been prepared by the inner management caucus (without a mandate from the rest of the collective). They had, no doubt, recalled those two members who were officially on leave to support them in their endeavours to rid the shop of areas which they considered unproductive — *ie* Black History and Politics, Worker Writers, Jewellery, Political Badges and Remaindered Books. Anyway, we were never to find out their plans because we were sacked without notice and forced to leave the shop half-way through the meeting without any coherent discussion of our grievances.

Ten minutes after our ejection, we three sat in stunned silence in a nearby pub. We'd been outmanoeuvred, having naively assumed that all those who had wounded us with their insensitive behaviour would see that we had a clear-cut case, realise the error of their ways, and at least apologise to us. Just one woman had.

Two weeks later, our sister Lorine returned home and I broke the unpleasant news to her that she no longer had a job even until January. Realising that our case was severely weakened by our resignations, we all then decided to consult our union representative, wanting at least to be able to claim unemployment benefit. He, in an attempt at arbitration, gave information that we felt to be confidential, to the remaining collective. Two months later, we succumbed to press pressure, and a story, complete with many factual errors, duly appeared in a local listings magazine. Hidden in the sludge of 'unbiased balanced reportage' this gem emerged: the bookshop complained that "their attempts to adopt progressive employment practices towards Black people have not been appreciated".

We who resigned (and were subsequently dismissed on the spot) are lucky to have gained the support of many ex-workers, who had either left quietly or been forced out for similar reasons to ours. Now the shop has been taken over by a completely new collective. Maybe — as a result of our challenge —those women who got rid of us have learned to not use the cut-off, unemotional methods of the patriarchy on women who they consider inferior or invisible because of race, class and sexual orientation.

Now I live in Manchester with Alexander aged nine and Damien aged four. We all live in a large, comfortable, very expensive to run semi-detached house, which I will be selling shortly. By the time that this is published, we will have moved away from Manchester where I feel that I have long overstayed my welcome. Since leaving the bookshop I have been unemployed but have done voluntary work on the Black Women Research Workers' steering committee of a child sexual abuse survivors' group. Recently I resigned because I felt that I could no longer work with some of the women who verbally attacked my love for my two children. Some of these women claim that the only valid feeling women can manifest, if we are being honest with ourselves, is misery and depression, due to our all-encompassing pain caused by male sexual abuse. According to them, suicide is probably the only real solution to our problem of living on a planet which contains men. I've been accused of denying my own and others' pain, and also of trying to set myself up as an exceptional individual because I have defended my two children who, I am trying to make certain, will not grow up into male abusers with an urge to dominate women and other children. I hope they will instead look for and find positive ways of being male in a culture where "male supremacy" has all but destroyed manhood.

I can't accept that there is no hope for these two boys and that I should reject them, because I'm trying to teach them to direct their power towards the service of life, not be afraid to feel their own sensitive women-selves, and to always be in touch with the earth, their Mother. They have always prayed to the Great Goddess (therefore having to put up with much hassle from other children at school who are being brought up to worship a male god), and consider this as natural as breathing.

Meanwhile, I smoke too many cigarettes and feel that I must withdraw for a time from women's politics while I sort out the practical difficulties of our lives — finding a new home, job and childcare. According to Tarot tradition and Numerology, this is my High Priestess year — the year when I get on my path, and there will be no more obstructions to the movement of spirit in my life.

As a Black woman living in Europe, life has never been easy for me. When I first became involved in the women's liberation movement it was almost exclusively white and almost exclusively middle-class and tended to ignore its own racism and classism. Many of the white women I knew then had no contacts with any other Black women or any working-class women. That was their problem, not mine. It still is their problem; white women have to take the initiative to fight their own and other white women's racist attitudes, middle-class women have to deal with their own classist attitudes. Heterosexual women have to deal with their own heterosexist attitudes. There are, of course, differences between Black women as well which have to be explored and discussed. In the meantime, many white feminist organisations continue not only to deny us access to services and resources, but also to work within a philosophy which is only relevant to white society and denies the experiences of Black women. This is inexcusable. We cannot change the course of planetary destruction now facing us — the direct result of 5,000 years of patriarchal rule — and create a future dedicated to life unless we challenge the existence of power imbalances between women, and recognise that we all have to struggle on behalf of those women who are most oppressed. When every woman recognises that she is part of the sisterhood then we can have hope for the future.

FEMINISM AND MARRIAGE

Griselda Pollock

Feminism and marriage.

There is nothing but antagonism between these two terms — or at best irrelevance. But then, this really depends on what we mean by marriage.

All through my twenties — from the late 60s and the beginning of contact with the emerging women's movement — I inveighed against marriage as an institution. It reduced women from independent legal status to that of dependent on a man, took away their name, their financial rights (to tax rebates for instance). And in those days women still needed a husband's signature to hire a TV or get a mortgage.

But 'getting married' or 'marrying someone' also stands for an attempt at a relationship between two adults — a woman and a woman as much as a woman and a man. It means commitment to seeing through the difficulties of two people living together, and sharing the ups and downs of their lives and their personalities. In this sense, marriage can take in many more relationships than those legally defined as such by a marriage certificate. I think it is important to keep a clear distinction between the social structure and the personal relationship (though of course the point feminists have made is that the latter is defined by the former, and I would not want to claim that individuals can stand outside of the larger frameworks which shape their lives). But making this distinction is the way I make sense of having taken the surprising step of getting married.

There can be no doubt that marriage is one of the institutional forms of women's oppression. Historically, marriage has functioned to control and regulate women's money, power, sexuality, pro-creativity, identity and labour within a heterosexual economy. In contemporary societies marriage typically makes love and attraction the price of the domestic package. In return for someone else earning a wage on the labour market, women get to service that bread winner, bear his children and raise them. In systems which designate one sex as sole childcarers and domestic labourers, this is what marriage means as a lifestyle.

If marriage had in any way meant sacrificing my hard-won place in a world of work and money, I would never have contemplated it. I did not have to buy that package of domesticity, and so being married has only meant the occasional irritation as some official form tells me to show it to my husband. I entered into this state in my thirties in partnership with a man with whom I wanted to have a child. I have an established position in my field of work as an art historian. The academic year allowed me to take maternity leave combined with long summer holidays, breastfeed my child and then return to work with remarkably flexible hours. In the first year after our son was born I worked till mid-afternoon and was able to spend afternoons at home with my child. But I still remember vividly the experience of my first 12 hours entirely alone with the baby after my partner had returned to work after his short time off. After one day I knew I would never survive this as a life — I could do it for six months as a gift to my child. But it was only the prospect of returning to work which made this period bearable.

I could watch with some detachment the way I was engulfed in the radically different rhythms dictated by a child whose routines and demands played havoc with the order of time in the public world of work and non-parents. I could fully understand the appeal of giving up the impossible struggle to reconcile a woman and a child with that other world. I could see why women involved with children enter another realm of childcare and food preparation and cleaning and washing and cleaning and washing and picking up and doing it all over again. But it was the privilege of my status in work and the value attached to the job which meant I could afford to employ another woman to help me with childcare. We have had three nannies over the last five years. I have sought out women who had a training and saw their work as a chosen profession. For some time I felt shy about employing a nanny and euphemistically talked of "the woman who takes care of my children". But this then deprived that person precisely of her professional status in her job. Our first nanny asked me exactly what relationship I wanted her to have with our child — it was painful to give him up to someone else, who would have to be close to him in order for me to feel happy when leaving him with her. It has so far worked really well and the children have loved their other carers. I have always, however, wanted to remain the *special* figure represented to me by the word 'mother'.

I do not think that my situation makes it possible to say 'marriage can work'. It is not anything about marriage-as-an-institution which makes it work. Money, which I earned, and the position I had fought for at work, made this escape possible. Behind that lies educational privilege, class and race and many other factors which gave me a chance to work out a lifestyle with a partner and children that did not imprison me.

Being married, having a child and needing all the supports which those events demanded, I joined National Childbirth Trust groups, mums and toddlers groups, and made contact with many women quite different from the feminist circles I had hitherto inhabited. These women negotiated their married, single, or non-married parenting situations in varying ways. With some I tentatively discussed feminist critiques of the assumption that all women love being mothers and are naturally good at it. But for many women I met, having children and caring for them was a positive choice, planned and organised with considerable skill and competence. I am left puzzled. For many women, marriage is both seen to and really *does* provide status in the world, a job they want to do, a way out of another kind of dependence in the families they were born into.

The oppression and subordination structured into marriage are an expression of the overall status of women in our culture. But a blanket feminist condemnation of marriage for all women of all classes, races and sexual groups tends to lose sight of the emotional and psychological field marriage also inhabits, and which the social system exploits. Women marry formally, or make lasting commitments informally, and have children because they *desire* to. The social forms available to heterosexual women to express that desire, and the legal and financial implications of those forms, capture that desire. (For lesbian women there is no social acknowledgement for that desire.) The oppressive and regulating force of the social terms is revealed when conflict arises, and women's lack of power is starkly exposed to men's socially reinforced dominance: when relationships break down.

If a woman can retain money, job, then she has some means to defend herself against loss of power in the private domain. She continues to exist in the public domain and is able to enjoy the life she has chosen in the private. I suppose this is what I think has happened to me, and to many other feminists who are either legally married or live in long-term partnerships with or without children.

In the 60s and 70s many experimented with non-monogamous relationships and multiple or successive relations. Personal experience, and that amazing stream of literature produced by women struggling to make wholly different lives, kept bringing me back to the sobering thought that we were trying for a way of life against the grain of our psychological preparation. There was no antidote in politicised morality to the terrible pains of jealousy, because we were psychologically formed in patterns of love and rejection which Freud analysed as foundations of sexuality and subjectivity in the European nuclear family. I do not mean to suggest that we are stuck like this. But I feel there has been an important shift of emphasis. We have become kinder to ourselves. We have tried to understand and acknowledge the force of our psychic patterning in this society — which is not wholly negative — so that we can negotiate the varying stages of our lives instead of trying to force ourselves into absolutely different moulds by force of will and political conviction.

I married out of a recognition that came to me painfully, after a decade of experimentaton and a high rate of failure in relationships. I did deeply want, if not need, the stability of a commitment to long-term sexual and emotional fidelity. I did want the comfort of an attempt to make a framework of solidarity around me. But why marry and not just live together? Frankly I loved being liked and wanted that much. I was knocked out by the fact that someone could publicly make that commitment to me as a long-term partner. I suddenly found myself able to make a similar decision about Tony. It felt like growing up and knowing what I needed and wanted, ending a false romantic fantasy and recognising what a real relationship implied.

We also decided to have children. I wanted to do this in a relationship which I felt might see them through the time they needed people who cared for them to be around in a simple stable way, one that would not leave me — or Tony — with all the difficulties of single parenting. This passes no judgement on the many ways women and men choose to raise children. Given what I felt I lacked in my own childhood, I determined to do my best to give my children a world of continuous love and support through joint parenting. Emotionally, being married warms me, and this makes possible my work in the public sphere. I work better. The way sexuality and relationships ploughed up the field of my life in my twenties and early thirties was distracting, disruptive, and plunged me into prolonged and painful depression. What I entered into by marrying, however, was not a retreat from feminism. It is a feminist, a political situation.

It probably sounds odd for me to say at this point that my partner and I are trying to make a feminist marriage. That comes back to negotiation, remaking actual structures as we live them with some acknowledgement of our needs and vulnerabilities. It is very hard, and I think my children and their father bear the burden in some ways more than I do. To have both the joys and pleasures of parenting — actually more than that, mothering — and yet have the kind of backup and support which means I can go to work every day, have the intellectual and emotional space to write, travel and lecture, accept invitations to go abroad, take up career opportunities, requires total co-operation.

Several years ago I went to Australia to work for three months as a visiting lecturer at the University of Queensland. This involved the whole family moving on my initiative and income. It also involved my partner's complete commitment to be involved fifty-fifty in childcare throughout his summer vacation. (Normally we both get a six to seven hour working day through paid childcare and share the rest.) Tony's worktime was much altered by the fact that we worked alternate mornings and afternoons, meeting on campus at midday to swap over the children. Our arrangements caused considerable interest. People usually started a conversation by asking what had brought my husband to Australia, assuming that it was *his* work which had brought us out. They found the fact that he so completely shared the childcare for me to work, quite as shocking a challenge to their assumptions as the fact that it was my job that brought us here. This experience was important. It is not just what I do that is feminist but the public effect of the whole relationship.

My partner does not 'help' with domestic and childcare responsibilities. That horrible term leaves unquestioned the idea that this work is fundamentally mine because I am a woman. He is the domestic organiser, he shops, plans menus, cares for the house more systematically and with more commitment than I do. After the birth of my first child, he relieved me of almost all housework so that I could care for my son while having time to work, to reassure myself that I was still a functioning productive person. I wrote more in that first year after the birth than I had for many previous years. I, however, took advantage of my husband's generosity and still do, ambitiously driven to do too much and thus undercut my partner, the children and our household in favour of my career interests and work responsibilities. Tony's work history has been marked by Thatcherism; forced out of teaching in the social sciences at the beginning of his career into unemployment, he retrained, worked commercially for some years and is now back in teaching computing science. Now, after a long time of interruptions and redirections, things are coming together in his work and I will give him as much space and support as he gave me. The division of home-based jobs is now negotiated on the basis of our own particular needs at different times. This can only be possible because of what we have struggled to work out before, to overcome any automatic sex-based divisions.

The hardest place for making this shift came with our relations with the children. I wanted the world — to be their mother, to enjoy absolute primacy over their hearts, to have them turn to me as the rock of their lives — while wanting all the freedom to work, travel and go out. Tony and I planned to share parenting. But to gain freedom from the domestic mothering package I had to give up something that I had not anticipated wanting so much to keep to myself: the closeness that only full-time mothering and being with the child can bring. I have not yet reconciled the desires of motherhood and the equally powerful passions of feminist scholarship and the world of work. I long for a feminist literature to help throw light on this particular dilemma.

Getting married brought me some positive bonuses. It has meant entry into a family — the one Tony and I have made and the ones we came from — my siblings with their children, his sister and his parents, cousins and so forth. When I first got involved with Tony and visited his parents, I tried to imagine myself becoming part of a Jewish family, where 'family' was so different from what I had experienced before. I remember clearly thinking I couldn't make this work, I could never play the part of daughter-in-law, I wouldn't make it in a network of relationships that suddenly gave concrete meaning to feminist theories of women as objects of exchange in a kinship system. I felt a total outsider. There seemed to be an unbridgeable gap between this community and my Bohemian, leftish, alternative, feminist life-style. But I was embraced by loving acceptance and deep respect for relatedness and loyal ties. When allowed in, welcomed with warmth and love into a close-knit family, caring for each other, treating the others with respect and their hopes, fears, successes as important, I feel I have gained greatly and have learnt a lot about decent, caring and loving human relationships. A side-effect has been a renewed closeness with my own brother, sister and their families.

This act of rejoining the family was accompanied, however, by a terrible breach. My immediate feminist community attacked and condemned me for having got married. In part it was because I had done it privately, not letting them know. It is hard to explain why I did not see the necessity to make a feminist statement about my sudden political 'volte-face'. I think now that my silence represented a withdrawal from a certain kind of feminist community with whom my links were weakening personally and politically. The women's group seemed no longer to be able to negotiate personal clashes politically, and my decision did not feel as if it could include those women. My decision came from the pressure of other feelings, projects and ideas for my life; in no sense less motivated by feminism, but no longer in those particular collective ways typical of that earlier moment of women's liberation. The major forum for discussion of getting married and having children had become Tony and me — a woman and a man. A stark clash was developing between a political commitment to women as a whole and a personal commitment to an individual man. I was sure that my women's group would, as it did, only offer me a blank negative about 'marriage'. So I took first my personal life, and then myself, out of that arena. Now I know more feminists of my age and generation — even from this original group — who have made the decision to marry, whether in recognition of a long-term relationship and its struggles, or in anticipation. In 1981 there was no one to talk to about making my decision, though I was defended in the group by one very wise woman who pointed out that the oppressiveness of marriage depended on specific factors like economic power, age and status. She herself was married, and offered me a model of someone calmly and politically working that out as one of the many possible ways of feminist living.

I was also attacked for allowing myself as a *public* feminist, known through my writings and teaching, to give credibility to an institution feminists opposed. I now wonder whether there is not a positive value in confusing the codes of femininity as well as simply attacking them. My students, awash with anti-feminist media steroetyping, gain a respect for feminism by encountering a forthright teacher who integrates a critical perspective on the oppression of women in every field with a conventional way of life (married with children). Publicly speaking feminism while being a wife and mother represents one vital aspect of feminism, a part that is set to critique and change rather than abolish some women's legitimate desires and pleasures.

Looking back over 20 years of feminism allows us to consider the revolution that our early iconoclasm and energy has forced us to live through. It also helps us to attend to the actual ways people are taking that revolution to the heart of their daily lives. I find that putting together working as a feminist teacher and scholar with living in a community made up of my partner and our children presents political issues every day of the most important and fundamental kind. I hope that feminists who live like this, with men and with women, legally or informally, don't get written off because we choose to struggle on what seems like such a contradictory terrain.

STILL REVOLTING

Penny Holland

When I received an invitation to contribute to this book my feelings were mixed. I am not someone who is generally approached to write articles. My name appears as one of many on a number of papers and letters written during the late 70s and early 80s, when I was a revolutionary feminist, but I have always felt that my contribution to the movement has been largely verbal. As a working-class woman, even with the benefit of further education, the issue of writing has never been straight forward — can I? should I? who is it for? And, anyway — I'd much rather sit down and have a conversation or collapse in front of 'Coronation Street' after a normal day of work, childcare, housework, meetings, blah, blah.

So? Which way round shall I do this? Start in the present and work back or vice versa?

1968 — I was 13, in my second year at a girls' grammar school, in love with my (female) form teacher and in the throes of adolescent suffering. My suffering had nothing to do with guilt about my sexual leanings, but everything to do with the fact that I thought this particular crush was doomed to be unrequited (not true in fact — but that is another story). Adolescent passion aside, I was blessed at school with a handful of wonderful women teachers, and although at that point in history I was not aware of a blossoming Women's Liberation Movement (or the need for one) I think some of them might have been. They were open to the most probing of our 60s-conditioned questions (the favourites being "Do you believe in sex before marriage?") and brought positive images of women in their own strong selves to the classroom. They fostered an atmosphere in the school that made most of us feel we could be whatever we wanted. Education was the key. A woman with education could take her place in the world alongside any man — that was the essential message. In retrospect I'm grateful for that illusion. It inspired me and gave me a few years' grace. I think I would describe myself then as a baby feminist who already saw lesbianism as a logical extension to close female relationships. Heterosexuality and its traditional roles for women never seemed obvious or inevitable to me.

I first became really involved with women's liberation in 1975, when I was a student at Bristol University, and by 1978 I was up to my eyeballs in the movement, and, as a revolutionary feminist, up to my eyeballs in the acrimony surrounding what was to be the last national conference in Birmingham. It is strange to reflect that 'revolutionary' feminism had only seen the light of day a year previously at the national conference in London. An intense year for those of us involved, with two major conferences (Edinburgh and London), workshops, writing and throwing ourselves headlong into debates with all comers on whether men (not just patriarchy or patriarchal capitalism) were the enemy. Revolutionary feminism (and thus revolutionary feminists) were blamed by many for the fury and anguish which left the plenary of that conference in total disarray. I remember returning to London with my lover (also a rev. fem) in a van with other women we lived near in London Fields (the Hackney lesbian ghetto). The journey was largely silent and it felt like we had been sent to Coventry (no joke intended).

For me it was an exposure to politics at a level I'd never experienced before. The women's liberation movement was the only forum I'd been active in. I'd not had anything to do with 'the left' in any of its guises, and before revolutionary feminism I'd been an 'individual' feminist, not aware that were options on supporting particular lines (socialist feminism, radical feminism, anarcho-feminism). I was stunned by the accusations that were flung at revolutionary feminists at the time — of manipulation, setting up areas of conflict, and ultimately of deliberately splitting the movement. Whatever else we did in our revolutionary fervour I will always defend us against that level of accusation. Perhaps we copped the understandable paranoia of women who *had* been in the male left — we were passionate but we were not sneaky or as sophisticated as we were accused of being. We were plotting the overthrow of male power not the WLM. I think I was terribly out of my depth.

I do not believe that such a small though vociferous group of women, collectively active for only a year could alone drive in a wedge so deep as to fragment the WLM the way that happened in 1978. I think we served as a focus for tensions, frustrations and anger that were around anyway, and that perhaps we pushed the already straining bonds of sisterhood beyond the limit. I still in all honesty do not understand why Birmingham was the last national

conference. In general, I believe that the movement outgrew itself
and had begun to draw in larger numbers of black and working-
class women who had not been represented among the founding
sisters. These new women found a movement which did not speak
their language and only partly addressed their issues. The umbrella
of the seven demands was not big enough to keep us all dry.
Although revolutionary feminism rocked the boat it was the failure
(or inability) of the WLM in the ensuing few years to take class and
race on board and make the step from seeing the world as sisterhood
versus sexism (the simplification is not intended to be insulting),
which eventually sunk the WLM boat, though not feminism.

Birmingham was only the third national conference I'd been
to.

I find is easier to explain why I stopped being a revolutionary
feminist than why I became one in the first place. I guess that once
you've decided, as I had, that men are the enemy, the only real way
forwards is armed feminist revolution. It became clear to me that
this was not about to happen — women were not about to leave their
men in droves around the world and seize power — did I ever
seriously think they would? I should point out that these were my
personal mental processes in late '79 early '80, not a line of debate
within revolutionary feminism. On top of this I was starting to
recognise more clearly my oppression as working class, and
revolutionary feminism could not stretch to accommodate the
experiences and feelings I was uncovering. I started to feel that I was
just toeing a party line rather than being part of a developing idea or
theory, became angry, disillusioned, isolated, and eventually
withdrew.

Birmingham was not the only feminist event of 1978. In October
there was a very bloody Reclaim The Night demonstration in Soho.
This march was a revolutionary feminist initiative organised as part
of a co-ordinated international protest planned at a lesbian summer
camp in Sejero in Denmark. It was my first, though not last,
experience of police brutality. The march was relatively small but it
certainly wasn't sedate. We hadn't just gone along to register distaste
at the sex industry — we were angry and actually wanted to threaten
that industry, if only for a few hours. The police hadn't taken us as
seriously as we were taking ourselves, and consequently they found
themselves in some difficulty — about 12 officers got backed into a
corner outside a strip joint. They panicked and fought their way out
with truncheons, randomly striking out and seriously injuring many

women in the crowd, some of whom had already withdrawn to the sidelines of the fray. They became sitting targets for the wounded and threatened male pride of the keenest police thugs. The police refused to call for ambulances. I escaped injury and spent the rest of the evening accompanying women to hospital. It was a terrifying evening. I probably realised for the first time that night just how much of a threat we constituted and how real the violence of opposition to feminism could be.

I realise that in describing these events I don't really describe what my life was like then day to day. *Intense* is probably the briefest description. I was living in a squat in London Fields with my lover and best friend (one person), where we had moved from Bristol in the summer of 1977. Yes — I had graduated from schoolgirl crushes to the real thing. At the Bristol Lesbian conference in February 1976 I had discovered that feminism and lesbianism went together for other women — hundreds of them. My lover and I had left the genuinely warm, supportive and active embrace of the movement in Bristol (sadly and reluctantly) to be at what we had thought would be the thick of things in London. That's how things were then — for many of us the movement was the be all and end all — it determined how and where we lived (actually it still does for me). London was in many ways a BIG disappointment, and I hankered after Bristol and my friends there for at least three years.

Yes, there were loads more feminists in London. Yes, we could belong to a revolutionary feminist group. Yes, there was lots happening. BUT. Apart from revolutionary feminists, no-one in London seemed particularly excited about being a feminist. I can remember being made to feel terribly green and wet-behind-the-ears by London feminists, because I was so keen and fired up by everything. They generally seemed very cool and took it for granted that hundreds of women (predominantly lesbians) could live as communities with their own political and social centres. There was a thriving subculture in which it was possible to totally immerse yourself, apart from work and shopping (I exaggerate only a little). Many of us were separatists, which meant that we did not have men in our homes and did not engage in relationships with men at all (fathers and brothers included). Our life-style demonstrated that women can be totally self-sufficient and do not need men. I thought this was all amazing, but to many of the women I met in London it was all 'old hat'.

I was working until June 1978 as a clerical worker, but gave it up because it clashed with my other job as a full-time feminist. Life was a fairly endless round of meetings, conferences, demonstrations, actions, pickets, going to court with women who had been arrested during various actions. And for recreation there were women-only plays, discos, films, parties, socials, benefits etc. Much of this subculture still exists in 1988, but not on the same scale. Holidays even! In 1978 my summer holiday consisted of a week at a karate summer school (mixed — but we went as a lesbian contingent from our ongoing class), followed by 10 days at the Danish lesbian summer camp. We had friends all over the country and all over the world (still do, actually). The lifestyle was as intense as the politics.

Things started to change for me at the end of 1978 — a personal mirror to some extent of changes within the WLM. I started to identify some of my feelings within the movement as having a class basis: it wasn't just my parents who were working-class; it was me! My lover broke her leg, which grounded us to some extent, and an old lover returned from two years in India and Bangladesh, bringing with her a whole new agenda of personal and political issues for me/us to deal with. My life started to move beyond the bounds of the ghetto.

So, where am I now in April 1988? Having in the intervening decade done personal and political battle with a range of issues and lifestyles, trying to straddle the straight world and the lesbian feminist world, I have returned to Hackney. As a lesbian mother I now need again for myself, my lover and our child the protection of a lesbian community. I live with the lover who returned in 1978. We met first at the Newcastle national WLM conference in 1976 and our twelfth anniversary is a few weeks away. We are not squatting. We have a flat and a mortgage. We are parents. We have been in the same jobs for the past seven years, Adi as a women's health worker in a collective general practice, me as an administrator and women's development worker in a community education centre. I am still a feminist, I am still a lesbian, I am still fighting.

I feel that my life now is a fusion of things I/we fought for in the 70s. I live just with my lover and our daughter, because I felt I'd gone as far as I could and learned as much as I could from living collectively. Our home is open — we are still part of a network of women and there are often women staying. Our inside flat door stays open for visits from the neighbours upstairs (three men, two gay) — important social contact for whichever one of us is at home childcaring while the other is at work or a meeting. My major relationships and networks are with women, but not to the exclusion of the odd male friend or relative. My separatism broke down through my work, which became my chief political forum. I wanted my life to be visible and accessible to women outside the feminist network and separatism would've kept me apart from the working-class women I wanted to be close to. I have always been out as a lesbian and a feminist at work, and I believe that has changed some of the people I work with for the better, as they have changed me. I have had lots of support and very little shit. The WLM of the 70s did change the lives of women in this country in ways I think we sometimes underestimate, for example, the women I work with have generally known about women's aid, rape crisis and assumed them as a resource (a tiny example — there are hundreds). But individually I feel that my work in the 80s has benefitted more women directly than my work in the 70s.

And the mortgage? That, too, is the result of battles around class in the 70s and early 80s, when working-class feminists made it clear to middle-class feminists that parting with privilege included parting with cash. When the house that a group of us lived in was sold, the owner shared out the money and I demanded enough for two of us to put down a deposit on another home. Downward mobility was a middle-class concept that I didn't buy.

Motherhood. How the hell can I deal in a paragraph or two with such a massive part of my life? The movement of the 60s and 70s enabled us to choose to become parents. I suppose I assumed for many years that being a lesbian meant being childless, unless you had children from a previous heterosexual relationship. Also for me, for some time, and for many women still, choosing to be a lesbian is partly about choosing not to be 'burdened' with childcare. The movement took a stand against imposed motherhood and I often remember the abortion campaign slogan: Every child a wanted child, every mother a willing mother. That is exactly the option that we and other lesbian mothers of alternatively conceived children have chosen. We spent two years in a group with other lesbians discussing every facet of conceiving, having and bringing up children before we went ahead. I am so happy that we did and I think that our choice ensures that our lifestyle and politics remain just as radical as they were in 1978. Our daughter was conceived by artificial insemination with sperm from an anonymous donor and is nearly three. Adi and I regard ourselves equally as co-mothers. We made a decision to have a child before we decided who should conceive it. As Adi is a few years older than me and her family at the time more receptive to the idea, the experience of biological motherhood fell to her. Our daughter knows whose tummy she came out of and has different but equally close relationships with each of us. Our responsibilities towards her are the same. As far as the three of us are concerned she has two 'mummies'. Frankly I think we make pretty wonderful parents, as do all the lesbian mothers I know. In the normality and routine of day-to-day parenting I often forget just how different and radical our choice is. The personal is political.

But this is 1988 — the year of Section 28, pretended families, the gathering backlash and a society transformed beyond recognition from that of 1978. Not a time to be positive about anything for very long. I am scared. We will not have another child — we can better protect one against what is coming. What I miss most from 1968, 1978 is a sense of optimism. We believed we could and, in fact, did change society. I am a little short of that sort of belief nowadays. I no longer know how to be politically effective outside work — I even joined the Labour Party — I wouldn't call that effective. At least going to demonstrations and meetings makes me feel less isolated, less scared, even if they change nothing.

To leave on a more positive note — Adi's father, a Communist Party veteran of the 30s, reminds us on the bleakest days that in the shifting sands of political history everything is never lost: two steps forward but only one back.

I wish us all the courage and comfort in each other to face the struggles ahead.

BORDERLINES

There are borderlines on the map of the world. Then there are borderlines in the body, in the mind (between conscious and unconscious, between 'mad' and 'sane'), between one world and another: between the maker and her work, between the living and the dead. All the writings in this section cross some or many of those lines.

It wasn't until the book was quite finished that I saw I'd had another reason for putting these writers together. Each of them shared with me some part of my life which wouldn't normally get written down in a feminist autobiography.

Like Thelma, I carry the awkward legacy of Irish Protestantism (though my mother comes from the South, not the North). Like Birgit I went through years of illness from the mid-70s (mine taking a physical form), and like her I struggled unwillingly to a spiritual deliverance.

I share with Christian the huge fact of inherited privilege (in my case not social but financial) and the sudden deaths of father and brother in almost the same ways. Like Janet, I carried family secrets which my mind is only now unlocking. One was a paternal inheritance from generations of vanished and assimilated Jewry — this book would have been straighter and narrower without it.

I also have a sister, very close to me in age, and in working with Alexis and Alyson Hunter I recognised a complication and intensity to sisterhood which sometimes get missed out when the word is used in its political sense.

Finally I share with most of the women here the desire to sharpen a skill, to communicate with more people than can be reached in conversation. On a good day in 1978, a feminist conversation could stretch to include 3,000 hearers. Nowadays audiences have to be fought for.

RESTORATION BY NUMBERS

Janet Lesley

1968

"Hold still."
The hand was firm, insistent, steadying.
"But I can't see."
"Be patient, they haven't started yet."
"But?"
"Just wait."
"Lift me up, lift me up."
"Lift me up please?"
"Lift me up PLEASE."
"I can't you're too heavy, hold still."
The child momentarily silenced looks through a sea of legs, listening to the low expectant murmur of voices. Voices and legs without faces. They're up there somewhere, the faces, way up there in the dark, so far it hurts her neck to look.
She feels eyes on her and turns to stare, to stick out a tongue, to pull a face.
The boy smiles. The hand holding hers relaxes.
"Come and play," he dares.
"I can't."
He disappears into the darkness, missing the tongue, the twisted face. Hand free! She moves to follow.
"Come back here, give me your hand." Her arm is yanked hard.
"But I want to play."
"Come back here, you know you can't."
"But I . . ." The boy is a shadow in the distance.
"They will knock you over and they will laugh at you, stay here where you'll be safe."
She stands still. Safe.
"They're putting the Guy on now."
"I can't see."
"I'll lift you, just for a minute."
"Is he my daddy?"

"Of course not."

"He's wearing wellies, I can see them," she strains over a sea of heads.

"He might be my daddy." Hopefully.

"He lived a long time ago."

"The gardener wears wellies? Is he my daddy? Are they putting the gardener on the bonfire?"

"No silly, its Guy Fawkes, you know who Guy Fawkes was don't you?"

"I thought he died last year."

"He died many years ago."

"Well why are they burning him now then?"

"He was a very wicked, evil man."

"Do naughty people get burnt?"

"No just wicked, evil people."

"Ssh, look they're lighting the bonfire."

"Let me down, I don't want to see." She begins to struggle.

"Hold still, you'll fall."

"I don't want to see, I don't want to look, let me down, let me go."

"Stop it, stop wriggling."

"Leggo . . . put me down," outraged.

Flames fold around him. The crowd cheer approvingly.

"Leggo, I hate you." She slips down suddenly. The hand closes around her, gripping, crushing. The crowd has closed, there are no gaps between the legs.

"You are wicked, now stop it or I'll put YOU on the bonfire."

The man on the bonfire screams, loud and deep within her head. She throws back her head, joining her voice to his, and hopes he can hear her above their cheers.

"Give her to me." Arms lift her level to a face, a shoulder to hide on. "And I'll speak to you later."

Inside she is safe. The voice with a face, smiles, soothes, reassures as she is gently undressed.

"They killed a man," she explains, the tight streaks of her tears dissolving into a warm flannel. "It might've been my daddy . . ."

"It wasn't, I promise, here, clean your teeth."

Climbing into bed she is told "It wasn't a real man they put on the fire, it was a Guy . . . you know what a Guy is don't you?"

But she knows, she heard him scream. The light goes out.

"When can I go home?" she whispers.

"This is your home, you belong here."
"Because I can't walk, because I haven't got any legs? I've got to live here coz I got burnt don't I?" she says to the dark.
"Yes that's right, now go to sleep."

I was very lucky someone wanted me.
"People do not usually want a child with a handicap, you should be grateful."
Proud to be wanted, afraid to want back, I left the children's home.
"It would be better if you called us Aunt and Uncle," she said. "We do not want people to think your disability is our fault." They introduced me as "our daughter".

Once in a crowd, a man dared to accuse them. "How could you have done this to your own child, it's unnatural at your age . . ."
She denied me. "I am not her mother."
He dismissed me. "I am not her father."
"It is not our fault," they said, moving away too fast. "She is not really ours." They had a daughter, but I had no parents. Following hurt.

"It would've been kinder to have put you down at birth," she said, not unkindly. Had she forgotten, surely she knew. I had not been born disabled. There had been an accident, a fire. Or did she know that I had been punished for something awful I had done as a baby. I never questioned a month-old-baby's capacity for sin. It seemed reasonable that these decent people should not be condemned for a wrong that was not theirs.
I was eight.
I understood.

"We will teach you many things and make you a better person," they promised, "the world will forgive you if you do well, and do it cheerfully."

"There is no such word as can't," they shouted, "You are just being defiant."
When my body shrieked 'can't', I punished it for rebelling.

They taught me well in '68, gave me a script for every occasion,

showed me how to hide myself in achievement, and protect others
with my humour. I learnt quickly. If I grew up wanting very little, I
would get everything I wanted.
"You should be grateful," they said.
I was.

1978

Eyes shift, uncertain, disbelieving, realising and then denying.
"But?"
"Are you sure?"
"You couldn't be."
Thinks. "She shouldn't be? Should she?"
"But how?"
Pinched smiles touch mouths that later would console, condemn
before hesitantly congratulating.

I knew my pregnancy would elicit some strange responses. As my
body shaped and changed to accommodate the new life within me,
so my mind steeled itself for the inevitable apprehension, surprise
and disbelief. I should've known there was worse than that. I
could've known, at least have been prepared, had fear, pride and
awe not caught me, held me, and lulled me.

My foster mother's voice was steady. Her revulsion and contempt
certain. She offered no compromise. Acknowledgement and
rejection.
"You were never grateful," she closed.
We were never to speak again.

> She sees, through the blurred mist of the anaesthetic, a half-formed
> figure shaped by a shadow. He had granted her peace in the creation
> of his imperfect self, but now he was there. She knew, even before the
> in-laws came to accuse, before the nurses gently reminded her. They
> said she ranted and raged, blamed him for the pain in her stomach,
> the dryness in her throat, and the bile on her tongue. He had allowed
> the bruises to yellow and fade, so they said she was lucky to have him,
> such a strong able-bodied man. They expected she was grateful.

My baby, so tiny, so fragile, I knew if I touched him I would break
him. One day he would grow and I would fade. He would break me;
I would let go, but never forgive.

> Muffled scuttering, thumping, crashing. Muted anger breaks to a
> scream. The children huddle together, the two eldest crouched,

rocking, clasping knees. The boy stands apart from them, stepping from one foot to another, a fist tight-balled in the small of his back, a hand clutching the waist of his pyjama bottoms. The infant stands still, silent, supported by the boy, listens without understanding. Waiting, uncertainly, as always, for it to end. A bottle breaks, a shadow passes. Cold. A door slams. Silence. Movement, shuddered breath, cries caught in the back of a rawed throat. They get up, moving towards a shuffling figure. The face is distorted, bloated eyes reddened with tears, mouth twisted, swollen with black blood, caught in the corner, paled on the teeth. Beneath the blouse, torn away at the shoulder, a purple bruise thickens and spreads.

The infant backs away screaming. This woman is broken.

1988

As a child I carried with me fantasies I believed to be memories, and images of moments I had never experienced. In furtive dark whisperings, I exchanged pasts and futures with other lonely and unwanted, disabled children, our lives and our lies overlapping down long silent dormitories.

By 1968 I had been fostered and begun to live a reality that was not mine, watching myself grow in their prejudices, with eyes that mirrored their contempt.

1978 was the year I liberated myself from my fosterparents' arrested expectations. An act of rebellion, to assume an identity that had been denied to me, I married and had my first son.

The years leading me to 1988 have been a time of convergence. The infant screaming as her mother hurts, the rejected little girl by the bonfire, the wife beaten to a rage, the young mother afraid to love her children. All are reconciled. The she and the I are fused.

1981, The Year of the Disabled, happened without me. I was having a baby. All over the world disabled people rallied and organised, planning and shaping a new future for the thousands of us still denying our reflections in shop windows and crossing streets to avoid each other.

For me, change happened slowly, evolved in the form of a friendship that never questioned or resigned itself to the limits of my self-prejudice. I stopped condemning and began to listen, stopped averting my eyes and began to seek out. My disability moved out of the medical text books and into political consciousness. I followed.

Since then I have been actively involved in different disabled organisations, working towards change, challenging prejudice (including my own) and combatting apathy. Moving forward. Unlearning.

In the absence of a positive role model, I had wasted several years of my working life contained within jobs that exhausted me only with their monotony. Then in 1986 I heard of, and went for, a job working in Manchester City Council's Equal Opportunities Unit. It was just the job for me. I could do it, I would do it, and do it well. There was so much I wanted to do, so much I would do. The job was mine!

I didn't get it.

It took me several weeks to get over the disappointment. Months before I could resign myself to my "allotted" career as a typist.

I decided it was not meant to be. I had been silly to aspire to such heights and I would NEVER apply for an Equal Opportunities job again.

Their loss.

The Housing Department advertised for an Equal Opportunities Officer. I was one of the first to apply.

Working for the Housing Department has given me the opportunity to make progress on all the Equal Opportunity issues, time to talk, time to listen and finally time to change.

Recently I have begun to check my direction and to question my objectives. "Do the issues I am now working on reflect the aspirations of other disabled people?" "What of my own experiences as a disabled woman?" For me liberation meant so much more than the right to vote, to work, to maintain a separate identity from men.

It is nearly ten years since I had my first child. We live securely, my two children and I, and without thinking I had assumed that the battle to have and keep our children had been fought and won.

Sadly this is not the case.

A child dies at the hands of 'normal' parents.

We are watched.

A young mother struggles with an unwanted child.

We are monitored.

"Will we crack?"

"Can we cope?"

It is wrong to deny us our children's growing.

Is it fair to deny them our disability?

WRITING IT DOWN

Christian McEwen

I am a writer, an obsessive annotator and a keeper of journals. My mother tells me that my first word was "baba", and that I applied it indiscriminately both to myself ("baby") and to books. I don't remember that. My stories start in 1968, when I was eleven and three quarters. Father Christmas had left a shiny Puffin diary in my stocking, and because of that I know that I was 4′ 8″, with green eyes and brown hair, that my favourite colour was blue, my favourite hobby reading, and my favourite meal, "chicken with peas, roast tatties and gooseberry fool".

I lived at home: "Marchmont, Greenlaw, Berwickshire", in the big sandstone house which had belonged to my grandfather, and was a weekly boarder at "St Mary's Convent, Berwick", just over the river into England. School meant "Latin", "got exam results", "2 months till birthday", "boring day", and home was, predictably, more exciting: "built igloo", "crystallised primroses", "racing Kelso made 10/-". There were five of us by then: me and Katie, James and Helena and John. But by March of that year Isabella had arrived ("baby sister born. 7lbs 3ozs.") and suddenly, at twelve years old, I was a godmother. I took the position very seriously. But who was this new person going to be? I remember standing by her high old-fashioned cradle, drawing back the long white curtains and just staring. "Who are you?" I asked her fiercely. "Will I like you by the time you are grown up?"

That summer, standing out among all the usual entries: "went circus", "went Royal Highland Show", "picked fruit", "played croquet", "caught a fish", are two short references to a larger world. 5th June reads "Bobby was shot", and the next day, "Terrible Bobby Kennedy died after being shot". Far away in Paris, small black and white figures set up barricades and threw things, but I paid no attention. The exams were coming up. And anyway, I was infinitely more interested in Isabella.

She was my godchild, and I had wanted her to be a boy. After all, I wanted to be one myself. "Mary Christian is a girl/who'd like to be a boy", my aunt had written in my autograph book. Long before I knew anything about class, I knew I was not the eldest boy, I was a girl. Boys could be clever and brave and independent and as naughty as they wanted. Girls had fewer choices. Mostly, they were very, very good.

In the upper class households that I knew, these stereotypes were exaggerated. Boys wore kilts and sailor-suits; girls wore little dresses with satin sashes round their waists. Boys learned to shoot and fish. Girls didn't learn anything much, except perhaps a little flower-arranging. They did not inherit, they were not expected to have a career. Boys were the important ones, the ones whose choices were taken seriously. When my brother James was learning to shoot I insisted I be taught as well, though I was never much good at it. What I liked best was guddling, fishing by hand in the burn, bringing up little speckled trout to be fried in oatmeal for breakfast or high tea.

Katie and I were going to write a book about guddling: my words, her illustrations. But that September, shorn of the new baby and the younger children, my parents drove the pair of us down to Greece. There, on the hot sand, tucking in my petalled bathing cap, I felt beautiful and sleek and girlish for the first time. There was a yacht, with a captain and a mate and a handsome cabin-boy, and I stood around in corners and I yearned for him. His name was Ikis (there were those awful jokes, 'I kiss Ikis —") and he was 15 years old.

Three years later, we came back to Greece, and I did kiss Ikis, though very briefly. But it didn't make the difference I'd expected. By then I'd met a real live grownup lesbian for the first time, "She's excellent nice", and I was thinking seriously about my future. "I want to write books when I grow up and marry as well."

By 1978, at 21, my sense of these possibilities was much less optimistic. I had gone to Cambridge to study philosophy and theology — later changed to anthropology, and finally to English Literature. I had also had my first (disastrous) affair:

"I have been looking so long for answers. Of course I must just start, with the ignorance left in. I knew that at least 2 years ago. The last years seem like nothing. I just disappoint myself: over and over again. Bring in the ideals, like washing on a rainy day. Hide them somewhere and hope the weather will improve. What must I do to write? *Write*."

On the page opposite is a list of women writers, from Aphra Benn through Marie Bashkirtseff and the Brontes to Dorothy Richardson,

Laura Riding, HD and Sylvia Plath, "Who is missing?" I ask at the end. "What is wrong?" And then the imperative, "Shd. order."

The truth was, of course, that I did not know how to order. I had read the books (de Beauvoir, Germaine Greer), and as a 16-year-old in London I had gone to some of the early meetings, but that was not enough. At Cambridge there were no role models, no one who could show me what to do or how to think. What was this feminism anyway? Nobody seemed to know. King's had been an all-male college for more than 600 years. Mine was only the third year of women to be accepted. In the university itself, there was no Creative Writing, no Women's Studies Programme, and the percentage of women staff was very small. Among the students, men outnumbered women nine to one.

At the time, confused and ignorant, I did not make these larger social connections. If I could not write or think or trust my own opinion about things, then that, I was convinced, was my own fault. For a long time I lost track of my ideas altogether, and could only think by proxy, stumbling from quotation to quotation. The first few pages of my diary are a log-jam of different authorities: Gwen John, Samuel Beckett, Henry James, Montherlant, Nabokov, Simone Weil. I had a passage from James about a woman "both diffident and importunate, restless, discontented, visionary" which I was sure applied all too accurately to me. "Dear Christian," says the entry above it, taken from Gertrude Stein. "You are very sweet without hope. Hope is for you."

Where that hope was to come from I had no idea. But it was essential that it did. Things were getting serious. I had to save not just myself but Papa too.

"Papa came back yesterday from Greenlaw and gave Mama the bottle he had with him when he met her in the hall — but the other bottle he hid behind a tree and went back for. He was ill all today."

My father had been a manic depressive since I was about ten. By the time I was fifteen or sixteen it was impossible to conceal that he was also an alcoholic. In taking on Marchmont, he had taken on too much. There was no money to run the place, no sense of an extended future there. Every holidays, I listened and fought and argued with him, digging in my heels, trying to haul him back over the border into life and possibility. It never worked for long. I was only a girl, not the son who would inherit. I adored him, but there was nothing I could do.

Anxious for him, helpless, I retreated to my journal. By then I'd been writing one for ten years straight. I was used to keeping tabs on what I did. "Read *Finnegan's Wake* all morning." "To the UL for Dorothy Richardson's books." But 1977–78 was the first year I really used diary-keeping to find things out, to talk to myself and to make sense of what was happening. It was a tremendous relief. I had run across Marion Milner ("Joanna Field") in the University Library, and I learned from her about "A Life of One's Own"*, reading books that would "keep my heart up", and "letting my senses roam, unfettered by purpose". Because of her too I began to draw again, quick embarrassed sketches of the trees at home, odd symbolic watercolours full of wombs and ovaries and vaginas, and very black scratchy Rotring drawings of the pictures and sculptures that (again with Milner's guidance), I was beginning to look at and enjoy.

That summer I travelled alone to Italy for a month, and came home happy and alert and full of noticings. The misery let up, and I began to have room in my mind (and diary) for other people too, as here, describing Mary, the old Irish woman who lived downstairs:

"Mary, on return, seizing my arm, giving me tea and bread and butter in the kitchen. Telling me about her si-in-law with a blood clot, her bro. in Ireland ill. But also about the war, stockings 32/6, nylon, when they first came out, smuggling things through the north, 10 yards of silk around her waist, bacon rashers in the padded shoulders of her coat, butter in a handkerchief box, sliced small, stockings in the coat cuffs or worn 6 pairs at a time on her own legs —"

As I began to record the outside world more clearly, I found myself more open to the inner world as well. I dreamed of Nina, who was to become my first woman lover, long before I had exchanged more than a few words with her. And I dreamed too of the States, where I had been on my year off, and of my growing US self, in the form of a baby rescued from the burn by my brother James:

"A baby of Mama's, but born in America and fed on sweet corn so when it came to England it could not eat (not sweet) corn. James brought it from the Adam Bridge with a dipper and I held out my arms in a room that wasn't a Marchmont room. The baby had a soft dry head and I was just hugging it."

'88. Just hugging it. How did I know how to take care of that baby? Somehow I did. I returned to the States on a Fulbright Scholarship, and I studied English Literature at Berkeley, writing short stories

* *A Life of One's Own* by Marion Milner (Virago, 1986).

instead of a thesis. In the years that followed, my father died, then, in swift succession, my uncle and my brother killed themselves, and my sister was accidentally drowned. It was an extraordinary time. But somehow in that chaos I was able to keep writing, and through the writing I began to understand. I learned the patterns I had lived inside, and saw how best to use them. I learned to take the jealous little girl, the swot, the tomboy, the anxious conscientious eldest daughter, and to make them a grownup I could trust. She is the one who lives in New York now, and teaches Adult Literacy and Creative Writing, the one who has just finished editing two lesbian anthologies*. I don't know what I think of her exactly. She is a writer, she tells me, and some sort of activist. She likes poetry and fishing and the colour blue. She reads a lot and writes down all her dreams.

---

* *Naming the Waves: Contemporary Lesbian Poetry*, edited by Christian McEwen (Virago, 1988) and *Out the Other Side: Contemporary Lesbian Prose*, edited by Christian McEwen and Sue O'Sullivan (Virago, 1988).

MARK-MAKING

Alexis Hunter

Remembering a New Zealand 1968. Hot and sunny days, Vietnam Peace-ins with balloons in the park, beach barbecues with buckets of fresh mussels, skinny-dipping in strangers' swimming pools at night, feeling that the world belonged to our generation. We felt different from the powerless ones who had suffered World Wars and depressions, we would solve everything with Love and Compassion. The darker side to this new freedom showed itself only occasionally — the drug overdoses and the immediate problems of the sexual revolution, unwanted pregnancy (abortion was illegal) and moral confusion.

New Year in New Zealand meant the summer break from Art School, restoring an 1860 model *Pa* (Maori fortification) for the Waitangi Museum and starting a series of landscapes of the original site. The ambition to be a great New Zealand painter grew in importance and I would work feverishly at any hour, haunted by my clumsiness and ineptitude, having already discarded the security of marriage as claustrophobic and unstimulating.

I don't remember any sexual discrimination at Art School, although there was plenty outside it, but there were no grants and the male students could earn real money working the docks, shearing or working on the new Hydro-electric dams, while we could only pick up casual work in factories.

We demanded male life models and got them. We demanded women tutors and did not, but had sufficient women artist role models and were introduced to the work of Artemesia Gentileschi as an example of a reputation hidden by Art History.

In 1968 there was a backlash against the American Woman's Liberation Movement by the popular National press in New Zealand, who quoted bra-burning (ironically planned as a joke against the US media) whenever a serious attempt at change was made by women politicians or trade unionists. The brave members of the Woman's Liberation at University would stand and speak in the quadrangle surrounded by a crowd of jeering men. My feminism at the time was of gut feeling and reaction rather than theory, and the rank chauvinism outside art school was met by a swift uppercut or inquiry into the offender's sexual aptitude.

The Third-year women painters decided to re-enact a suffragette demonstration as the University Capping procession wound up Auckland's main street. Traditionally at the end of the procession the all male and white engineering students, dressed as joke Maoris in raffia skirts and lipstick tattoos, did a *Haka* (war dance) and then tried to carry off the women art students in a mock rape. So we prepared not only our banners — *Pills for Men — or support Your Bastards, Abortion on Demand — Your Daughter may be pregnant now!* — but ourselves, for the inevitable attack.

What I remember most about that march was the silence when we expected jeers. The public shouted at the other groups but fell silent as we passed by. The women's eyes caught ours, in accord. It was the most wonderful feeling, a feeling of wordless strength. The Haka began and women in front of us were beginning to be dragged off. We tore into the Haka — now the horrified men were vulnerable and silly in their skirts, which we ripped off down to their psychedelic underpants, opposition was met with a jab with a sharpened stave concealed under a banner or a swing of the heavy chains we had wrapped around our wrists, although somewhat hampered by our large hats and Victorian dresses. The police appeared, still trying to track down the banner with the illegal word "Bastards", and in the mayhem we ran off in all directions, meeting up in the Kiwi Bar Ladies toilets to drag off our costumes and sit calmly around a jug of beer. The rest of the procession draggled in, with the story of what had happened already magnified and mythified. It was glorious.

At the end of the year I discovered I had to let the creative gift come to me, not to chase it and bully it but invite it in with rigorous observation and loving sensitive mark-making. My personal life would have been a lot happier for the next twenty years if I had applied this reasoning to real people instead of to art! But this was the year of radical change — men were powerful and dangerous animals who wanted everything their own way. As they used us, so we must fight.

After a year as president of the Student Union, I travelled around Australia on an award, and in 1972 joined a Greek Cruise Liner through the Panama Canal to England. Appalled by the class distinctions in London, I joined the Artists' Union and was

Feminist demonstration, Elam Art School, Auckland, 1968
L to R: Alison Cavell, Christine Gregory, Alyson Hunter, Elizabeth Coates
and Alexis Hunter.

introduced to the Women's Workshop. We found that we were all making secret art about our lives, parallel to our more formal body of work. We started to concentrate on this 'art for women' and exhibit as groups, encouraged by the collective making of Judy Chicago's Woman House in Los Angeles.

By 1976 I had moved completely away from painting into narrative photography to best express the fears of women brought up against changes in their consciousness. I made images to be read on several levels, influenced by the Socialist feminism of the Artists' Union Women's Workshop, where we based our work on theory but wished to make it accessible to people who would not be familiar with the ideas or even with looking at art. I joined the Women's Free Arts Alliance and also made visits to New York to meet artists Nancy Spero, May Stevens, Miriam Shapiro, Betsy Damon, Mary-Beth Edelson and critic Lucy Lippard.

In 1978 I moved into a studio flat above a new housing estate in Regent's Park, needing an ordinary environment to set the 'heroine' of the photo sequences. It was a dangerous move away from the artistic ghettos that I had taken for granted for seven years, and I became very distanced from an audience, although my photographic work was being exhibited every month. I fell into the habit of illegal drinking 'after hours' in bars, because I missed the camaraderie of shared studios. It was the only way I could relax enough to sleep. Every conversation, every emotion was picked over for an idea; I began to think of my pictures as spells, and even became frightened of them myself.

I was invited to exhibit in the 1978 Hayward Annual — dubbed "the Women's Show" or "Ladies Night" by the press because it had an all-woman selection committee, it aroused an immense amount of publicity, some outrageously sexist and exposing virulent misogyny under the sophisticated exterior of the critics.

The two words 'Alexis Hunter' moved away from me, and I felt people who were introduced for the first time were surprised that I didn't have fangs. I had not realised *how much* the male observer projected inner anxieties onto an image; what to me were humanistic, evocative feminine symbols were read as brutal attacks on society.

I felt in 1978 that I had to 'adjust', took a job I hated, teaching graphics at a Polytechnic, and made changes to my personal life based on insecurity rather than real emotional involvement. The continual dredging of my own psyche for work was taking its toll

Ink drawing, Alexis Hunter, 1968.

Rather than be wise
Churning out words,
Better drink your sake,
And weep drunken tears.

Tabito

Alexis Hunter 1968

GODDESS, 1987 monotype, Alexis Hunter.

and although my own life looked tidier on the surface, it was going to pieces.

By 1981 I had moved back into painting from photographic work. The sublime balance of physicality, sensuality and intellectual rigour needed to produce good painting is such an exhilarating challenge that it has superseded problems of changing medium in mid-career.

A West End gallery started to offer me solo exhibitions, a pleasant change from the difficulties of dealing with the Arts Council. The Totah Gallery was very supportive of the experimental "biological feminist" paintings I was doing in the early 1980s, which were well received critically as they were in tune with Post-Modernism. I was given regular teaching days at Byam Shaw School of Art, and with an income from the gallery I was able to get off the dole at last.

On an artists' residency in the Lake District I realised the necessity of community, and returned to join a housing co-operative in London. My attitude to marriage changed with this commitment to a particular community rather than to political principles only. I met Baxter Mitchell, who was running the 'Falcon' Public House nearby, and we were married on New Year's Eve 1985.

It's not easy, painting, exhibiting five or six times a year, teaching, and helping with the continual problems of running an inner-city bar as well as living in a co-operative. But just when it starts being too much, I receive a grant or the opportunity to exhibit overseas — as I have at this moment of writing — and this gives me the space to analyse my work objectively.

TRANSPARENT POSITIVES

Alyson Hunter

Shaping my life up to 1968 was a childhood set in the New Zealand of the 1950s. Memories of white liners moving sloẇ.y away from Auckland Docks like icebergs, the crowd beneath the turning hulk singing 'Now is the Hour', paper streamers filling the air with rivulets of pink and green. Foreign merchant ships blew their fog horns at the stroke of midnight on New Year's Eve, the sound reaching out across the still black water of the harour — there would be an answering roar from the revellers round the Post Office in Queen Street.

Down from our white wooden house with its pink drive, startlingly round and golden oranges could be stolen from the dark green sub-tropical bush and eaten in secrecy in the mangrove swamp.

School I feared — wooden desks carved with welts of boredom, slates to scratch on, dunces' caps, forty-five pupils in the class, the folded leather strap stuck in the teacher's back pocket. I longed to be old, 12 years old, girls could not be strapped after 12 and it was the only advantage I could think of then that girls had over boys.

I was the archetypal tomboy, reading *Tarzan of the Apes* avidly by torchlight under the blankets at night, and building a raft out of carcasses and oil drums. The raft foundered in French Bay, and my thoughts turned to horses, boys and bicycles.

Out on the country road in my tight pink pedal-pushers, pink puffed sleeves, red eye shadow, pale pink lipstick — getting as far away as possible from the family on my silver and blue Japanese bike: miles and miles of unknown gravel roads through farms and orchards, getting back after dark with only the sound of the native owls and the wheels whistling on the cooling grey road.

The Young Anglican dance on a Saturday night was the high spot of the week — lines of girls waiting to be asked to fox-trot by shy boys in suits. Socks in your bra, threepence in your suspender belt, nail varnish on your stocking ladders. Cheong-Sams made from furnishing material, beehive hairdos, spangled nail polish, false eye lashes.

In 1960 my twin sister Alexis and I had our first exhibition of

TIME TOGETHER, *collage, Alyson Hunter, 1968.*

paintings in the Titirangi Coffee-Bar — house paint and wood varnish on hardboard, in company with steaming cappuccino in olive green cups, pine and hessian walls, men with beards and guitars, women with copper chains over black woollen sweaters pointed into twin peaks like Boadicea's breast plate. Adultery, whispering, drugs, folk singing, skiffle, jazz.

Our father (a socially-minded factory manager) took us to the Auckland Film Society — I remember anti-fascist films from Poland and Czechoslovakia, and also Fritz Lang, Eisenstein, Dziga Vertov, Luis Bunuel, Marcel Carné, and Jean Cocteau. Seeing these films at an early age shaped my politics and influenced my work in the 1970s. I accepted photography as a fine art form, and used the same ways of cropping and placing figures and objects.

At Auckland Girls' Grammar we had a lunchtime debate — Virgins against the rest. Being the leader of the former, I lost heavily. The other six-form girls, more sophisticated, decimated my argument of 'keeping oneself' when men were encouraged to become sexually experienced as early as possible. I couldn't articulate my idea of 'keeping oneself' for *oneself*, and being free of the rules governing marriage and living in a conventional society, the suburban death for sharp minds.

The film of James Joyce's 'Ulysses' was shown in Auckland — to segregated audiences, men only, then women only. So Molly Bloom singsongs her soliloquy to a theatre-full of women. I sit there feeling embarrassed and excited. Amazed that so many mothers and grandmothers have managed to arrive, by themselves, into one place, without it being a 'caring' situation, like a school, hospital or WI meeting.

By 1968 I was in my third year at Art School in Auckland, and far too arrogant to notice male chauvinism even if it was offered to me. I was majoring in sculpture but also selling my paintings. There was no problem with finding women role-models in New Zealand, from Katherine Mansfield's short stories to Frances Hodgkin's painting.

For the Rag Day parade I borrowed a tambourine and a drum, my friend Alison Cavell collected an array of Suffragette clothing and the third-year girls set off with our placards, one of which read *Pills for men or support your Bastards*. The police made us cross out the last word, but let us onto the main street.

After a day of running street battles with the engineering students I got back to the Art School Common Room — and the floor was a heaving mass of placards with painted arms and legs writhing underneath, a great 'Love-In'. I gazed at it stupified in my bonnet and long black frock, feeling very left out and confused with my own emotions about sharing sex.

I was also wary of drugs — could they rob me of my desire to create? Would I turn from my own strong style of realism to the flowing patterns of my fellow students? But these thoughts didn't stop me trying to drink every man under the table in the Kiwi Hotel, where I was still three years under the lawful drinking age of 21.

Walking around the city at night, sexual agression was shaken off with bravura — treating the harassment as a price to pay for independence. I thought it happened to every woman all the time. I suppose it did. I suppose it does.

I arrived in Britain in 1969, the tail end of 'Swinging London' disappearing like a conga dance up a street in front of me, too late to join in. My painting was faltering, the English light was so different, and painting considered then almost a blasphemy in Modern Art practice.

In 1970 I shared a studio with Ilona Bennet in London Bridge Road, and the Women's Workshop of the Artists' Union held its first meeting there. I remember disagreeing about crèches being set up in all artists' studios. I thought that women artists would need space away from children even more than male artists. I was shouted down as I had no children myself; then I remember being angry and saying that was my choice.

I joined Ilona at Night Cleaners' Campaign meetings in Kings Cross. The campaign was a sound one, night cleaning being underpaid and un-unionised, with unsocial hours. But the area frightened and depressed me. I was walking a tightrope myself, and I believed one had to be very secure to be able to help others. Otherwise it was patronising — using others to make a political point. I felt too foreign, too middle-class, to be justified in being involved. I realised I was too much of a loner to fit in with other women's ideas of what was wrong and right.

It was a time of separating from men and finding one's own rules. I found the undercurrent of dislike for males too strong, a destructive element. But I did feel that the women's movement was going to be the most exciting political change this century — that it could make some bloody awful mistakes, but could drag us into a new world for men and women. I felt that the hatred of men for women and women for men would always exist, but at least women could be armed with new ideas in the struggle for domination between the sexes.

At the end of the 60s I had set out for Spain in a blue Ford van with my lover, a sculptor and flamenco guitarist from New Zealand. My elder sister Linley came along for the ride. Andalucia was my first experience of real restrictions put upon female behaviour; I realised my luck at having been brought up in a relatively free society.

In Moron de la Frontera, a lithe gypsy dancer strutted on a door laid flat on the yellow earth — bare feet, flashing hands, turning head and hips — and my sister's heart was captured. Oh, woe the 60s! Linley — in your yellow mini skirt, your hands clasped over your knees, your spectacles and your MA in French Literature, always so prim and proper — take advice from the family black sheep, this life is not *our* reality. But advice always falters before love . . . In 1988, she is still in Moron de la Frontera. I was glad my raft foundered in French Bay, for freedom has its own prisons as well as its rewards.

In 1971, I was accepted into the postgraduate printmaking course at Chelsea Art School. Photographic etching was the medium I wanted to use — something sculptural, hard, graphic. Dealers sought me out in the King's Road wine bars, and my fate was sealed for the 70s.

In 1972, I was printmaking at the Royal College of Art. It was competitive, with sexual harassment a part of that. Everybody ready for the put-down, even the staff, and only one other girl in my year. But it didn't bother me; I was used to male company and liked the competition.

I was living in the East End of London and using Brick Lane as my subject matter, but for the RCA box of prints I made a feminist work from words in a thesaurus. It was thrown back at me angrily and I was told to make another one and not to be so "bolshie".

From the printmaking department there was a door into the Victoria and Albert Museum. I loved being able to wander through this magical darkened place, and various artworks became favourite things — clothing, shoes, altars, bowls, swords, tapestries, fans, sculptures. There was so much beauty — this was the best education one could have. The work I am producing in the 80s is influenced by these visits: trying to make art with a human element — yet finished — and yet capturing the fleeting world. I visited the museum again recently and it was like paying entrance money to visit a church, or even your own home.

Through the 70s I sold my photo-etchings to galleries and

WORKING WOMEN VERSUS THESAURUS, transparent positive, Alyson Hunter, 1972.

SELF PORTRAIT, CALIFORNIA, Alyson Hunter, 1981: the conflicts between teaching (financial), drinking (pleasure), relationships (love and care), and painting (oneself).

museums, married a nice Englishman, bought a fishing loft in Cornwall (a studio once belonging to the woman painter Dod Proctor), and ran a gallery in Highbury called Islington Graphics.

But by 1978 I wanted to give up using the camera. I felt I had betrayed my natural ability to draw, and so I became unsettled. I started what would be ten years of experimentation in my work, and these changes affected my personal life. I felt that to do new work I needed a new existence, to become at last a woman rather than a girl; and long limbs seen through the mist of alcohol in the buccaneering Swordfish Long Bar were what I chose.

I had to force myself into the 1980s by throwing away all the security I had built up in the 1970s. In 1981, I travelled through America, New Zealand and Australia, having a daughter in Auckland in January, this being part of the major plan of change. I came to realise how vulnerable women are with children, but the rewards in a beautiful child are profound. I like Sydney, but feel homesick for London and Penzance. My ties are cut with New Zealand; I feel a stranger there.

I keep working all the time and manage to exhibit and sell work. Being with another artist helps — only another artist could understand the particular pressures that need to be separate to work. In 1982 I was visiting Professor in Drawing at the University of California, and in 1983 I was back in London.

I don't know if having a child affected my work, or if I was going to have difficulty with it anyway. Mothers seem to have a sort of sixth sense always at work around children, watching for danger continually. I think men care just as much, but are more separate; they don't seem to have the same protective factor which stops me working with a child around. I can't concentrate enough on my work, and feel selfish if I do.

So my day has become cut up into segments of caring and working. I feel happy about it now. For me the changes I wanted in 1978 have come in 1988: to become a Tarzan, the successful alien — in my own way, in my own world. My daughter has *Sheena of the Jungle*, of course, and no problem with sexual identification.

Looking into the future from 1988, our daughters must be ready for their own fight as the world changes. The side streets and street corners have been won by three generations of women — but we must be careful of changes in the terrain, and not let our ammunition and arms become outdated.

We must not be put into retreat now, with so much won.

THE SPIRITUAL IS THE POLITICAL

Birgit Voss

How do I describe my spiritual development?

How far back do I go?

— Way back to my early years in small town southern Germany where my mother tried her best to bring my younger brother and me up in the Catholic faith as she had promised when she married — shock horror — a Protestant (einen Evangelischen) whom she brought home from the war. Little did the church fathers and faithful family members know: my father was not even a Protestant, he was and is an atheist.

I have always had a very strong sense of justice and the idea that my father (and all the other heathens in the world) would smoulder in hell fire while my mother, brother and the rest of the Catholic family would live it up in heaven simply did not seem fair. That was my first big doubt in my faith.

But Catholicism held out until about my sixteenth year, when doubt and rejection of all my inherited values set in. I was deeply shocked that my parents did nothing to prevent THE RISE OF HITLER ("Why did you not hide in the crowd with a loudspeaker and shout nonono when he asked the people if they wanted total all out war?"). I loved them dearly yet I felt so ashamed of their past, my German heritage. I left home and tried to forget where I had come from as soon as I had finished schooling.

A young man offered me shelter and adventure in England, so to London I came at the tender age of 19 in 1967. What a disappointment it was, though. Bands did not play in the street, the sun rarely shone, despite flower power and love it appeared cold and primitive. I could hardly communicate and depended greatly on my young man for translations, security and home comforts. But it was a brand new life without the constraints of parents' or neighbours' disapproval. Nobody said anything even when I chose to walk the streets in my nightdress. Quite a change from living in small town

Durlach, where everyone felt free to comment on any unconventional aspect of anyone else's appearance or behaviour.

So in 1968 I had just arrived in Britain. I was "in love". I was young. I was pretty and willing to sell this prettiness to the public. I tried modelling and hoped to be a millionaire within a few months. I shaved my legs into babyface surfaces, I put on false eyelashes, I learnt the catwalk. But my career as model was cut short by a photographer who pinched my nipples in an effort to make my pout look more sexy. That was too much for me and the end of my dreams to get rich fast. Instead, I asked my young man to marry me and this saved me from having to struggle for the necessary work permit. I began earning my living as a 'Girl Friday' in an office for a proud £14 a week. My young man — husband — started his studies at the London School of Economics and together we were drawn into the mind-expanding events of '68.

I was interested in love, peace, hippydom; a new and better, more moral way of living altogether, together. One of our projects was taking apart an old car and rebuilding it. I learnt a great deal about car mechanics, but I barely concerned myself with the future. Life was to be lived, here and now, righteous causes had to be struggled for. Women found their voices and demanded liberation. I joined one of the early CR groups in 1970, and my young man, still fully in love, supported my views and moves.

But then my mother was found to be seriously ill. She died with me by her side in the summer of '71. It left me with nothing to find for comfort. My father's and husband's nihilistic views did not explain the feeling I had of something leaving, something being around, something going when the last breath was squeezed out of my mother's body. I was confronted with questions which had been irrelevant during my carefree time of free love and living here-and-now. Why do we all die? What happens to us? Is there life after death? What sort of life? What would my death be like?

These questions would not leave me. On top of my grief, my terrible loss, came a very deep fear: that of my own inevitable death. I was young but that is no guarantee for life. I went through a very difficult time. Anxiety states could not be squashed with Valium, my doctor could not reassure me — despite visits to the surgery about once a week — that some evil cancer was not lurking somewhere in my body ready to consume my life. Sleep was difficult to find as drifting off reminded me of dying and the terrible fear would immediately descend upon me, strangling my breath, paralysing my limbs, making the room spin around, and making me sink deep into a bottomless sweaty terror.

It was during this time that I started reading about different religions; I re-discovered prayer but tried to address my praying to a god (in his benevolent white flowing beard) and a goddess (rosy cheeked and motherly). I also discovered Jung, Yoga, eastern philosophies, rebirth. I started practising the yoga, breathing and meditation. Eventually I dared to let my fears have their way.

One awful night when I once again woke up just before sleep could set in and I was convinced that my death was right there, I decided, OK. So be it, let it. I did not struggle against it but made myself comfortable in front of the fire, a purring cat by my side; trying to regulate my breathing, I let it wash over me. Something happened because when my consciousness became clear again, when the shuddering had stopped, I watched a most beautiful sun rising. A brilliant, clear joy filled my whole being. I felt at peace. Somehow I knew that dying did not matter. I would do it easily as everybody does, and life was — is — indeed for living. I knew my fears and anxiety had gone. I was free and blissfully happy.

The next thing that happened was that I got pregnant. I conceived during my menstruation (which is not very usual) and I saw it as a gift, a small miracle. 'The wheel of life' continued. My mother was gone but I would have a daughter. A kind of rebirth.

Since then I have had no doubts about my existence being meaningful. My visualisations of God, however, kept changing. The old god–father image was very strongly imprinted in my psyche, I deliberately had to make a goddess out of him in my conversations, debates, arguments and prayers.

Still, my 'god' was kept in a closet during the 70s. It was a private affair. I would not own up to her-him-it in my political groups, where Marx or Mitchell or Marcuse or Shulamith Firestone had the word. But it was my faith as well as my sense of justice that gave me the courage and strength to act, to be daring, to live in a commune, to become a lesbian, to cut the wire at Greenham Common.

In 1978, I found myself and my five-year old daughter homeless. Desperate, I was, with already two offers of council housing rejected. The poky two-bedroomed flats in some huge estate did not appeal. With the encouragement of women from the Haringey Women's Centre (which I had helped to set up) and a lover and friend, I decided to take the plunge and squat a house. The first night was spent keeping warm in front of an open fire on a borrowed mattress from the women's centre, with one of my sisters helping me to guard the house, keeping watch, keeping other squatters out and keeping our spirits up. It took a great deal of courage but this small beginning was the seed of a housing co-operative which, with lots of luck and much collective work and effort, now owns 11 houses and provides homes for 36 adults and 10 children.

Now, in 1988, I live in one of our purpose-built communal houses with my 15 year old daughter, three other women and two more children. It is a beautiful, comfortable, precious home which I treasure and love sharing with the others, especially the children. I have been working for the Inner London Education Authority for twelve years. As things are presently, my redundancy entitlements might amount to £3,000 or thereabouts. I don't like the idea of losing my job. For the past year I have worked in the support service giving teachers help in their development of anti-racist, anti-sexist and class bias-free ways of teaching. It's a great job and important work, but sadly Great Britain's present administration has no heart for justice and no money for humanitarian changes and challenges to the privileges of a few.

However, when I am free of my nine to five (or more like seven to ten) paid job I shall have more time to develop other areas of my work. I am a member of Women World Wide, a co-operative that promotes things women anywhere in the world have produced. There are about 90 shareholders in the co-op, and four other women who regularly come to the meetings. The co-op is still quite young — a year and a half — and a great many things have been created already, but our aim is to change the world economy and there are still mountains to be moved. So, if any women out there reading this are into moving mountains . . . stop looking elsewhere: help move this one!

I am now also treasurer of the London Women Working for a Nuclear Free and Independent Pacific. And of course I still belong to a consciousness-raising group — a German-speaking one now. At last I have owned up to my roots.

*

I have had several experiences which for lack of any other explanation I call spiritual, psychic, or religious. Some of my contemporaries would call these 'craziness' or 'mental disorder' and from the outside it may well have looked like it. All in all over the past 13 years I have had five such experiences, each one teaching me so much about myself, life, the universe and my particular task at this particular time. They were times of intense learning and reshifting of 'data'.

During my first 'spell' I became aware of the enormity, depth and stranglehold of my guilt. The event which triggered it off was my first extra-marital relationship. I was engaging in the sin of adultery and my sense of guilt literally paralysed me. Only when an elderly doctor (who looked like god to me) gave me a kind of 'absolution', could I move my body again. But the exploration of guilt did not stop there. I found out my guilt about working for abortion law reforms, guilt about being German (the Jewish holocaust), guilt about being female (evil Eve), guilt about being alive (original sin). The sheer weight of all this guilt was squashing me and tearing me apart. I spent a couple of days in a mental hospital and eventually worked through it. Guilt no longer rules my being and I have learnt how the Christian religious dogma has kept me chained and unfree.

In my visions a world exists where sharing and caring are the cornerstones of being. Greed will have vanished as will have hunger, lack of shelter, rape and wars. Nothing is there for us to own, everything is on loan. My faith is that this is how we can, will and must live (if life is to continue on this planet). Everyone has choices. We can choose to change ourselves to be fit to live in a peaceful, co-operative world. Having changes so much myself in the past 20 years I know from my own experience that it is possible.

At the end of '87 — beginning of '88 — I went on a retreat during the Xmas holidays. I learned to meditate in a group (I had always done so on my own before), and discovered that I had a great deal in common with Buddhist philosophies.

I am excited by the activities around the London Buddhist Centre: some of these are women's co-operatives (a typesetting business, a shop, a vegetarian restaurant), some are mixed, like the housing co-operatives. There are several communal living projects, both single-sex and mixed. In these 'Right Livelihood projects' people are attempting to create ways of living according to their ideals. This is what I have been trying to do, too, in recognising that the personal is political and that the changes we want can be created here and now, within oneself and with others. We do not have to wait until 'after the revolution'. The revolution is now. I was impressed when visiting these co-operatives by a sense of unity which reminded me of my own treasured discovery of sisterly solidarity.

I remember well the blinding fury, the brilliant anger, the sense of betrayal I felt and shared with many of my sisters when, through consciousness-raising, we unravelled the patriarchal plot; I remember the joy when we allowed ourselves to feel love for women instead of the negative feelings normal in a misogynistic society. Before we can find love, before we can share it and love others we have to find the love we have for ourselves. I believe that without a feminist perspective it is very difficult indeed for women to create this love for themselves.

For me there is no difference in my travelling on the 'spiritual path' and my pursuit of feminism. My feminism feeds my spiritual growth and vice versa. It was important for me to find the Goddess and to dethrone God-the-Father, so that the understanding of living without God as a being could develop. The ideal of Buddhahood, each individual's potential for enlightenment, makes sense to me, although my visualisation of the spiral path to enlightenment is a horizontal one, not the phallic one described in one of the Buddhist texts I've read. My involvement with the Friends of the Western Buddhist Order is a recent one and I have no idea yet how much I will let myself get drawn in. Some sexist language in their publications has made me aware of how they collude with the status quo. Also, out of 320 order members, only 50 happen to be female. I ask myself why? And how does that effect the communications and the running of the organisation?

How does it matter? I intend to find out.

A recent development — the discovery of some abnormal cells in my body — has added yet another dimension to my life. Now I use some of my meditation time for visualising the growth of healthy cells. I also visit a colour healer regularly (as well as the conventional colposcopy clinic) and I am learning to eat vegan food. I have enjoyed good health so far; learning to live with potential disease, pain, dependency, my physical form getting more worn out, older, less reliable, is — possibly — the next challenge in my life. I have accepted being mortal (I made a will ten years ago and took out some life insurance so that my daughter will be materially secure). But accepting being in need of care, losing my independence, seems quite difficult.

THE STRENGTH OF TOMORROW

dedicated to my mother
Zouina Ben Halla

Maggie Nichols

I was born in Scotland. My father is a Highlander and my mother is half French and half Algerian Berber. The older I grow the more important these different parts of me become.

We lived in Soho for a large part of my early years in London, and the clubs I went to from the age of 13 were not Youth Clubs. An ignorant policeman told my dad that the people who went down them were the "scum of the earth" and the "dregs of humanity" but they were family to me.

At 15 I got a job as a Windmill Girl, and then at 16 I started singing in a strip club in Manchester. I was desperate to sing jazz but discouraged by the cynical white male musicians on the jazz scene. Yearning and terrified all at once, I was a sitting duck for many of the men who thought nothing of taking advantage of my naivety and eagerness to belong. Luckily not all the musicians took advantage — there was a brilliant pianist called Dennis Rose who took me under his musical wing and I started singing with him in a pub off the Caledonian Road. He was in the forefront of the revolutionary bebop movement in Britain, and developed many musicians besides me. He went a long way towards making up for the casual disrespect and sexual abuse I suffered from other musicians.

In 1968 I was 20 and living several lives. I was still deeply involved with the Soho clubs community. I went down the lesbian club The Gateways, I was doing occasional gigs in pubs and hostessing in a drinking club off Regent Street. By this time I was living back home, which was now a Peabody Estate behind Grosvenor Square, but as I wasn't a student or close to anyone politically active, the momentous demonstrations on my doorstep passed me by. I remember feeling affected by them, but knew of no way in.

I had been abroad for about a year, dancing and hostessing, and when I came back, a fundamental change had taken place in the world of jazz, influenced by world events and musically by Afro-Americans like John Coltrane, Ornette Colman and Eric Dolphy, as well as by Black South Africans now living in London. Whereas

improvisation had been based mainly around chord changes, it was
now harmonically and rhythmically freer. Ronnie Scott's Jazz Club
had moved to Frith Street and his first club in Gerrard Street, now
called The Old Place, had become home to a lot of the newer music.
I was so excited by what I heard, and felt convinced that I could hear
a voice playing an equal part in this musical revolution, but I didn't
have the confidence to articulate my feelings beyond enthusiastic
hinting. At last someone mentioned that "John Stevens uses voices"
and I went to hear him, up endless flights of stairs in a wee room
called The Little Theatre Club.

It was a mind-blowing experience. I couldn't understand how this
large group could sound so new and adventurous and yet so
coherent. How did they do it? A couple of months later I was doing it
myself with John and Trevor Watts. John set up a springboard for
improvisation that I use in workshops to this day; a piece so simple
that people can easily miss its limitless potential. I sang the first note
that came into my head and Trevor played a different one on the sax.
We repeated our notes according to our individual breath cycles,
while John played beautiful resonating textures on a gong. After a
while we were improvising completely, and I couldn't believe the
feelings of liberation. I was also singing in a strip club in Old
Compton Street and I danced and whooped my way round there in
the rain, elated, I opened out beyond belief. It was a real
breakthrough and I sang with the Spontaneous Music Ensemble
throughout '68 and some of '69.

In November '68, we played in Berlin at the Total Music Meeting,
the first European Improvisation festival, which was set up as an
alternative to The Berlin Jazz Days. Held in a large rock club, there
were two stages which provided continuous music and the place was
packed. We were put up in a dormitory in a Youth Hostel, with cold
stone floors and no hot water, but it was magic; so much exciting
music and conversation; my first taste of promotion to "one of the
boys". It was there that I met Julie Tippetts, who was singing at the
main jazz festival with Brian Auger and The Trinity, but it wasn't
until a couple of years later that we established our amazing musical
relationship which has got stronger and deeper over the years.

Looking back, I realise that the only women musicians at the
festival were singers, and that me and my mate Annette carried
John's percussion back on the train and boat, while the other "boys"
flew back on the plane. Still, I wouldn't have missed the experience
for anything.

I changed radically in the years between '68 and '78. In 1970, my daughter was born, and our relationship has been a constant source of inspiration and frustration, guilt and understanding. What I have learned as a mother fighting to survive in this hierarchical, sado-masochistic system has changed me profoundly and deserves a chapter or book of its own. All I can say is that the discoveries of our precious, contradictory relationship are contained in everything I've written here.

Later in 1970 I was encouraged by the youth leader and administrator of Oval house to start giving music workshops there, in spite of having no teaching experience or qualifications. I used workshop pieces I'd learnt with Spontaneous Music Ensemble, and some of the workshop participants showed me wonderful exercises that were part of the revolutionary developments in theatre in the 60s and early 70s. Because of the way I started teaching, I developed over the years a method of integrating different ideas and exercises to suit different needs, combined with my discoveries as a performer and a social being. It helped me demystify the creative process and share discoveries and skills with others. Quite a few people who've been to my workshops are now running their own. You don't need formal qualifications, but you do need to respect creative ways of working and the people you work with, and to understand that learning is a mutual and continuous process.

At the Oval House, I also acted in fringe productions and joined a local rock band. It was in the coffee bar there that I found a dog-eared copy of *The Female Eunuch*, which I borrowed when no-one was looking. The chapter 'Fear, Loathing and Disgust' showed me that what I'd been through was not just personal to me, but profoundly political. I was moving towards feminism, including acting in a Michelene Wandor play, when I was "diverted" by the Socialist Labour League (forerunner of the Workers' Revolutionary Party), which I joined in 1972. Leaving school at 14 had made me nervous of students and intellectuals — I got an excellent education through the party in economics, history and philosophy and most importantly, connecting them all, dialectical materialism, described by Engels as "the science of connections and the universal laws of all motion and development." It was the dialectical method that enabled the SLL to grasp the essence behind the appearance of constantly changing world events.

When Nixon took the dollar off gold in 1971, they warned that the post-War boom had ended and that the class struggle would intensify as attacks on living standards and rights increased. They were called alarmist, but world events today bear them out. The theory and practice of materialist dialectics has made an enormous difference to my personal life and to the way I practise music, individually and collectively. It was also crucial in deepening my understanding that the personal is political. Although some Marxists might disagree with this essential truth of the women's movement, in Lenin's *Essay on Dialectics* he writes "The opposites are identical: the individual exists only in the connection that leads to the universal. The universal exists only in the individual and through the individual." This applies equally to the personal and the political. In spite of their consistent fight against bourgeois ideology and formal thinking, the SLL leadership separated the personal from the political in a formal way, by treating sexual politics as a diversion.

A combination of factors led to my "retreat" from the party around 1977. One of the main ones was my conditioned inability to confront leadership where I disagreed with it, and there were also the enormous pressures of trying to survive as a single parent on Social Security. Although I did very few gigs, I wrote some of my strongest songs during the years I was a party member, and its influence is with me to this day.

In 1978 I was still doing workshops at the Oval House once a week, and I wrote in my diary, "What a flowering of strength and musical creativity and independence. No more waiting for the musical knight on the white charger to shape me musically and fire my soul . . . real musical interaction, real influences and the discovery that learning is a mutual process."

Something had happened in 1977 that determined how I was in 1978. I went to see Gay Sweatshop in a play about lesbian mothers and custody. "I liked it a lot . . . one woman in particular . . . she was great in it and I really found myself so drawn to her. Afterwards I was able to look right into her eyes and she looked right back and smiled and I felt quite shaky and excited. If I could have gone off with her there and then I would have. For a while the thought of any man, however gentle, felt clumsy and heavy."

Through a lesbian relationship of a different kind from what I'd experienced in the 60s, I started reading feminist books with fervour and experienced the slightly frightening exhilaration of my first women-only gatherings. I went to a conference concerning "The Liberal Takeover of the Women's Movement", and was accused of being part of that takeover because I spoke passionately about the Grunwick strike and class politics. I persevered and discovered other women raising questions of class, race and later disability. "We've started a political revolutionary feminist group; one that doesn't avoid the question of class, but is fighting to draw from the best of Marxist theory and practice and to use dialectical materialism as a thing for us. We went to Grunwicks and had a tremendous discussion with the women there. We began to link the class and sex questions; production for need and not profit and women's control of reproduction ... We talked about it in terms of concrete examples like child-raising, medicine, drug companies (Thalidomide etc), and profit, enforced sterilization and racism. It was a very lively yet serious discussion and we learnt a lot and got a lot across."

I also began to understand the political nature of lesbian feminism as a threat to male supremacy. Some male musicians certainly reacted in a very threatened way, no doubt wishing I would remain content with my status as "one of the boys" and not make them uncomfortable. After a particularly sharp and upsetting argument with eight of them, I wrote a song sitting up in a Bed and Breakfast late at night:

Oh you backward men
with those fantasies of yours
the sexy young chick there for you to fancy
packaged just for you to revel in
It's natural you say it's what she wants, is asking for
It's what she's there for
Male identified invention
heaven in the female shape
keep an eye on her by fixing her in your appointed place
and hell for you the ugly woman the old woman
who is she
I don't want to see her through your eyes
I won't define a woman by her age her shape her size.
I see women trapped I see women breaking through
and when a woman wakes up I see her struggle to
refuse your definition of her
She doesn't want to laugh she doesn't want to cry
at all your anti woman jokes no more.
She is angry she is realising
that what she felt but locked inside
is now what she knows and will not hide any more
and as we women reach for one another
we must reach for her.

The argument had an impact on the musicians; the next day they revealed intimate details about themselves and their sexuality and one of them picked up a paper and said "I see what you mean about the *Daily Mirror* being sexist."

Until then, most of my intimate musical experiences had been with men and now I wanted to explore improvisation with other women. I was a founder member of Ova, a six piece women's band that was one of the first to include improvisation with its songs, but I wanted to go deeper, so at the end of 1977 the Feminist Improvising Group came into existence. After our first gig in October, I wrote: "Very exhilarating . . . women really identified with the roles we were working through; harassed mother/housewife (me), angry, patronised child (Corine), straight, demure symphony "lady", "Hip chick", "dolly bird" and how we sort of questioned them and rebelled against them through the music . . . I think some of the men felt really threatened by it. It was a challenge to the sort of dry, intellectual abstractions of a lot of male improvisers."

There's no doubt in my mind that FIG had a strong impact on improvised music. We performed the connection between the personal and the political; we explored the relationship of the concrete and the abstract. We improvised theatrical sketches and made personal and political statements. We challenged patriarchal bourgeois levels of technical and improvising skills. When we did women's events we would often be sharing the evening with folk and rock musicians, and at first women found what we did strange. But invariably our commitment to communicate and demystify improvisation, as a process relevant to all our lives, connected with women at these events.

I was still singing with a women's rock band that I'd joined in 1977. I had been criticised by some feminist musicians because of the band's male manager and desire to become well known, *ie* "commercial". New as I was to the women's movement, I took my politics into the band. I took the contract to the Musicians' Union to have it checked, and as a result we didn't sign. I raised feminist and socialist issues and was open about my sexuality. We all became friends, and things were going well musically until a new pianist and her boyfriend joined forces with our manager. Loads of "unaccompanied" women were coming to our gigs and the manager was heard to say that if he didn't watch it we'd get the reputation of being a dyke rock band. In March '78 I wrote "Alan told me today that I wasn't communicating with the audience (*ie* flirting with the men) and that

I wasn't a rock singer. He gave me yesterday's and today's money and that was that."

Most of the women were very upset, but in the end felt it would be easier to get another singer than another keyboard player, in spite of the enthusiastic audience response to the band as a whole. Again I wrote "I was sacked by Alan because I'm political . . . I never rammed it down anyone's throat, but I didn't avoid discussing with the band. I didn't keep an unprincipled peace and it upsets me that it's been made out that it was for musical reasons. The more I think about it the more needled I get." I noticed that the feminists who had criticised me before stayed silent and continued going to the band's gigs.

In spring '78 Julie Tippetts and I did our duo album 'Sweet and S'ours', which we are very proud of to this day. All the tracks were composed spontaneously by the two of us, and as Julie wrote in the sleeve notes for the album, "We feel that this album shows many sides of our natures, both as working partners and as dear old mates." FIG also got the chance to perform at women's festivals in Eindhoven and Copenhagen. At the end of the tour I wrote: "Well, it's all over and it's all just beginning. I've discovered what I always felt, that improvisation can be communication in a powerful and moving way. It's these wonderful women improvisors and loving friends that have tested it out in practice with me." I also wrote "I think it's important we play in different combinations and not just the same splinter groups. It's important not to develop favourites because that's where the problems start."

As FIG worked more, some white male musicians were anxious to divide and rule, and picked out favourites in the group, while criticising the others according to their subjective ideas about musical "aesthetics". I have come to hate that word as I have encountered so many people who use it to disguise their prejudices behind a pretended objective position. Recently, having decided where to pin a brooch on a lapel, my musical companion Shirley Hall exclaimed: "That's aesthetics, Mag." I could have hugged her, because sometimes I forget that the academically-educated don't have a copyright on what works creatively. Bourgeois standards carry a lot of weight, even in so-called alternative artistic circles.

The internal doubts, divisions and disintegration of FIG came about later than '78, in the early 80s, but the question of women doubting themselves and each other is an ongoing one. We challenged male standards and were undermined by them, but the lessons I learned from trying to work in revolutionary ways are with me today in 1988, particularly in an open women's workshop performance group, Contradictions, which I initiated in 1980. It's a way of working rather than a fixed group, and many smaller groups have come out of it, including Salmag'n'Shirl, an improvising trio which occasionally performs songs written by all three of us.

My commitment to improvisation — a process that reflects the immediacy of each new moment and connects with what you bring from the personal and collective past — is in everything I do. When I sing songs in '88 that I first sang in the 60s, they have a different content and form because of the years of exploring improvisation contained in how I sing them. Often people think that totally improvised gigs are composed, and improvisation has inspired me to compose, too.

I love workshops. In 1978 I wrote that I wanted ". . . workshops to break down the barrier between or understand the interconnectedness of 'everyday life' and 'music'. It does happen in the workshops but outside these four walls it has to be so subtle or they'd lock us up. It's legitimate, respectable as 'art' but not on the bus or the street thankyou very much."

In 1988 I have discovered old truths in a deeper, newer way. I prepared these notes for a recent workshop:

> *Exercises to relax and give confidence*
> Finding a common focus for a diverse group
> Learning to listen actively as opposed to passively
> The challenge of simplicity
> The relationship of the individual to the group
> Risk-taking from a position of relative safety
> Learning from each situation, from each other
> Unlearning mechanical methods of music making
> Music as a social force made by social beings.

Creativity is a political question. It is no accident that when people fight back, their creativity expands and those who struggle against enormous odds and survive are the greatest improvisors. We are in the middle of a rapidly deepening global economic crisis and the consequent threat of nuclear war. The world debt runs into trillions and the International Monetary Fund demands that each government slashes services, drives down wages, starves the poor and smashes individual and collective resistance. We can be passive in the face of these attacks, or we can join the international revolutionary resistance and struggle to find the most effective ways of fighting both individually and collectively, for a world where human beings can live in creative dignity with their basic needs provided.

We need unity of a principled kind, where different organisations and sections of society don't have to dilute their policies or compromise who they are, The kind of unity inspired by the miners' strike of '84 and '85 where many different groups, such as The Lesbian and Gay Support Group and Camden Black Workers, supported the miners and found the working-class women of the mining communities ready to grasp the necessity and significance of forging links between all those in struggle against the government. On this April's demonstration against Clause 28, these links were carried forward by the presence of Women Against Pit Closures and trade unionists including the seafarers currently fighting P&O for the defence of trade unions and safety standards. There are no "single issues". Each of these fights is our own. It is a matter of life and death that we unite, but we can't sweep our differences under the carpet. We have to sharpen our understanding of difference so that we can grasp what connects us.

In a small but significant way, this is what many of us are exploring through music workshops, and in fact about ten of us held a workshop before the April 30th demonstration. We started with a warm-up and improvisations, and out of that came many musical and verbal ideas which we improvised around on the way to Kennington Park. As a lesbian mother, I was moved and proud that my daughter was there, singing by my side.

There is also much to learn through personally political relationships. I have been in a three-and-a-half year relationship with my lover Sue, continuing an ongoing struggle against romantic masochism and passivity, and learning again that friendship in love doesn't destroy magic. My closest friend and comrade, Vicky, has shared the discovery that female friendship, based on nurturing each other's growth and creativity and fighting out differences, can strengthen you and make you more effective politically.

Writing this has been exciting and frustrating. Exciting because I have realised I am capable of it and frustrating because I've had to leave so much out. I would really like to write a book!

There are no guarantees in these constantly changing times. I am full of fear *and* hope and I want to have the courage my mother had when she refused to sing for the Nazis and risked her life trying to get her Jewish lover out of Compiègne concentration camp.

The Strength of Tomorrow
Oh the past is such a heavy weight to carry
Sometimes seems like things are never going to change
It's like a long cold winter that seems without an end
but in the earth are the changes that bring Spring through
fresh new life fragile and unsure
Its got the strength of tomorrow
strength of tomorrow
streeeeength of tomorrow

Yesterday is dead and today is always dying
cos change is the one thing you can rely on
Breaking out of the old skin, couldn't cling anymore
fresh new life fragile and unsure

Its got the strength of tomorrow
strength of tomorrow
streeeeength of tomorrow

We've got to get ready today.

Maggie Nicols
© 1976

THROUGH THE NET

Thelma Agnew

There is something about parents that is unanswerable. They know you weren't like this when you were nine. It irks, being cast as a product of left-wing propaganda: me at 18, a great big sponge lying around college common rooms and soaking up the influences. In *1968* universities may have provided a free radicalising service, but I was in no fit state, at two years old, even to appreciate what I was missing. The 80s brand of subversive should at least be credited with a little conscious effort. I prefer to think of my politics not as an environmental hazard, but as a long-pursued, lovingly given-into temptation.

Good feminists (and Smiths fans) are born, not made. But they do need somewhere to practise. A third form Religious Education class, for instance, with the teacher explaining that Eve was made out of Adam to serve and comfort him, and all women are Eve. With the same dispassionate air he describes the nails going into Christ's wrists — the hands could not have supported the weight. I think: he's serious; there are probably a lot of them about. Four years later I met quite a few of them at university, stripped of divine authority but furtively certain, beneath their Oxfam coats, of the natural order of things.

My home town, like anybody's home town, was short on space. I left Larne for the University of Kent at Canterbury in 1984. This was no wing-flapping exit from the nest; more like a defection. In 1984 I did not just go to university, leave home, fancy a change of scenery — I went in search of a Whole New Reality. (If you're going to do something you're ashamed of, it's as well to have a grand motive.) My first introduction to reality had been in 1978. Tenth Anniversary newsreel — Civil Rights marches, the shock of seeing troops *arrive* (instead of being there forever). The Troubles showed up as a matter of cause and effect, a man-made disaster. Not an ongoing natural phenomenon.

I used to joke that had there been a University of Cornwall, hanging by its fingernails from Land's End, I would have migrated there instead. But not so. I was tired of living on the edge. I wanted somewhere that was near, smugly near, the centre of things. Canterbury was symbolically, if not literally, the farthest possible point from Northern Ireland. It was the kind of place where God, due to unforeseen circumstances, felt unable to attend but wished everyone well. I depended on the centre of Anglicanism to be indifferent to religion.

Imagine my distress, dear reader, to be constantly engaged in conversation with "And are you Catholic or Protestant?" A decade or so earlier, a visiting tough young nut from Belfast had demanded to know whether I supported King Billy or the Pope. But even properly coded, the question had struck me as indecent. In English student mouths, I suspected a request for news from the frontline. In that first week of smile-you're-at-university, Northern Ireland appeared to be running a close second to what everybody did for their 'A' Levels. I could deflate expectations and declare boredom before bombs as the bane of Irish life. Or I could offer up whatever anecdotal material I possessed. Guilt struggled with eagerness to please. It was exhausting and it was irritating.

I had not come to an English university to talk, or even think about 'the situation'. I had come to find an outlet for my furtively developed feminism (I was already on intimate quoting terms with Simone de Beauvoir), and to get a closer view of 'real' politics. Real politics had always been that great televised event, Left v Right. For the troubles to be fitted into such a format seemed . . . inappropriate. I'd grown up in a community that did not consider the British Government an imperialistic oppressor, but a shifty-eyed slacker, all too likely to clear off home at the first opportunity. I'd adopted a position of lofty neutrality, muttered *tribalism* against years of Twelfth Day parades, said (quietly) I hadn't a drop of Orange blood in me. It took English curiosity to make me realise I was not, in fact, Switzerland.

In my new enlightened environment, where Ulster Unionists were regarded as *Sun*-reading Ayatollahs, I found myself afflicted with a growing need to explain, defend, their need (and mine?) for a British identity. This was not made any easier by the simultaneous discovery that I had an accent which was lovely, really, and that I was so wonderfully expressive it must be the Celtic strain. England insisting I was Irish. I'd been used to piously objecting that Irish jokes were jokes against ourselves. But I knew the difference. Being born in the north, being born a Protestant — these were disqualifications that could not casually be disregarded. When left-wing acquaintances graced me with the highest level of oppression, and assumed I was a Catholic nationalist, I felt obliged to own up. Running away from Ulster did not mean I was prepared to appropriate Ireland. Virginia Woolf's comment that a woman has no country struck me as rather heartening. You and me, Virginia.

Even feminism had its catchphrase 'Irish Women', which left me falling through the net. 'Irish Women' featured on posters in support of the armed struggle. I wondered if they included RUC widows, and made a conscious decision not to ask. Part of feminism's original appeal was what I persisted in regarding as its internationalism. I would give no energy to politics that could be sub-sectioned into Northern Ireland. The experiences that shaped my version of sisterhood were common to any small-town girl. I used to think that Woman = Adam's Rib (women from men, for men) was *just typical* of a country where Pope-as-Anti-Christ still had a certain currency. I know now that I overestimated the rest of the western world's capacity for lateral thinking.

Undergraduate revolutionaries (even in the job-obsessed 80s, not everyone is there just for the degree) are usually prepared to give to the common good all the stocks, shares, and property not yet in their possession. Of course, one of the advantages of empathising with the proletariat is that you don't have to socialise with it. It rarely attempts to get a word in edgeways or follow you into the bedroom. Feminism expects to be taken personally. It usually is. You have designs on my manhood: you have designs on my girlfriend: you are an insult to my mother's memory. The latter variety of taking it personally will interpret a nut cutlet as a vicious and unwarranted attack on his pork chop.

For future members of the moral majority, university is a testing time. The most sensitive will wake in the night, wracked by doubts . . . if you laid all those minorities end to end, there might be . . . quite a lot of them. The average Thatcher Youth is however quite capable of rising to the challenge. On good days he explains (to those girlies who think they're feminists but aren't because they're not ugly) that Women's Groups are sexist. He is pleased with himself for knowing that word and for being able to use it in such a clever and original way. Feminism hoist by its own petard. Sex-ist. When not feeling quite up to that level of articulation, he contents himself with carving pictures of genitalia on library desks. Meanwhile, deep in the library loos, his female equivalent adds to the paranoia surrounding a lone lesbian symbol on a toilet wall. In the tradition of *"Well I like men"* ... *"So do I"* ... *"All my best friends are men, my boyfriend is a man and I am going to marry a man"*, comes ... *"Sod the miners"*.

A fair proportion of students are at one with the government in believing that educational institutions have no business running around inciting people to think. This refusal to think is alas, unequalled by any reluctance to talk about it. The energy I spent during one-to-one 'discussions' during those first few months: I demand a refund. The southern English do not temper hostility with politeness, they express it through it. It can take fifteen minutes to realise you're being flayed alive. The only honest survival technique is to take to the Women's Group, the Women's Committee, several campaigns, and a couple of speeches at Union General Meetings. It also helps to don leggings, men's jackets and (especially if you have defective eyesight) little round glasses. Always make sure the enemy can see you coming, they only get really nasty if they catch you out in uniform. The horror of the first few weeks in student society is due to the necessity of speaking to people. By Christmas, everyone has picked up visual shorthand and knows exactly who you are. Ex-students don't miss the protection of university, but its constant exposure.

I suppose it might have been amusing to have celebrated graduation by putting away my marching shoes and starting a collection of houseplants. But 1987 was hardly the year for it. I howled at Thatcher's victory, quite as sincerely stricken as any of my comrades from Kent. English politics had, over the course of three years, lost the quality of an anthropological study — and come close to home. For years Northern Ireland has been a collection of 'special circumstances', abstracted from the Overall Achievement. Now the Overall Achievement goes from strength to strength in the absence of Scotland, Wales and a good slice north of Watford. I used to bemoan my country's social and sexual intolerance as regrettably behind the times: women having to cross the water for abortions, homosexuality only recently and grudgingly legalised, moral guardians with 'Keep sodomy out of Ulster' placards. Now, as Alton's Abortion Bill and Clause 28 progress through the British Parliament, it looks as though Northern Ireland's anachronism was really the original 50s classic.

I'd like to give England the benefit of the doubt and attribute its recent backlashing fervour to an uncivilised minority. Certainly there are a great many people protesting that it wasn't always this way. There is much wailing and gnashing of teeth and evoking of the spirit of '68. At the risk of sounding heretical, I'm beginning to doubt that the spirit of '68 was ever generally imbibed. Perhaps you had to be standing in exactly the right place, at exactly the right time, with your mouth open very wide. There may be a touch of pique here, admittedly . . . at 22 I'm the late arrival at the party who insists it can't have been very good, since it finished so *early*. But the established Left really is most provoking; forever disappointed in the under-30s, insisting they gave us the best start in life and we've gone and squandered the inheritance. Truth is, they over-estimated how much they had to give, and we're spending it in a way they didn't expect.

Dropping out is not an attractive prospect when there is no guarantee of ever getting in. Dropping out is a placebo for a society with full employment. I suspect the 60s' line between party time and politics was blurred. What held it all together was a generally rebellious euphoria of goodwill. Today's nice middle-class young man is not likely to be disillusioned with the system and is more than passing fond of his Alessi kettle, while the politically active 80s youth is inclined to fight for specifics. Thus dies the fabled unity of the movement.

It is not even what we do, or fail to do, that is so disdained by the '68 generation. It is what we represent. People are usually blamed for the decade which they happen to grow up in. I refuse to believe that the Thatcher revolution is about pandering to monied, jaded youth. Channel 4's commercial breaks — beautiful young things being treacherous in boardrooms and languid in loft conversions — are important not because they exemplify a new reality but because they have entered our dreams. Your average 60s guru does not approve. The root of his objection is not money. No decade has ever been indifferent to money for more than 15 minutes on a Sunday afternoon. Not thinking about money requires a level of self-absorption requiring therapy and usually getting it. The epithet most frequently and damningly affixed to the 80s is 'Designer'. The Left may be the most affected, but it's not alone. The British have nurtured an image of themselves — soft-slippered, eccentric and tolerant — which the 80s are burying.

I can't pretend to mourn two utopian decades in which, from the vast TV consumption of my infancy, there were no women. Hands shoot into the air. Alright I will concede the Liver Birds, but only as an exception that proves the rule . . . like Mrs Thatcher. Mostly it was Likely Lads, Butch and Sundance, and acres of Clint Eastwood. With a great concentration of will an image re-emerges of Katherine Ross smiling and Susan George screaming. The favourite 80s stereotype, a sort of pin-striped suit on heat, is preferable; if only by a (perfectly coiffured) head.

THE GEOGRAPHY
OF HISTORY

This is one small segment of a net of feminist groups and connections, covering the British Isles and stretching out to neighbouring countries. Put enough of these pieces together and they cover the globe.

There are writers from all over the UK (and beyond) scattered throughout this book, but these particular women cover a wider field than most; different laws, different language for some; notable feminist itineraries for all.

You can see here how threads intersect. Zaidie Parr and Rachel Bodle link their different histories in one article; Gay Jones and Jo Somerset wrote their accounts separately, but they were both active in Manchester at the same important time.

It was a time when conflicts between women started to pass beyond the realm of the political and take on the form of territorial contest. Now the dust has fallen but we're left with a Balkanised landscape. The French notion of plural 'feminisms', the American political 'communities', the left Labour 'sections' and 'committees', could all be summed up in advertising jargon: what we have here is a process of *market diversification*.

The movement's media reflect this strikingly, with different patterns of exclusion or advocacy no longer argued over [any more]. Peace reigns, but only at the price of suppressing issues of censorship and political priority. Perhaps this too is part of history. The pamphlet age is over, and the imagination and creativity now go into culture and the arts.

In the meantime feminists all over the place go on meshing words and theories as well as practical actions together — not sure at any moment when they might get the chop. But in the end, as Rosie Brennan shows, there's maybe nowhere else to go but up.

TWENTY YEARS IN THE LIVES OF ZAIDIE AND RACHEL

Zaidie Parr and Rachel Bodle

R: I met Zaidie when I joined the feminist news magazine *Women's Report* in 1975. We kept in touch for several years after Zaidie left the collective to follow a course in Birmingham, but we had not seen one another for some time when we came together again to collaborate on this contribution. We agreed to document separately selected aspects of our involvement with, and feelings about, the women's movement over the past 20 years. Here we compare notes.

Z: I left home for university in 1967 but my journal still reflects the fractured perspectives of adolescence. Romantic spirituality rubs shoulders with tortured self-searching and notes on revolutionary change. Despite the suffocating sexual ignorance of my girlhood, by 1968 I had established a relationship with a male postgraduate student. This was based on the premise that as either marriage or living together were inherently oppressive, then by maintaining our domestic independence we would find emotional freedom and sexual pleasure. And so, for a time, we did. We went with other students from the college film society to the Vietnam Demonstration in Grosvenor Square. We were all separated in the turmoil created when the police charged the crowds. He returned much later than the rest of us, with film and camera both carefully safe, but shaken by the unexpected violence. We spent time, shocked, analysing police tactics, winding down. Later that same year one of his flatmates who was gay told me that he thought him a male chauvinist pig. I did not understand this new vocabulary; it was the first time I'd heard it used.

I spent most of the next year supposedly attending Rouen University. This proved difficult — most of the time the students were on strike and lectures were cancelled, while Fascist groups from the local town roamed the campus and put the boot in, in full view of passers-by. I found it hard to concentrate on approved texts and spent most of my time reading political satire. In retrospect I see many roots of my politicisation here.

My mother died that year. I hadn't understood her illness and it was a shock. Thereafter her relatives had little to do with me — they no longer considered me part of the (patriarchal) family. I was bewildered by my isolation.

R: Like Zaidie, it seems that in 1968 I was still a girl, although that year I attained the 'age of majority'; moved from full-time education to a full-time job; and committed myself to a husband and a mortgage. The surge of student activity in the late 60s didn't have a marked impact until my final year and, unlike Zaidie, I didn't participate. I did not appreciate the problems I would face, newly married and living far away from family and friends. Struggling for recognition at work, I leaned heavily for support upon a young man no better equipped for his part than I was for mine. I've never been so lonely as I was at times during the next three years. These bad times were interrupted when we moved to Philadelphia, where my husband was to study. It was 1972; the year of George McGovern and early rumblings from Watergate; the women's movement more visible with the first issue of *MS* magazine. Working on campus, I made new women friends. They showed me the sights of the city and Pennsylvania County; we prepared meals together, played cards in the sun together . . . and talked. We discussed our growing up, our relationships with family, friends and lovers, issues raised in the news and by articles and books we read; we joined other local women to establish a women's arts centre. At the end of the year I was sorry to leave, but I had found the Women's Liberation Movement (WLM) and hoped to find support through it at home.

Z: 1972 was significant for me, too. In the spring of that year my best friend Jenny sold me a copy of *Nightcleaners' SHREW*, and invited me along to the consciousness-raising group she'd recently joined. Despite the harrowing experiences of other women's sufferings which we discussed in the group, I remained in an intellectual fog for some time, unable to make the connection between my own feelings of oppression and the experiences of other women. I was on the point of leaving but was prevented from doing so after another women in the group confronted me on the need for commitment. I went on to participate in picket lines, Womens' Day Marches, leafletting the Ideal Home Exhibition, Gay Pride Marches, and the eventual production of a *SHREW* with irreverent cartoons mocking men. One day I nervously went along to the Soho office of the Womens' Liberation Workshop: I saw and purchased a copy of *The*

Myth of the Vaginal Orgasm. This mystified me — I was out of step again. Not only a whole new vocabulary but new sexual expecta-tions as well. I was dubious but made suggested adjustments to lovemaking, which brought an uneasy realisation that perhaps men might not, after all, be indispensable.

In 1973 College sent me to Avignon to teach as an *assistante*. The contrast between the students was pronounced. (There is no grants system in France.) Those who came from wealthy backgrounds wore staggeringly expensive clothes and did very little work. In class they were arrogant and disruptive and I had no idea how to control them. Then there were the church-mouse-poor scholarship students and those others who, blacklisted after their activities in May '68, found it hard to earn enough money to pay their way. I had more empathy with them and tried to support them as a teacher.

I was in the throes of a first lesbian infatuation which, whilst euphoric, had disoriented me. Although I was losing my hard-won heterosexual status, I did not think I could, in all honesty, lay claim to an exclusively lesbian identity. I decided I must be bisexual. After giving a lecture on Women's Liberation In England, I joined a women's group that was just starting in the town and made friendships there that remain strong today. We had a lot of fun. We hit town in one woman's car, wolf-whistling and yelling insults at men on foot; we called on a lesbian household to find the occupants like creatures from another world — plastered with thick green mud as they'd chosen that day for a beauty session . . . The group focused on the by now nationwide Movement for the Liberation of Abortion and Contraception (MLAC). The police, faced with mass opposi-tion to the punitive abortion laws, could not arrest everyone, and we knew a nurse in town who wanted to set up a local MLAC group. A male doctor was on 24-hour standby but I don't think he was ever needed. Cannulas, illegally imported from the United States, were used for the vacuum aspiration method of abortion, with a pump rigged up on the kitchen sink. A table, decked out with clean bedlinen, served as operating couch. My role was to call on women's homes (mainly working-class tower blocks in the suburbs) to offer them two appointments. They were counselled first, both women and their menfolk (a political activity in itself) and then the secret abortion was arranged. As a result of the Campaign the law was successfully reformed the next year, but not to the extent that feminists would have liked.

In 1974 I returned to England and a temporary job as receptionist for an International Planned Parenthood Federation research project on early menstrual-extraction/abortion, but politically I felt at a loss after my time abroad. My Need to Belong was further thwarted because bisexuality was now deemed "ideologically unsound". I began to identify with Radical Feminists who said (like Robin Morgan) that providing you womanned the barricades it did not matter whom you slept with. But that year 'The Clit Statement' was reprinted from an American journal, *Off Our Backs*, in the London Women's Liberation Workshop Newsletter; the message was basically that heterosexual women were the enemy.

R: My lifestyle back in England was very different from my earlier isolation. Although, like Zaidie, I did not feel comfortable within some of the groups of women I met, I made a few friends and at that time was not unduly disturbed by peripheral differences of approach or analysis. Much of my energy was directed towards reviewing my living situation.

Early in 1973 I became pregnant. I hoped it would be possible to combine my working with having a baby but until I discussed the 'problem' with my sister I had no idea how to manage it. At that time she was working for low pay in a job she didn't enjoy: she had no close relationships and was able to move away from the north of England: and she was feeling broody. She was keen to help me out — so she moved in.

She and I soon became friends as well as sisters. Although I wanted to share ideas from the movement with my husband, he was uninterested and it was my sister with whom I talked. As time went on we shared more and more and, when my son was born, together we learned how to meet the needs of a somewhat fretful infant. In the spring of 1974 she and I took the baby on a short holiday to Philadelphia. The holiday provided an opportunity to reassess the pattern of my life; I described to my friends how I lived, what work I did, and — on one occasion — my marriage and what it meant to me. What I said sounded so ridiculous that from that time I questioned whether I should stay with my husband. On my return home I suggested a separation though I neither expected nor wished him to accept the idea. I was hoping for some recognition of the distance between us and a joint attempt to bridge the gap. It didn't happen. Over the next few weeks we divided our possessions and in the middle of 1974 my sister, son and I moved out.

It took some time for the hurt and disappointment to heal. My self-image comprised: female, white, 5′ 6″ tall, and married. I had been half a couple, and I had to recover a sense of myself as a complete whole. Thereafter my relationships with men have been more guarded affairs where space is carefully reserved for Me — to be alone or with other friends. I have not avoided intimacy (or pain!) but I have never again allowed my sense of self to get lost.

At first in a rented flat, and later in a mortgaged house (complete with dry rot), my sister and I became very happy together. We tackled the money problem by establishing a common fund for household expenses and then each having pocket money. Her friends considered her lucky to have found such a comfortble way out of her tedious job. My colleagues at work thought I was lucky to have someone on site to share the care of my son. I was under less stress, and doing less housework, than any other working mother I knew. (At the same time, I was more involved with my son than most working fathers!) At times we lived as one family, shopping and eating together: at other times, in order to accommodate other relationships, we gave each other more space. My sister had a daughter in 1977. Our children flourished; each one had one of us as their special parent, and the other of us in reserve. They had the attention of an only child, and the companionship (and rivalry) that comes from fellow siblings. In return for the energy which my sister and I, supported by our friends, put into the household, it provided us with a stable base and safe refuge.

Z: In Autumn 1974 I joined a Women's Aid group local to my place of work (now Social Services). The women in the support group came from many political tendencies and backgrounds — Radical, Christian, Communist, unaligned Socialist Feminist, International Marxist Group, plus women who'd come through the refuge; they were inspiring in their efforts to keep that refuge open and I became part of the common purpose. We ran what was probably the most underfunded refuge in the London areas, but many came to us from Erin Pizzey's Chiswick Family Refuge, and seemed to prefer our democratic approach. Eventually our refuge received substantial funding from the GLC — ten years later. Conditions there are quite luxurious now.

Later on I moved and joined Women's Aid in Birmingham. Lacking a refuge, we squatted a National Trust house that had been ear-marked to become Birmingham's first American-run private hospital. The squat was rather an ambitious project for such a small group and the resultant publicity meant that local women could not feel entirely safe there. But many did come to the house, or rather mansion. Women and their children disported themselves all summer in the spacious rooms and garden. It was a glorious moment.

Meanwhile I was (inappropriately) involved in Women's Aid at national federation level, trying to work towards more overt political campaigning, to reach out to more women. But there was not the will to do this: it would have over-taxed the federation's resources and threatened their much-prized charitable status.

R: While I was living with my sister, our babysitting needs meant it was not possible to be part of the same women's group unless the group met at our place. I was the one to move on, so that my sister, who needed day time support, could remain in our local group (which itself gave birth to a Women's Aid group). I was a subscriber to *Women's Report*, and in May 1975 I read a small notice amongst the details of movement activities: "*Women's Report* Collective welcomes new members". I arranged to go to one of the weekly meetings, and met Zaidie!

Z: I was recruited to the *Women's Report* collective at the Edinburgh National Women's Liberation Conference in 1974. It proved an intellectual challenge: the first time I'd been in a group where such rigorous criticism and debate prevailed on all aspects of feminism.

R: Within the collective our lives adopted a two-monthly cycle: from monitoring and clipping newspapers, through to writing, proof-reading, publishing and distribution. At weekly meetings throughout the cycle we discussed practical and theoretical aspects of the process. The whole machine was well-oiled by the enjoyment we got from one another's company. The healthy laughter as we saw opportunities for cartoons; and the hysterical laughter which kept us from tears as the deadlines loomed ominously close. As each issue was (miraculously) completed we shared food and drink at a celebratory get-together.

Z: *Women's Report* became a vantage point from which I could safely observe the mutations of the Movement. I cocooned myself there, finding routine, ritual and meaning in the regularity of magazine production.

During my time on the collective I went to China on a three-week tour organised by the Society for Anglo–Chinese Understanding, which is how I met Emmie, a new kind of feminist and socialist alert to every idea and so alive to experience and political change. We were all very lucky to be allowed in as the Cultural Revolution was still going on.

But China was not the Utopia we'd naively expected. Goods were rationed and commune finances controlled by central government. The smooth-talking guides and cadres were very distant cousins of the older, plain-speaking women and men who'd helped to create the Revolution. Now Ting-Ling (a feminist writer) was in prison and we were informed that post-revolutionary China had no homosexuality and no physically-handicapped children either. We did see a factory employing mainly blind people, who'd have been beggars before the Revolution. Facing up to the reality of Third World poverty around us, and the tremendous positive changes that had been wrought, we thought it ill-behoved us to criticise — the main political activity in the affluent West. We heard witness accounts of suicides, humiliation, and worse from Overseas Chinese whom we met clandestinely, but we kept our concern and disillusionment to ourselves on our return and I never referred to it in *Women's Report*.

Emmie was to die only four years later. Her death was another unnoticed statistic in the silent epidemic of cancer amongst young women. She was 32. The way she had lived out her feminism had given me hope which went when she died. (By then I had left *Women's Report* and moved up to Birmingham for two years to train in social work at the University there. In revolt against reactionary assumptions on the part of the lecturers, women on the course set up the first Feminism and Social Work group, which began a series of yearly conferences.)

R: I also found security within the *Women's Report* collective. We comprised a range of political ideologies: there were socialist feminists, radical feminists, as well as others like me who were wary of the demands and resposibilities associated with claiming a label. Some of us were involved in other groups or campaigns as well. Being part of this group enabled me to feel more confident about how I fitted into the movement — and how the movement fitted into my life. Within the collective I felt able to contribute to 'the cause' in a practical way, without threat to the compromises I needed to reach in my personal and working relationships with men. However, all good things must come to an end . . . By 1979 the style of reporting in the "straight" press and on radio and television had clearly changed. The flow of new women to replace those who moved on from

Women's Report had dried up. Rather than drown under an unmanageable workload, those remaining planned a final issue to go out in style. The cover showed a small band of feminists in a rowing boat (called 'Autonomy') rescuing members of the collective from the sea around a sinking ship.

1979 seems to have marked the end of a phase for several aspects of the WLM. From 1970 to 1978 there were national conferences each year but there was no national conference in 1979, or ever after.

My first national conference was Edinburgh in 1974. I remember the discomfort and cold of the hall where I hardly slept; the serenity of the Edinburgh streets which I explored whilst other women were still in their sleeping-bags; the warmth and ease of the women with whom I later shared workshop discussions. At my first conference I hardly noticed the political divisions amongst the participants. In subsequent years, although I still enjoyed the togetherness of our conferences, I was also aware of powerful undercurrents of tension. Disagreement about the 'means' led to doubts as to whether we had a common (or even compatible) 'end' in view. I don't think we had.

The last national conference I attended was also the last national conference of the Women's Liberation Movement — Birmingham in 1978. I was unable to stay for the whole weekend and missed the unpleasant plenary session on Sunday. The Saturday was bad enough. The sisterly warmth between women from all over the country seemed to get lost in the crowds and formality of organisation necessary when 3000 people seek to share the same inadequate space. I had some positive experiences: as I hawked copies of the magazine around, I was warmly greeted by several *Women's Report* readers: but in the evening I felt alienated by the noise, smoke, and lack of consideration shown toward the harassed conference organisers. My day-to-day life in a mixed society was less oppressive than that day.

Z: I was living in Birmingham when the last National Women's Liberation Conference was held there. I was an associate of Revolutionary Feminists, whose tendency had emerged over the last two years. Some of them stayed in my household for the duration of the Conference. (This did not go down too well with the men who lived there.) I believed then that the outspoken approach of the Revolutionary Feminists who stated that Men were the Enemy (as opposed to the wishy-washy approach of Socialist–Feminists) might lead to a more rational democratic campaigning structure in the Movement.

I had perused *Feminist Revolution* by the American Radical Feminist group Redstockings, and also the Radical lesbian Rita Mae Brown's *Plain Brown Paper*. I was rather taken with Rita Mae's simplistic (but taboo, to feminists) idea that Women's Liberation could benefit from being structured like a political party or federation. I hoped that if we had an agreed political programme, reprobates like myself who'd seemingly failed to find the Holy Grail of Political Lesbianism might yet find a way to be Ourselves, but still of use to the movement. But the Revolutionary Feminists had no more intention of tinkering with the Movement's structure than any other feminists, being preoccupied with theories, like overthrowing male power by Anger, which I found increasingly obscure.

I felt that the Movement, my new "family", had let me down. I was just as much an outsider as I'd ever been. Old-style Consciousness-Raising had long since given way and a rather more "Maoist" model had emerged. It was OK now to criticise other women's politics and lifestyles — it showed that you really cared about them, and wanted to set them on the right path. I indulged in it myself. The Cold War was alive and well and in the Women's Movement.

The theme for the last conference was: "How do we oppress each other". Although oppression between women was rife at the conference, and one of Monica Sjoo's beautiful paintings was slashed on the sly, oppressions of class, sexuality, educational privilege, race, language and disability were not seriously analysed. Revolutionary Feminists wanted to discuss our oppression by men. With most of us mystified and frustrated and with our allotted time in the building running out, things came to a head at the Plenary. With women screaming and fighting over the microphone, 3000 women in one smoke-filled hall, — it was impossible to see, hear, or know precisely what you were voting for.

Despite this telling débâcle I still entertained hopes that the warring factions could be helped to reconciliation. I saw the Movement as timeless and I had no understanding of its historical context. Feeling compromised by my earlier support for one faction, I hoped to help organise a subsequent conference where the rifts could be healed. In 1981 Rachel and I called for another National Conference in a letter to WIRES, but only two women acknowledged our suggestion and no-one came forward to organise it with us.

R: My motivation for joining with Zaidie in suggesting a further conference was purely selfish. There was no single-issue campaign which seemed sufficiently pertinent to me, and I had always avoided any group which seemed to have an overly theoretical or idealistic approach. Just as *Women's Report* had provided a practical way of using my feminism without introducing threatening changes to my precariously balanced lifestyle, so too would involvement with a conference planning group. The conference could help us communicate, see the strength of our number, or to face the weakness of our disunity — and I could be a catalyst, involved but remaining unchanged ... Recognising the enormous stress placed on any group (particularly after Birmingham) attempting to organise within our amorphous structure, I now think I was being somewhat naive!

At present my energies are divided between those I live with, my job, and a few friends (a small number of women and an even smaller number of men). Within our household the predominant struggle is not the battle of the sexes, but the battle of the sex-hormones: whilst I'm finding out how to accommodate increasingly uncomfortable symptoms of the pre-menstrual syndrome my son is contending with the mood swings of adolescence. He and I are living with a man friend — a warm and comfortable relationship of 5 years standing. Within this friendship I have been free of emotional hassle and as my son has become more independent I have been able to plough more energy into my work, as a statistician with British Coal. But the social changes which have made it possible for me to sell my labour and win status in a male-dominated environment have done little to ease the domestic burden imposed by motherhood. Superwoman is an oppressive image created during the years when the Women's Liberation Movement has been active. It sometimes seems that the achievements of women this century, including our own, have done nothing to redress the imbalance in the social contribution required from men and women. Time with those of my women friends who also have management responsibility tends to be spent in discussing our staff's welfare — I don't believe that men in equivalent positions have the same preocupation with nurturing their staff. Perhaps we live within a constantly shifting society which can accommodate numerous legal forms without changing the bottom-line for women.

I like to hope that more fundamental changes are taking place, albeit slowly. On a good day I can foresee my descendants 500 years hence (is that long enough?) in a society with greater value placed on women and the qualities currently ascribed to us but denigrated. I don't think that I, or any of my sister feminists, could become sufficiently mature or civilised to live in this future. It will take generations of progressive child-rearing to achieve a society where there could be a peaceful and egalitarian existence for both sexes and all races.

On a bad day I can still find it possible to believe that women and men may come to share power equally — but on a bad day I foresee a society not improved by the change.

MAKING CHOICES — SCOTLAND AND THE WOMEN'S MOVEMENT

Aileen Christianson

My life, like anyone else's, doesn't fit a tidy pattern of development. But random memories do in the end make a kind of pattern. At the time they interwove or separated with no necessary connection to the external "historical" world of 1968, 1978 or 1988. Only in 1978 does my joining of Edinburgh Rape Crisis Centre as a volunteer coincide with the pattern of this book. My feminism and my self found in that a passionate and complete expression of what came to be for me *the* cause: the fight against male violence against women and girls. But its roots lie much earlier.

My commitment to women's issues is central to me. As central is my commitment to being Scottish, all the stronger for being based not on blood or birth, but on involuntary immigration. I was born in Wales in 1944; my parents (both Geordies, of Welsh/English and Swedish/English ancestry) brought my sister and me to Croftamie, Dumbartonshire, in 1946. That's my first political influence. I didn't grow up Welsh or English, but wasn't allowed quite to feel Scottish either.

My mother taught at the village school and couldn't leave me at home, so I began school at three. My years followed not the calendar, but the academic year and, by chance of an August birthday, my own. I appear on a wonderfully symmetrical photograph of the whole school in 1947, Miss Ferguson at the top of the school steps with her 28 pupils ranged below and me, tiny with wrinkled socks, in the middle of the front row. We are all in old and much-worn clothes, looking like refugees — children from another age. That childhood was a mixture of the freedom of fields and streams, and of strict discipline in the house, the hair brush on the bare bottom for misbehaviour. Once my mother hit me in class, formally on the hand, for getting my sums wrong, my earliest astonished memory of the concept of fairness rigorously applied.

In 1952 we moved to Helensburgh on the Clyde. We went to a private girls' school, St Bride's. In my twenties I realised that I had benefitted from growing up without the complexities of the daily presence of boys, and with women in positions of power and authority. My diaries record with embarrassing detail for the next few years the food, the household tasks, the rows wih my sister, the lessons, the girlfriends in and out of favour, the endless speculative lists of boys' names, music on the wireless, and library books.

The school and my parents decided that I should go to University (the first in my family to do so), not to Art School as I vaguely fancied, and certainly not to be a typist. I intended to be a great writer and knew that writers were supposed to type their work, and thought I could earn my living while I learned about life. My English teacher thought I should learn about other great writers at University first, and I turned out not to be a "great writer" after all.

Helensburgh was a conventional West of Scotland town. From it I learnt a wish to be different, "interesting", *not* a Helensburgh type. I rebelled against it, not my parents, *Manchester Guardian* readers, liberal, strict, who apparently assumed we would earn our own livings and not be supported through marriage (more of the norm then). My personal experience of anything other than white middle-class Presbyterian values was not great. But I was a voracious reader, learning more from books than life, it seemed: Trevor Huddleston's *Naught for your Comfort* and Alan Paton's *Cry the Beloved Country*, both about South Africa, and Martin Luther King's *Stride Towards Freedom*. The Montgomery Story. I admired and identified on a childish level with Rosa Parks who began the Montgomery bus strike in 1955 by refusing to give up her seat in the white part of the bus because she was exhausted. I often had sore feet, got tired very easily, and deeply resented having to give up a seat on the bus just because I was a child. I loved Mary Renault's *The Charioteer*, a romantic exploration of homosexuality in World War II; their treatment was as unfair as the treatment of blacks — I knew that too from a Gollancz yellow-covered book, title long forgotten.

The first American nuclear submarine arrived in the Holy Loch, not far away, in 1961. My first political act was to join the CND march from Glen Douglas, where we'd picnicked as children, to Glasgow in 1962. I wasn't allowed by the Headmistress to go on day one, past Faslane, then a shipbreaking yard, now a nuclear submarine base (all the places of my childhood seem to have bombs under them or floating beside them). Too conformist to go without permission, I joined days two and three, feeling very young and terrified anyone I knew would see me. But when I read an article in *The Economist* about the new mass movement of CND I felt part of history.

After five years at Aberdeen University, I moved to Edinburgh to be research assistant on a joint Edinburgh-Duke (N. Carolina) Universities' edition of the collected letters of Thomas and Jane Welsh Carlyle. If I'd been a man I probably wouldn't have remained in such a non-career, non-tenured job; but 20 years and 15 published volumes later, now called research fellow and associate editor of the edition, I'm still there — caught not just by inertia and, latterly, lack of jobs elsewhere, but also by enjoyment. My interest is more historical than literary, along with the excitement of following a hunch, correcting an old inaccuracy, tracking down a difficult piece of information or the identity of unknown people, particularly women.

Gradually I've gone against the feminist grain in my assessment of Jane. Interpreted as a great man's oppressed wife by many (including Thomas himself after her death in 1866), to me she came to seem more of a magnificently skilled manipulator of her own life as material for her letters, which are both funny and painful. She had no radical sense of women's position (unlike her friend Geraldine Jewsbury) but she had a sharp capacity to undercut pretensions, particularly Thomas's, and presented vivid pictures of her life with herself as heroine. Each new year of their lives brings new people and events to be traced. If my post is axed as part of the University cutbacks, I'll miss them as they've become like family — often irritating but familiar and part of me.

In 1968, the year Malcolm Muggeridge resigned as Rector of Edinburgh University because the Students' Representative Council had decided the Pill should be available at the student health centre, I got my first prescription. That summer our flat rented its first TV; and the image I remember most is the Black Power salute from the Olympic medal rostrum. In 1969 I joined the Defence of Literature and the Arts Society, founded to fight for *Last Exit to Brooklyn* (a book I wouldn't defend now) by John Calder, its London publisher. He arranged to meet two of us at his club one day — I had to wait outside as women weren't admitted. I thought it funny but nonetheless noted that he assumed we would be male. In contrast to that early unthinking involvement *against* censorship, I take a different view now. I'm still uneasy about aspects of censorship (*who* decides), but if pornography damages women, as I'm sure it does, it should be censored. If page 3 nudes are used against women, as I know they are, they should be banned.

1969–70 was my year of political involvement. It began with

helping organise against the rugby tour of the South African Springboks, and getting thumped around the head along with many others trying to get onto the pitch when they played Scotland. Then a sit-in began at the University against Barclays Bank interviewing at the careers office; excitement and support grew when comments on students' race or class were found in the careers officers' files. The spring term was in turmoil as sit-in followed sit-in. I was quietly involved — as a very junior member of staff I could have been sacked. I noted a shift from the original anti-apartheid purpose, to something nearer the students' hearts, themselves, and a pre-dominance of men talking and women listening.

Next a group of us ran an independent candidate (male) for local election on a platform of grass roots democracy — up and down the tenement stairs delivering leaflets, knocking on doors. We lost, of course, but fulfilled an election commitment and laid the ground-work for a Residents' Association. My year ended with me co-chairing its inaugural meeting. I then sighed with relief and retired into 2 years of what was probably the only *really* destructive relationship I've ever had.

In December 1970 I read Germaine Greer's *The Female Eunuch* with delighted recognition. Here was the analysis of my place as a woman in the injustices of the world; of all those feelings I had had about women's position; of my cantankerous sense that I was as good as any man, whilst emotionally finding it hard to feel confident in my intellectual capacities when in opposition to theirs. In the early 70s I crept in the back of the first Edinburgh Women's Liberation Conference but didn't stay very long. I didn't go to any of the reading groups springing up — I wasn't a joiner, I said. Meanwhile the relationship ground its way through communal living and relationships (his). My rejection/escape was followed by a kind of nine month breakdown where everything seemed com-pletely bleak. Being with more than one or two people at a time was unbearable. Licking my wounds in the Aberdeenshire hills I felt fully for the first time that I *was* Scottish. What else could I be? I rebuilt a new person from the broken-up insecurities of the old, and found I came out much the same, but with a new acceptance that I was what I was.

On my emergence I went to the Scottish Homosexual Rights Group Teach-In, and spoke from the floor with my heart thumping. (Homosexuality was still illegal in Scotland.) I felt more at home than I had at the Women's Conference, stayed all day, and left

moved and excited about the injustice of it all, feeling that the
heterosexual couples walking around outside were the abnormal
ones. I turned 30 in the States. I took part in various Scottish
"literary/political" conferences. I shared an allotment, bought a bike
for transport, and stopped smoking. I had one very close woman
friend, and lots of other, mainly women, friends. In 1976 I joined a
consciousness-raising group. No revelations about the world; I was
stunned by the drama and trauma in the lives of the American,
Australian and German women in the group, compared to my
douce West of Scotland past, and bemused by the word "feminist"
which was much bandied about. The American was involved in
setting up Edinburgh Rape Crisis Centre. I listened with interest and
kept well clear, envisaging the pitfalls and much too scared of the
new and strange.

Winter, 1978–79: my life produced a kind of flowering. Ten years
earlier, another anti-Springbok campaigner (now a Labour MP)
remarked exasperatedly that I was "an issues person". Meant as a
put-down, I now accept it as true, and the reason why I never had
joined a political party — despite considerable, if fluctuating,
interest in straight politics. In 1978 I found my issue. The
consciousness-raising group had ended (the one Lesbian woman
was fed up with that status and suggested its end was overdue).
Almost absentmindedly, I joined the Rape Crisis Centre, which six
months after opening was desperately short of volunteers.

That winter I also made several new friends, all lesbian (being the
token heterosexual at many a gathering), and cautiously began a
relationship with a young lawyer I had met in the library. He turned
out to be passionately Scottish, to have the same philosophy of
"fairness", to accept the feminist analysis of women's position (and
the idea that he automatically benefitted just from being male), and
not to be appalled, as all before had been in their different ways, by
my inconsistencies as a strong woman who would also be a
quivering wreck, sometimes simultaneously.

At the same time I was learning about collective working and not
to call 'women' 'girls'; reading Susan Brownmiller's *Against Our Will*
and being overwhelmed by the strength and clarity of its picture of
male violence against women; feeling terrified of the emotional
demands in supporting women who had been raped; but learning
by doing.

I was also excited by the campaign for the Scottish Assembly. We
won the referendum too narrowly, in part scuppered by the Labour

party's lack of enthusiasm (or virulent opposition from some, including Neil Kinnock). The Scottish National Party (SNP) in fury helped vote out the Labour government in London. The election of Thatcher heralded, as it turned out, a change to all the old political rules and assumptions. Scotland subsided into its normal state of powerlessness and resentment against the English. And I stopped being a loyal Labour party voter and became a tactical voter with SNP leanings.

I decided this same winter that what we needed was a history of women in Scotland, and that I should write it. So for the next year I continued in a ferment of new friendships, new ideas, new commitments, and a random programme of historical research. Half way through the year I was hit with fear and insecurity about my membership of the Rape Crisis Centre, but felt too ashamed to leave before the year was up — "Aileen can't even commit herself to a kitten", a friend had said earlier. By the time the year was up, I'd begun supporting women and learning enormously from them, became fascinated with the law and its peculiar intricacies, and forgotten my fear.

Since then I've found collective working isn't easy. Rows blow up over perceived imbalances of power, over class, over sexuality, over lack of commitment, over personality clashes. The wheel is constantly re-invented as the collective re-forms round new women. But with dogged stubbornness, problems can be worked through. What I'm too frightened to do for myself I'm capable of doing for the Centre, and with other women sharing responsibility, all kinds of impossible tasks are made possible.

I mostly put feminism first, Scottishness second, but I discovered that "anglocentrism" (the English belief that they are the centre of the universe) also affected the women's movement. Scotland has a different legal system from the rest of the UK. When I offered in 1981 to write an article on our laws on rape for *Spare Rib* I also had to include English law, about which I knew very little. One of the main points was that rape in marriage was theoretically illegal in Scotland (in 1982 the first prosecution established this in practice as well). In England and Wales it is still not a crime in 1988. With my article at the back of the magazine, *Spare Rib* printed a piece at the front saying how shocking it was that rape in marriage wasn't a crime in 'Britain'. It continues to be a source of irritation when Britain is used to mean England (or England, Britain), and Scotland's different laws or experience — sometimes better, sometimes worse — are peripheralised or ignored completely.

It has been more helpful for us, as other centres within Scotland have been set up (only Glasgow Rape Crisis predating Edinburgh) to look to joint meetings with them for support and campaigns; and not bother overmuch with "National" (*ie* English) campaigns. In 1987 we helped to organise a Scottish conference in Glasgow for women working against violence against women. To the 300 of us meeting from all over Scotland it didn't feel as though the Women's Movement had broken up. It felt very powerful that after ten years of work we had survived and accomplished many changes.

The recognition of widespread sexual abuse of children has been due almost entirely to women who came to Rape Crisis Centres as incest survivors, and helped us and then others to recognise its extent. Cleveland notwithstanding, the abuse can't ever be hidden away again, even if we're only at the start of learning how to deal with it. The feminist analysis of male power and the role of violence in sexual abuse, our insistence on the *responsibility* of the man rather than the old "victim blame" — extreme and dangerous ideas in 1978 — are at least partially accepted today.

I gave up my Scottish women's history, though I hanker after a Scottish women's dictionary of biography instead. I've now survived 20 years in the same job, nearly ten in the Rape Crisis collective and a relationship with the same man, our reserves and interests meshing unexpectedly well, still not living together. I remain reluctant to be too close emotionally, and suspect this may be the reason I never did yet become a lesbian, despite feeling it was a positive choice. Men always remain that bit apart — that safe distance for me — would a woman? At 40, I made a positive decision not to have a child.

What happens in the 90s, for other women as for me, I put my faith in what we've built continuing, though we'll have to fight for it. Older is bolder.

GROWING UP

Sally Collings

So I've been grown-up for twenty-years — that is my first, amazed reaction to looking back at 1968.

But what is it to be grownup? That is a question that has fascinated me at many points in my life. In 1968, as an 18 year old at grammar school trying to sort out who I wanted to be, I certainly didn't think of myself as grown up. Even ten years later I don't think I had really learned to take myself seriously enough to feel that. For the first half of 1978 I was caught up in what now seem fairly unhappy attempts to have politically correct, non-monogomous relationships. I spent much of the second half deciding to have a baby, but even in making that decision I'm not sure I really felt myself to be grown-up.

Now, many changes later, in a job I like and in which I am valued, as a mother of an eight year old who is a source of delight, fun, pride and challenge, I at last feel with my forties only just round the corner that I am — more or less — grown up. (The process of growing up a bit more now, seems quite interesting and exciting, and certainly not as difficult and painful as it seemed at some points in my past.)

*

According to my diary, written sporadically from the age of 14, my main concerns in 1968 were 'A' Levels and sex. "I shall not sleep with a boy unless we are engaged — I think, though I'm not sure" I wrote.

This was a constant debate amongst us girls during breaktimes in the winter — we sat in the cloakrooms out of earshot of the boys and talked endlessly about who we thought "went the whole way" and what we thought of them. If any of our gang did, they certainly weren't letting on. The prevailing opinion was that virginity — just — was the right thing. Long discussions with my boyfriend seem to have been a thinly disguised attempt to persuade me to have sex with him.

The girls I went around with were a pretty tight-knit gang of eight. Though we sometimes went out to the cinema in groups of twos or threes, or to the Youth Club dance, our lives centred around schoolwork. We mostly wanted to go to university and our attitude to what we might achieve in our own lives came more from a youthful arrogance than any understanding of the world. We didn't realise at that point just how restricting it might be to a woman, and so we didn't limit our sights.

When I went to be interviewed for a journalism course I said I would like to be a foreign correspondent. The three male interviewers exchanged dubious glances and asked me to name some women foreign correspondents. I couldn't name one and I suddenly realised what they were getting at — how could I, a woman, even think of choosing such an obviously male specialism?

My friends and I were trying to grapple with politics and what we considered right and wrong. We went to a Shelter meeting in the poshest part of Bristol and felt out of it because we came from the suburbs, and cross with them for making us feel out of it. There was a French *assistante* at school who shocked and impressed us by discussing Vietnam in our French conversation class one afternoon along the lines of 'better Red than dead', and then making us promise not to tell anyone what she had said. We had been brought up to think Communist was a dirty word, but we admired Yvette tremendously — she was almost saying she was one. After we left, I went with one of the boys from school to a Spartacus League conference. By the end of the year — now on my journalism course — I was going to demonstrations, but with only rather a hazy idea of what it was all about.

I am shocked at how unsophisticated we were then. Though we couldn't avoid politics totally, we were still children and at 18 led a very sheltered life. The debates of the day barely impinged on our lives and the first stirrings of 'Women's Lib' hadn't even nudged us.

*

In contrast for much of the next ten years my life was centred around the women's movement, as we came to call it. By 1972 I was right in the thick of student politics — having gone to Warwick University partly because Germaine Greer was there — and through till 1978 I was immersed in feminist and left-wing debates and action. I had become — or realised that I was — a lesbian. Noticing women who were openly calling themselves gay, I saw it as a possibility for myself. I liked the idea of having a woman as a partner, to make love with and to share ideas and struggles; and luckily straight away I fell in love with a woman with whom I could do that.

Looking back at those years I get glimpses of some of the ways things have changed for the better. When we first started having Women's Liberation meetings in Coventry we were very unsure. We once decided to have a party, and were so unused to parties without men that we hardly dared to enjoy ourselves. Sometimes boyfriends would come into the meeting at the end to pick someone up and listen to the last ten minutes of discussion!

But it was the heyday of the Women's Liberation Movement and we were really trying to change the course of history. We tried everything from zapping discos which had topless dancers to writing letter after letter to local papers, leafletting shopping precincts on every feminist issue, setting up bookstalls outside mother-and-baby clinics and even chaining a man to the railings outside Parliament in celebration of the Suffragettes. We talked and thought and wrote a lot, too, trying to figure the world out.

But for me 1978 was the year I decided to try to get pregnant. I wanted to be involved with the world of children and felt that my only sure way of doing that was to have a child of my own. I thought I would be a good mother, following many of my own mother's ways; but I also wanted my child to grow up understanding feminism and sexism, and hearing directly from grown-ups at home what we thought was wrong with the world. I wanted to see if it was possible for me to have an honest, open and mutually respectful relationship with a child, and do other things I wanted to do as well as being a mother. I also wanted to experience being pregnant and giving birth.

I was living in London, and along with other women who had made the same decision found a group of gay men who gave us their sperm when we needed it. It was a very exhilarating time for me — I was quite sure about what I was doing and felt I could take on the world.

I did face criticism from many sides, including some from past allies, lesbian feminists who felt it as a betrayal of their dedication to other women for us to give in to what they saw as society's pressure to have children. They felt that we should put all our energy into the movement. I, and friends of mine, took the arguments seriously but although we discussed them a great deal we didn't change our minds.

I made some of my strongest friendships with women I became close to while we were all trying to get pregnant. Our support group was a source of enormous strength. We could only have done all this in the context of the women's movement, because we had learned through the years what groups like that could be. In the end I and another lesbian in the group were there when each other gave birth — and our children are growing up as friends too. It seems important, as well as fun, that we keep in touch with other mothers and children with the same background and experiences. That's another thing feminism has meant to me — making sure I'm not isolated is a very good survival technique.

*

Perhaps the changes in the last ten years have been the most marked of all. Becoming a lesbian mother has drastically changed my life and, just as any mother will tell you, it is impossible to imagine beforehand quite what it will be like to have a child. I enjoy my son, we have a good relationship as I had hoped, but I am much less involved with other children than I originally wanted. I cannot even know how much my son has affected the course my life has taken.

I feel just as strongly about issues and injustices in the world, but my priorities have changed over the years. I value a quiet life, and now want to put energy into growing up myself. After years of thinking that focusing on personal changes was a way of ignoring politics, I have come round to the idea that I need to make a few changes in myself as well as trying to change the world.

We now live by the sea, almost in the country. My lover and most of my close friends live a few hours away. In London it seems that I used to spend most of my time outside work with other lesbian feminists — nowadays my friends are much more of a mixture. At first I found this difficult, but now I find it positive to be with people who question some of the beliefs I have taken for granted for many years. It makes me continue to think and change.

My need to change the world is mostly met by working with Citizens' Advice Bureaux. The service helps individuals put their rights into practice, and also tries to influence social policy. These are things I believe in and I enjoy getting involved in debates nationally about setting priorities, how money is to be spent, the future of legal advice and so on. As manager of one bureau I am responsible for its tone, work standards and training, watching people develop skills and move into more difficult jobs. Here I can make a contribution to something I value and enjoy myself at the same time.

The frustration in my work is that individual rights are being eroded year by year under the present government. The job we do at the CAB is to interpret the law and tell people the rules. I have to go along with that while the whole of the benefit system is slowly being dismantled. Poverty among claimants makes them feel very separate from people who have money to spare. I worry that children growing up today will learn to value profit and selling more than people and ideas.

What saddens me about the 80s is not the demise of the women's movement as it was — feminism has gone in many directions and I see most of that diversification as a positive force — but the overall political climate. We are products of our times and our thinking is often restrained by what we can expect to achieve. Some of us who have been grown-up for 20 years or more have moved into less energetic ways of trying to put our beliefs into practice. Maybe that is to be expected. But will the next generation be inspired enough to keep on trying?

I desperately hope so.

A WELSH PATCHWORK

Rosanne Reeves

For many generations Wales has been a cultural patchwork. Inside the small nation (only two and three-quarter million people), the Welsh language communities of *Y Fro Gymraeg* cover Gwynedd, Dyfed and parts of Clwyd and Powys; the Anglo–Welsh industrial valleys of the South are in Gwent, West and Mid Glamorgan; the Anglicised areas are South Glamorgan, the northeast coast, southern Pembrokeshire and the borders.

The goodwill which exists in the South Wales valleys towards the Welsh-speaking *Fro Gymraeg* is self-evident in the number of parents who now wish their children to receive a bilingual education. Between 1970 and 1984 the number of children taught through the medium of Welsh rose from 8,260[1] a year to 19,345 and this growth is continuing.

During the 70s rural Welsh-speaking Wales suffered a culture shock from an influx of outsiders still referred to by the majority of locals as "those hippies". Then as house prices in Wales' declining and neglected economy failed to rise with the British average, the rich and elderly from England came to take their pick.

Today in Dyfed — once a Welsh-language stronghold — every other house and farm is owned by an immigrant. In the late 50s the local primary school I attended had as few as one child in 25 from monoglot English families; at the present time only 13 children from a total of 150 speak Welsh at home. The village Congregationalist *"Ysgol Sul"* (Sunday School), as recently as the early 70s, boasted an attendance of 40 children but is now virtually closed due to dwindling numbers.

It is estimated that during this decade 500,000 people will have moved out of Wales and another 500,000 moved in.

But Welsh, English, Anglo–Welsh, rich, poor, old or young, one fact remains — half the population of Wales at any one time was and is — female.

The struggle to save the language has had some bearing on the development of the fight for equality — if only to slow it down. The argument would seem to make sense: the language is dying, but women are here to stay. Therefore Welsh-speaking mothers have hurled themselves tirelessly into the thick of the campaign for Welsh-language nursery education, assisted by other women eager for their own children to learn Welsh from the cradle and have an opportunity which they missed themselves.

Today the *Mudiad Ysgolion Meithrin*[2] (nursery movement) — is thriving, though there is perhaps one irony worth mentioning in passing. While every *Ysgol Feithrin* as far as I know is run by a female supervisor and a female assistant, the head of the movement (who holds the only job in the whole organisation with a relatively good salary) is — a man.

This speaks chapters for the traditionalist attitudes which have clung throughout the 60s, 70s, and 80s to some of our female language campaigners.

To redress the balance however "*Cymdeithas yr Iaith Gymraeg*"[3] (The Welsh Language Society) founded in 1962 mainly by men, has virtually been taken over by women. Today the head of administration and the organiser for North Wales are both female. One woman has just come out of prison for peaceful direct action against a government building, and as I write another has been gaoled.

By 1968 I myself had left for London. One may well ask, what use was a Welsh literature degree in London? Well, very little. And so, while the battle for the language was raging in the aftermath of the drowning of Cwm Tryweryn (in order to provide English towns with water), I sat and wrestled with short hand and typing in a classroom at St Godric's College. My career as a secretary lasted all of 18 months when I decided to participate in the "Infant School Induction Course for Graduates" run by the ILEA. After two and a half years teaching in a school in Plaistow in East London, I left well equipped to launch on my next career as a mother.

Meanwhile, in Wales, alongside the *Mudiad Ysgolion Meithrin* the all-pervading "*Merched y Wawr*"[4] — (Girls of the Dawn) were gathering force. This society is very similar to the Women's Institute and there is hardly a village in Wales without a branch. Activities include weekly meetings, usually with a guest speaker who specialises in a subject of general interest, invariably non-political, but always through the medium of Welsh. The head of this organisation, (an elected non-paid job) is without exception — a woman.

But of course, all those women working for the language did not remain immune to the rise of the women's liberation movement. The discussion, self-help and direct action groups which sprang up all over Wales in the 70s made an ideal forum for the exchange of information and ideas, and the creation of a common bond. Contingents from Wales visited the women's peace camps at Greenham Common[5] from all walks of life, and indeed it was from Cardiff that the very first Women for Life on Earth march to Greenham set out on August 27, 1981.

Other organising groups like Welsh Women's Aid[6] shared with the women's peace movement an integration of the traditional and the innovative. As Women's Aid refuges gradually spread from urban to rural Wales they became — almost overnight — full to bursting point; and so, the myth that Welsh men in Welsh language communities did not beat their wives was shattered once and for all.

Nowhere was the fusion of diverse cultures better illustrated than during the miners' strike of 1984, when the whole of Wales was caught up in the plight of a community under threat of extinction.

Here for the first time in the history of the valleys the miners' wives left their kitchen sinks and fought side by side with their menfolk. Women's support groups from all over Wales and abroad rallied to their calls for help; cultural, linguistic and even sexual barriers were forgotten as it dawned on the thinking people of Wales that they were all in this together. The future was at stake not only for Welsh mining towns but for Welsh rural communities, (as has been proved retrospectively with the closure of two creameries in Dyfed); the survival of the language and the freedom of Welsh women were also in the hands of a power-crazy London Central Government and its dictatorial policies.

Even though the battle was lost and the women returned to their old kitchens — these were new women. Poems, songs and stories written by miners' wives and daughters as a result of the fearful events of the previous 12 months bear witness to their permanent politicisation. Some months later women took a prominent part in the Quarrymen's strike at Blaenau Ffestiniog in North Wales. The history of that confrontation was recorded by the women of the Quarry Workers Support Group in the book *We Stand Together* (*Safwn Gyda'n Gilydd*) published by them in 1986.

In 1975, the International Decade for Women had begun in Wales with an exciting milestone in the women's movement and also a new departure for a Welsh traditionalist publishing house. Gwasg

Gomer published *Asen Adda* (Adam's Rib), an enlightened collection of the thoughts of six Welsh women on the world-wide revolution on their doorstep, and their message to their sisters was — to take matters into their own hands, since this was "our battle about our rights".

By 1978 I had spent another five years in London, and four in Brussels, where I ran a playgroup for two-year-olds, arranged a Welsh class for the Welsh-speaking children of the capital and organised a small office on behalf of the four political parties of the Bureau of Unrepresented European Nations — EL from Alsace, PNV from the Basque Country, the Breton Nationalist Party and Plaid Cymru from Wales.

I celebrated the beginning of the International Decade for Women in Brussels by attending the Tribunal on Crimes Against Women — a large scale ambitious conference which drew women from all over the world. The posters I bought at that event still grace (or grease, by today) our kitchen walls.

By the time I returned to Wales in the late 70s the consciousness-raising discussion groups of the late 60s and early 70s had started giving rise to positive action.

In 1977, *Rhiannon*[7] was launched, the first-ever feminist periodical in Wales — an informed magazine concentrating on specialist articles, practical advice and a listing of feminist events in Wales. The editors of *Rhiannon* were very much aware that Wales is a bilingual nation and made efforts to include Welsh-language articles in every issue — a tribute to the success of friendships and understandings between women of different cultures formed in earlier years.

In stark contrast, it seems, the male-oriented *Socialist Worker* selling on the street corners of many Welsh towns today has failed to grasp this one basic fact.

A more downmarket, grassroots publication which also appeared in the late 70s was *Megan* from Swansea. The paper was typed, photocopied and stapled together with an uninhibited freshness of approach which compensated for its amateur appearance. It is a pity that both magazines had to fold as the women working on them channelled their valuable time into other urgent directions.

Since then there has been further expansion in the world of women's publishing: a new Welsh-language monthly called *Pais*[8] (Petticoat); the first-ever Welsh-language collection of poetry by women *Hel Dail Gwyrdd* also published by Gwasg Gomer (an

Anglo–Welsh counterpart may well be published within the next two years); a special issue of a literary Welsh language periodical, *Y Traethodydd*[9] devoted entirely to the analysis of Welsh literature by women; a Wales Women's Directory,[10] and the first bilingual Welsh Women's Diary.

This development has been matched by similar advances in other fields such as accountancy, film-making, the performing arts, photography and acountancy.

Mrs D Mary McGarry & Co have become the first and so far the only all-women chartered accountants' firm in Wales.

Red Flannel[11] is a co-operative film workshop based in Pontypridd. Red Flannel hold screenings with local groups, are establishing a video archive to cover historical and contemporary lives of women in the valleys, and have a commitment to making at least one campaign film tape a year with local organisations. The first of these was the Penrhys Gingerbread Group. The workshop has received funding for the next four years from Channel 4; their first television film *The Welsh Mam*, shown last June, looked at the economic and social influences which formed the role of the Welsh Mam within the life of the valleys, and at the way that role is changing with the rundown of heavy industry.

Deadlier Than the Male[12] organises regular feminist entertainment at the Chapter Arts Centre in Cardiff, where women interested in reading their poetry or short stories, singing their own or other people's songs are warmly welcomed by a supportive audience — mainly women but with a sprinkling of men.

Ffocus[13] is a group of women documentary photographers who aim to set up a photo-library with particular reference to women in Wales. Their first project, the bilingual exhibition, *Who Cares for the Carers*, was completed in March 1987 and has been touring the country ever since.

The South Glamorgan Women's Committee (a sub-committee of the South Glamorgan County Council) is the first of its kind in Wales. During the past few years the Women's Committee has helped to initiate many projects and publications, notably the South Glamorgan Women's Arts Festival which by popular demand has become an annual event.

At this time changes began to take place within the Plaid Cymru Women's Section.[14] Since my youngest child was now three years old, I was able to take part in this group's progress from a tea-making, fund-raising organisation to a real political force within the party, and for two years I became its convener. Such were the strides taken that by the General Election of June 1987, nine women candidates stood for Plaid Cymru compared with four for the Alliance, two for the Labour Party and the Greens, and none for the Conservatives.

Members of the Women's Section by today form a majority on the editorial board of the party's quarterly magazine *Radical Wales*,[15] and I and another woman organise its marketing and advertising. The new editor of *Welsh Nation*,[16] Plaid Cymru's monthly paper, is also a woman.

As the demand for feminist writing in Wales reached marketable levels, the time seemed ripe for a commitment and so in 1985 two groups of women, unaware of each other's existence, embarked on two publishing ventures — Womenwrite Press and HONNO.

Womenwrite Press[17] is a Community Publisher aiming "to publish books that illuminate all aspects of women's lives in such a way that the value of this culture can be understood by everybody". In 1986 it produced *Homeworking — an information booklet for South Glamorgan* and in 1987, *Women in Wales: a documentary of our recent history* and *Living Fire Poems* by Merylyn Davies.

HONNO[18] is a bilingual community co-operative, aiming to publish all kinds of works by women with a Welsh connection. Many who do not speak Welsh ask what its name means. It has no English equivalent. There are three ways of referring to "her" in Welsh: "hon" means "this one here", "honna" — "that one over there" and "honno" — *that* one (who isn't here at the moment)". Similarly for "him" there are "hwn" "hwnna" and "hwnnw".

Members of HONNO's working committee (myself included) come from all over Wales and meet regularly in Rhaeadr. In order to raise initial capital we invited the women of Wales to buy shares at £5 each, and were delighted with the response — 250 shareholders and £4000 in a space of 12 months.

Male-dominated publishing circles in Wales were taken by surprise when HONNO appeared.

"Why?" they asked. "Why women only?"

The answer is nowhere better illustrated than in the recently published *Blodeugerdd o Farddoniaeth Gymraeg yr Ugeinfed Ganrif* (Anthology of Twentieth Century Welsh Poetry). Of the 170 poets included — only six are women!

Fortunately HONNO simultaneously published *Dangerous Women*, a collection of poetry by Penny Windsor, and — surprise surprise — four months later it was sold out; a rare event by any standards in the field of Welsh and Anglo Welsh poetry.

HONNO's first two titles, for its launch on St David's Day 1987, were *Buwch ar y Lein* by Hafina Clwd, a young Welsh girl who left home in the 50s for a teaching post in London and a reprint of an English-language book first published in 1857, *An Autobiography of Elizabeth Davis: Betsy Cadwaladyr — a Balaclava Nurse*, edited by historian Jane Williams with a new introduction by Dr Deidre Beddoe. The second Welsh title, in Summer 1988, was a reprint of the classic *Sioned* by Winnie Parry.

In spite of all this ground gained since the 60s, women's progress towards equality now seems at a standstill. Oppressive government measures have forced working mothers back to their homes and others to low paid part-time jobs, while single parents have been driven to the brink of despair.

But the one consolation and the one creation which cannot be destroyed by any government is the Welsh women's network, connected strand by durable strand over the last twenty years of campaigning, giving us hope that it will always be there to bring women together in times of crisis.

Footnotes and Resources

Rosanne Reeves is marketing co-manager for *Radical Wales* and Plaid Cymru community councillor for Dinas Powys as well as a founder member of HONNO.

1. Figures from the Welsh Joint Education Committee research dept, Cardiff, South Glamorgan.
2. Mudiad Ysgolion Meithrin, 10 Park Grove, Caerdydd, De Morgannwg.
3. Cymdeithas yr Iaith Gymraeg, 11 Stryd Lochaber, Y Rhath, Caerdydd, de Morgannwg.
4. Merched y Wawr, Penlan-Merwyn, Aberporth, Aberteifi, Dyfed.
5. More information in *Arcade* issue No 20 and No 26, C/O 25 Westbourne Road, Penarth, South Glamorgan.
6. Welsh Women's Aid, 38/48 Crwys Road, Cardiff, South Glamorgan.
7. Copies available at South Glamorgan County Library, Cardiff, South Glamorgan.
8. *Pais*, 40 Stryd yr Wyddfa, Penygroes, Gwynedd.
9. *Y Traethodydd*, Ionawr 1986 (January 1986 issue) Gwasg Pantycelyn, Lon Ddewi, Caernarfon, Gwynedd.
10. *Wales Women's Directory*, Greenhouse, 2 Trevelyan Tce, Bangor, Gwynedd.
11. Red Flannel, 13 Market Street, Pontypridd, Mid Glamorgan.

12. Deadlier Than the Male, c/o 75 Fidlas Road, Llanishen, Cardiff, South Glamorgan.
13. Ffocus, c/o U Print, Chapter Arts Centre, Market Road, Cardiff, South Glamorgan.
14. Plaid Cymru Women's Section, 51 Heol yr Eglwys Gadeiriol, Caerdydd, De Morgannwg.
15. *Radical Wales*, 25 Heol Ilton, Penylan, Caerdydd, De Morgannwg.
16. *Welsh Nation*, 51 Cathedral Road, Cardiff, South Glamorgan.
17. Womenwrite, PO Box 77, Cardiff, South Glamorgan.
18. HONNO, Ailsa Craig, Heol y Cawl, Dinas Powys, South Glamorgan.

I WAS A TEENAGE *JACKIE* READER

Jo Somerset

In 1968 I was 13. My friends and I were full of *Jackie* magazine. We ogled the boys from the next-door school out of our classroom window. I was going to get married when I was 26 — long enough to have a few years in a suitable career before devoting myself to my husband. Tony Blackburn woke me every morning with his cheerful chatter, and I started to moon around after a friend of my brother's, who seemed only slightly interested in me. The talk at school was all about who had got off with whom on Saturday night.

That was the fantasy world in which I lived. The reality, which I tried very hard to ignore, was quite different. The overwhelming feeling I have of those days is loneliness, being desperate for someone to talk to. Earlier in my life my older brother had been my best friend. Now we were starting to go around together again, sharing our adolescence, his friends and my friends all in a gang. But there were some things I could not tell him.

I had two best friends at school — Pep and Clob. But somehow, although we spent hours on the phone to each other every night, I didn't know how I could tell my friends what I was *really* thinking and feeling. I had a reputation for being strong and self-reliant. People respected my privacy. They never touched me, nor pressed me to reveal my inner thoughts. How I wish they had.

How I wish I had been able to confide in someone my fears about being abnormal because I really *really* liked our gym teacher. I would have liked to tell of my relief when I found out that most girls had "crushes", and I would soon get over that phase. No-one ever spoke about their "crushes". Were we all too well brought up, or just terrified of being called a lesbian?

No-one knew that the summer before I had been subjected to my first grown-up kiss — tongue and all — in a dark cowshed on the farm where my family was on holiday. It wasn't my first experience of being interfered with sexually, and similar things must have happened to friends of mine. But everyone knows you mustn't talk about it.

No-one knew how I felt simultaneously excited and disgusted after my first session of 'heavy petting'. I never told anyone of the hands up my mini-skirt, or men's thighs that pressed next to me on the bus on the way home from school. I thought they were occupational hazards of being young and female.

How I wish I could have told.

Somehow I was optimistic. I looked to the changing times, the advent of rock music, long hair and bare feet. I read the *Birmingham Post*, knew students were in revolt in France and that there must be more to politics than Harold Wilson. I wanted to be part of the generation of hope, yet paradoxically tried to appear older — smoking, swearing and wearing ever shorter mini-skirts.

In fact, my head was full of contradictions.

*

Only 10 years later, I had become active in the Peace Movement, spent a year in the USA, dropped out of university, and come out of the closet.

For me, 1978 was the heyday of sisterhood. I lived with women, worked with women, socialised with women, sprayed paint and demonstrated with women. I was not particularly anti-men, but I had discovered a fulfilling way of life with women. I had a lover — 2 lovers (it felt compulsory in those days to have multiple relationships). I lived with one and worked with the other. I expected the kind of physical and emotional closeness from friends that I had been longing for for years, and started co-counselling to feel, express and make sense of the jumble of feelings inside me.

Sisterhood felt like it would go on forever. I didn't think anyone could take away the strength of mutual support we offered each other, the encouragement to take on challenges, the love and excitement that seemed to flow just because we were women bent upon our own liberation.

Working at Moss Side Community Press was my focus for over 2 years: six women sharing skills and expertise in a non-traditional trade. We were women who controlled our own business, banging out the leaflets, posters and newsletters for Manchester's radical scene. We shared tasks equally — dark room, plate-making, running the machines, and administration. We drank a lot of tea.

It was tremendously exciting. I remember showing my brother (by then a junior executive in a drugs company) round the Press and being delighted at how impressed he was. "You know much more about business than I do," he said. We loved that grimy, dingy, freezing little place. It was ours. The money we made and distributed in wages had been made by us. Even the grants which helped us keep going had been acquired by members of the collective. I had a fierce pride in our abilities and our independence.

Many of my friends were also involved in collectives connected with the printing, publishing and book trades. We had so much to say. I joined the Feminism and Nonviolence Study Group in 1976, but we found that there was hardly any material to study, so we decided to write our magazine *Shrew*. It was written, edited, typeset, pasted up, printed, marketed and distributed by our group. It seemed like the more we tried, the more we could do.

At home, my lover and my three other housemates and I cooked for each other and held each other's hands when someone was sad. It was not all easy, we had so much to learn about how to share our lives, whilst still being separate individuals. I know I took the others for granted sometimes, and ignored them at other times. And we were all much of a muchness: all white, without dependants and living a communal lifestyle. We were from working-class and middle-class backgrounds, but had found a common ground outside the constraints of traditional society. We did not think much about the daily grind of having to earn your living to support a family. Naively, I spurned what I saw as lavish lifestyles, not realising the level of financial and material security which I enjoyed, and which is everybody's right.

We tried. We became aware of the growing threat of fascism, limited at that time to small groups, but gaining a hold on the undercurrents of mainstream society. I joined Women Against Racism and Fascism and organised countless Public Meetings, leaflets and demonstrations. A group of us white women met for some very intense sessions to address the racism we had internalised by growing up white in a racist society. We called it the 'purge group'.

Of course, now I can and do criticise most of that activity, because I had very little contact with Black people in this fight against racism — how absurd. But I have to say that it was *because* of this involvement that I learnt about that absurdity, and learnt that any political activity would only be worth its salt if it took on anti-racism, just as I had learnt that all worthwhile political activity had to be anti-sexist.

However it soon became clear, even then, that sisterhood was not as simple as we had thought. My second year at the Press was fraught with divisions between collective members, and public meetings were called which involved most of the Women's Liberation Movement in Manchester. We were totally unprepared for dealing with a dispute about working methods, and it ended with half the collective leaving. We knew that similar bitter conflicts were happening in other cities. The unthinkable was happening: women were attacking other women. As well as revealing personal differences, throughout the country class politics and racism within the Women's Liberation Movement were coming to the fore, teaching the painful lessons that all women are not automatically united simply because we are female. The bitterness of the arguments made it look as if we had accepted the values of a woman-hating society and turned them upon each other. It has taken years to learn from these painful experiences.

*

Now it's 1988, and where do I find myself?

I'm working for Manchester City Council as their Women's Training Officer. I have become a Municipal Feminist — but already the aura of support for Equal Opportunities is on the wane. The concept has hardly had time to establish itself in its own right. Yes, I've achieved some good successes. 10 years ago, I would not have thought that women's groups would be meeting in work time, feeding our issues into official policies. I did not think that sexual harassment would become a disciplinary offence at work, or that applications for extended leave for women to visit far-off families in Pakistan would be treated sympathetically.

I am proud to have been a part of these progressive measures. I am proud, too, to have contributed to increasing young women's chances of becoming building apprentices; to have set up training courses which encourage women to increase their confidence in challenging sexism and the other obstacles that confront them; to have used my position to support the creation of separate Black women's space in a variety of ways; and to have taught male managers about the issues that face women in the workplace.

But suddenly, the scene has changed, and many of our victories are in jeopardy. The "people's politics", which a few radical Councillors had tried to incorporate into the Council's structures, is in decline. Thatcher's brand of Toryism has brought a relentless erosion of people's rights which the Council had been trying to enhance. (Interestingly, recently my lover and I remembered that in 1979 we cringed at the slogan "MAGGIE! MAGGIE! MAGGIE! OUT! OUT! OUT!!", because of its sexist overtones. But now, 9 years on, we agree with it, for we are being subjected in the late 80s not to Conservative rule but to pure Thatcherism.)

It is becoming increasingly clear to me that the political arena has shifted, and my activity must move from the Local Government base to resistance against Central Government measures. This cannot happen primarily in the Council framework — Councils have their hands full finding ways to discharge their responsibility to deliver services to local people, and cannot abdicate this duty. No, the resistance must come from the place where it has always been most effective: from the streets and people's collective will.

In concrete terms, for me it has meant being a part of that *inspiring* day on 20th February when 20,000 lesbians, gay men and our supporters gathered on the streets of Manchester to register our opposition to Clause 28 of the Local Government Bill which forbids Local Authorities from "promoting homosexuality" (whatever that may mean). It means getting involved, once again, in an anti-deportation campaign to stop a local woman and her 6 children from being forcibly removed from their home, and sent to a place where they could be in danger.

The backlash has not happened suddenly, but suddenly it is having a direct effect on *me*, and what shocks me is that most of the threats to me and my friends are appearing in the form of laws. The sinister implications of these laws go largely unnoticed, because they are very cleverly written. It almost feels like a battle of wits.

Two weeks ago, for instance, I went on a local demonstration to support the National Health Service and to draw attention to the way it is being run down. This is a popular cause, and the demonstration was highly successful, with several workplaces going on strike for the day to support the Health Service workers. What did I find out yesterday? That Thorn-EMI are taking four shop stewards to court, in an attempt to surcharge them for lost production on that day. It took me several minutes to work out why: because the two Trade Unions involved had not held a ballot to authorise strike action. So all the rhetoric about strike ballots existing to protect the rights of individual Trade Union members is hogwash — the reason is to enable employers to punish any Union that dares to step out of line. I kind of knew it before, but had not realised the full implications. Am I naive? Not particularly, but the lawmakers are very clever. I finally realise that I do not have the absolute right to combine with other workers and take industrial action.

It is not only a battle of wits, but also of wills.

Another example: in December 1987, five of us are having a meeting at work. Suddenly, one of my colleagues bursts into laughter. "I've just realised," she says "out of the five of us here, the Government is trying to outlaw three of us." We look around. She is Black, and has to decide by December 31st whether to register (and pay her £60) to be allowed to carry on living in this country which is her home; I am a lesbian, another workmate is gay, and we know that the provisions of the "promoting homosexuality" clause are just the tip of a sinister iceberg; our fourth colleague is severely disabled, and she has never had any rights under the law anyway. Our eyes finally rest on the boss. He is white, male, able-bodied and heterosexual. He escapes legal sanctions on his existence — until he tries to draw his pension.

On the home front, you could say I never had it so good. I live with a lover (who I am supposed to call a partner these days) in a good — fiery — relationship, and we'll be celebrating 5 years together this year. We both have a steady income, and in 1986 we bought a house with a garden, which we are endlessly repairing. Since my lover is disabled, I have learnt a tremendous amount about the politics and practicalities of disability, which I feel privileged to know about, and incorporate that knowledge into almost everything I do. Being in my early thirties, with a job, I notice a certain societal approval which I have not experienced before. I know it won't last, but I like it, and I am angry that this sense of esteem is limited to so few people.

From the insights I have gained about making political activity accessible to *all* people, I will never again support a form of organisation or life-style which involves dashing about, having 3 meetings a night, a conference every other weekend, and socialising at clubs in smoky cellars, or socials upstairs in a pub. That kind of behaviour excludes not only my disabled friends, but also anyone who is not 100% fit, economically independent, and with no-one to look after.

It is true that sisterhood is no longer the simple thing that it was in 1978. But the balance of power between women and men has shifted irreversibly in the last 20 years, and I intend to use that experience to keep making our movements for radical change ever more diverse. It is never all right to exclude people who share our aims (that's discrimination), but now the urgency is more pressing than ever. If we are to stop this trend towards fascism — and I will do my damnedest — we oppressed people of all shades and varieties need each other now as we have never done before.

Several years ago I gave up what I called 'mindless political activism'. Now, with my wits about me, I am politically active again.

I am not interested in protest any more, I want to be involved in actual change.

WORDS ARE NOT ENOUGH

Gay Jones

1968

In 1968, I was a first-year music student at Nottingham University, utterly unaware that I was living through an *annus mirabilis*, or even history. I was 18 and it was a wonderfully exciting time, though more for what was happening to me personally than for what was happening in the world around. I had chosen music quite deliberately, knowing that I had no idea what I wanted to do with my life. I wasn't brilliant or single-minded enough to be a practising musician in an overcrowded profession, but I didn't care; music was what I enjoyed most. Since music students *were* expected to be single-minded, I spent the next three years in a state of some tension between music's demands and my interest in other, more worldly matters.

I'd grown up in a family where world affairs were more easily and readily discussed than our emotional or personal relationships. Political activism of the socialist and pacifist kind — although without much class awareness — had sprung naturally from Christianity at home. We'd all gone on Aldermaston marches since they'd started, and I'd gone to numerous peace movement work-camps in my teens.

Perhaps that's why I had such a wonderful time finding out about myself and other people in 1968, but found it so hard to get involved in student protests. The protests, the rioting, the music, the political ferment, even the deaths, all seemed perfectly natural; and inevitable — it was what I was used to. But I'd grown up through the 50s and 60s feeling a bit of an outsider, and I couldn't suddenly include myself in the sense of novelty and excitement sweeping so many of the students. When I brought supplies to a friend sitting-in in the Great Hall one evening, I felt intimidated and slightly threatened by all the rows of sleeping-bags, the banners and the knots of students in the smoky atmosphere. Such strong, even passionate feelings seemed foreign to me — conviction was in my family's vocabulary, passion wasn't. At least, not overtly.

I was on holiday when the USSR invaded Czechoslovakia, and although it was upsetting, it also felt both distant and somehow inevitable. Ever since the French 'revolution' had collapsed earlier in the summer, it had become hard to believe that the State would not always reassert itself and win. Even the death of Martin Luther King — a childhood hero — that April had seemed sadly inevitable. I don't know whether I was being cynical or just passive. I'd got considerably more steamed up that June when three people I knew went to Moscow and dished out leaflets in Red Square calling for the release of dissidents. They hit the headlines, and I held my breath until — with astounding good fortune, in retrospect — they were thrown painlessly out of the country.

At that point, too, I'd never had a 'proper' boyfriend, or girlfriend, for that matter. Despite the fact that I'd been besotted with a friend right through school, I had felt very clear that I was just going through a phase! Despite all the talk and writing about sex that was in the air, and despite being aware that a certain amount of 'it' was going on at university, I found once again that it hardly touched me. I'd tried notching up kisses, brief encounters that did nothing except reassure me that I wasn't hopelessly boring or sexless, but it took an equally brief encounter in my first term to convince me that kissing could actually be pleasant.

So I spent 1968 longing for passionate romance instead, utterly failing to find it, but fortunately making good friends. Mostly women, of course, and one gay man, who spent three years living an entirely double life that none of us even began to suspect. It was still too early to worry about the fact that I found men difficult, strange creatures, hard to talk to easily, and that I really didn't know what it meant to fancy someone. So I buried myself in music, my new friends, dallied a little with the peace society and anti-apartheid — and watched world events with interest and some approval. Whilst somewhere deep down, probably sown by my unconventional and independent mother, was a tiny seed of awareness that women were in it all, too.

1978

I'd finished my course, done a year's teaching training (during which, memorably and prophetically, I'd been to an early Gay Liberation Front meeting), tried — and hated — teaching, narrowly avoided marrying the man I was then living with, moved to Manchester, worked as a secretary for several years, tried communal

living, discovered feminism, fallen in love for the first time at the age
of 26 — with a woman — and by 1978 I was living with another
woman in a household of five feminists, and was working at
Manchester's radical bookshop, more by accident than design. Busy
years, the 70s!

They are also very strange years to write about. I can't quite
reconcile the fact that the 70s, the years of the social contract, are
regarded now as such drab, disastrous years that paved the way for
Thatcherism, and yet were the most exciting and opening-up time
that I'd known. Even after the painful 1978 national women's
conference, I didn't have much sense of "the end of an era". I
assumed local events would continue even if national ones didn't.
Perhaps I'd come to feminism a bit too late to have a sense of
movement history, or perhaps when you're living it, you don't see it
as such.

At the bookshop, we kept saying, "The recession's really going to
start biting this year," but the takings kept going up, despite a nasty
hiccup that year which led to some of us signing on again. In our
study group on feminism and nonviolence, members gloomily
started to predict the reintroduction of conscription, but that didn't
happen either. And meanwhile, life was full of discovery — a very
time-consuming and challenging home life, and as stimulating and
satisfying a work life as I'm ever likely to experience.

Feminist politics were the centre of my life, despite working in a
mixed collective. I lived with four other white lesbians, from mixed
backgrounds although all middle-class by education and expectations. None of us were truly separatists although our lives revolved
around women. The original connection between us had actually
been the peace movement, which in the 70s concerned itself very
much with 'lifestyle' issues, sexism, ecology, nuclear power. We must
have seemed a very intimidating unit to the outside world, but we all
actually felt far from tough. We believed in nonviolence; none of us
drank heavily (then!); and three of us put quite a lot of time into Re-
evaluation Co-counselling, a democratic therapy method that had
worked out quite a sophisticated analysis of different forms of
oppression and how to deal with them. Two of us also worked on the
Manchester Women's Paper, an attempt to produce a cheerful, non-
didactic women's magazine.

We had been involved in anti-rape activities the previous year,
helping to organise the first Reclaim the Night march in Manchester
(when women took to the streets *en masse* with flaming torches to

demand that the streets be made safe for women, especially after dark). Some of us were also active in a local Women Against Racism and Fascism group. The National Front was a growing threat that year, and the Manchester Left was very active in response, although the WARF group was partly a reaction against the macho style of some of the Left groups. It was about that time that we started to say that we couldn't tell much difference between the National Front and the street-fighting men of the Left . . .

The National Front also paid some attention to the bookshop, although we finally got organised enough to push the men out of sight at the back of the shop if trouble threatened, partly on the grounds that the Front weren't terribly interested in fighting women. We also spent some time on issues of sexism within the shop. The women, in the course of a drunken and hilarious evening, drew up a statement accusing the men of mystifying the booktrade and especially the finances. We could, of course, have handled things better. Then, as now, it was easier to complain than to organise change calmly and confidently, although none of us were exactly wilting flowers. However, after a very tense and hurt meeting, a more disciplined approach to skill-sharing began — and with it, the beginning of my enjoyment of basic accounts work, and of taking myself seriously as a bookseller. After watching the agonies other collectives (and this one, later in time) have endured over internal politics, I can only think that we got off lightly. In between all of this, two of us joined with two York women to organise the first Women in Bookselling conference, helping to create a network that still flourishes for many of us.

The Feminism and Nonviolence Study Group spent 1978 planning and producing what turned out to be the last issue of *Shrew* — an irregular magazine that had originated in London in 1968, but had 'gone national', rotating through any group that wanted to put it together on a topic of its choice. Our group came from — and met — all round the country, although I and three of the other members were living together in Manchester. My memory is that somehow the whole group worked remarkably well together on that issue, over a period of about 18 months. We each identified areas we wanted to write about, discussed and edited the resulting articles together, typeset them under the guidance of a member based in Nottingham, laid it out on the floor one weekend in London, and printed and collated it in Manchester. It felt good. I co-wrote a rather worried piece about Northern Ireland, and an anonymous piece (it embarrassed me) about the perils for a feminist of trying to be 'nice'. The ultra-nice persona I'd worked so hard to construct for so many years seemed increasingly to be a liability and doubtless dishonest, although I wasn't sure what lay underneath. The article also enabled me to celebrate the events of two years earlier, when I'd "lost God and found Kate Millett". I'm still grateful.

The bookshop women took a stall, as usual, at the National Women's Conference in Birmingham; a painful and frustrating event of which I remember very little detail, except that the booksellers got very competitive about political correctness. Any woman selling things at that time was likely to be accused of ripping off other women — although, conversely, I also remember a distinct sense of shock at the consumerist attitudes of some of our sisters at these events. I sometimes felt more of a shop-girl on the stall than I ever did at the shop, and I think some of the women serving food and sorting out accommodation felt the same.

The pressure to be right-on and politically correct was at its height throughout that conference, and at the final notorious plenary session it was hard not to be swamped by all the anger and pain and guilt-tripping. My sympathies were mostly with the organising group, who received few thanks and endless criticisms for all their hard work, and I think many of us left in a state of shocked amazement and bewilderment about the 'unsisterly' behaviour. Perhaps that's where our euphoric belief in sisterhood finally died . . .

To complete my disillusionment, the first rumblings of a major feminist row stirred in Manchester towards the end of the year. It involved two of my household, one of them my lover, very closely, and I couldn't help but be involved. Three of the five workers at a women's printing press sacked another of the workers. She, in turn, called a public meeting for local feminists, the first of a series, at one of which a management committee for the press was set up (and included the sacked woman). The original argument about whether a feminist collective could or should sack a worker turned into a bitter struggle for possession of the press itself. Finally the management committee 'took over' the press, and locked out the three workers. It was quite a shock to the system to be involved — however peripherally — in lock-outs, stake-outs, vitriolic meetings and abuse, physical violence and the souring of friendships between women. My reaction, not uncommon in feminists involved in political rows, was to withdraw and avoid risking the rage, the destructiveness, the pain and the disappointment that we managed to inflict on ourselves.

1988

Now, in Plymouth in 1988, my specific feminist activity has shrunk to being a member of Plymouth's small and beleaguered Lesbian Line. For a few years at the beginning of the 80s, the Feminism and Nonviolence Group unexpectedly found itself in the vanguard when a specifically feminist anti-nuclear analysis became widespread. I'd joined CND in 1980 as the only way I could cope with the sudden restimulation of all my childhood fears of nuclear war, and when women's anti-nuclear groups developed so rapidly I put a lot of time into the peace movement, both in Manchester and Plymouth over the next four years.

Life now revolves mainly around the bookshop I opened in 1982 with a woman — another bookseller, from New Zealand — whom I had met in Manchester. It's been an uphill struggle, since Plymouth is deeply conservative these days, dominated by the dockyard and the military. The radical nature of the books is somewhat disguised by various colourful, even frivolous, items we also stock, but inevitably there are people who regard us as a hotbed of subversion, connecting us to CND, communism, man-hating feminism or the occult, depending on what threatens them most. The other side of the coin is the tremendous help and support the shop receives from a bewildering range of people: from all shades of Left, centre and green, from astrologers and healers through to Hunt Sabotaging anarchists and Quakers. Political and alternative groups have a hard struggle to survive here, but the rate of political rows and splits is correspondingly low! We don't get visits from the National Front at the shop, or bricks through the window; we have pickets by the Young Conservatives instead.

After eleven years in the book trade, I'm intrigued by the way that feminist publishing continues to flourish even when other political publishers collapse. I'm sure that women have a tremendous *need* to read. Barbara Cartland, Georgette Heyer and Mills and Boon may feed us delusions and false hopes, but I think they also keep hope alive and make life more bearable for many women. I suspect that feminist novels have a similar function in the 80s — but with one major difference. We have become our own heroes now, although

Our Heroine does fall enthusiastically and persistently into the arms of Ms — even occasionally Mr — Temporarily-Right. (Relationships are still central to our experience, even if the terms have changed.) The world of the imagination — and the need to decrease our isolation — become more and more important in these hard times.

There has been a recent spate of books on 'loving difficult men', or, better, learning to leave dead-end relationships. But there has been, perhaps predictably, no parallel enthusiasm for books by and for men on changing their relationships with women, or on learning to love and value them. However, in the last few years I've found friendships with men to be increasingly important. I still find men infuriating, difficult and sometimes downright weird. I wonder reluctantly if there *is* a real biological difference between us. But I also believe that differences between people are, or can be, a solurce of excitement and growth, not just threat and fear. Old patterns die hard — but allowing and taking risks over friendships with men as well as women is a change I've been very glad about.

Another change is that I've lived alone with my lover for most of the last six years. Full-time work has become so pressured that one other familiar person is all I can cope with on a daily basis. Much as I loved my Manchester household, the inter-relationships were inevitably very time-consuming and absorbing. Hospitality could be difficult, too; having someone to supper or to stay could be an extraordinarily intimidating business. Love me, love my household. Living with one other person makes it easier to maintain outside friendships. (There's less guilt involved in taking a lover for granted than an entire household!) And living so far down the south-west peninsular makes friends and visitors peculiarly important.

Recently, I've become aware of a lot of internal pressure to resolve long-neglected issues and to do things that are personally important. I've had to sort out a phobia about staying alone in a house at night. I've looked at astrology in an attempt to understand myself and other people better. Music, especially singing, is looming large again, and I wish my yoga practise was rather more disciplined ... small attempts to stay sane in a world that seems increasingly difficult and horrifying.

On a purely personal level, the tremendous political changes of the 80s have produced new insecurities in me where none existed before. Since the development of AIDS made us a useful scapegoat for the uncertainties and ills of our society, rising hostility towards gay men and lesbians has meant that for the first time in my experience I don't feel able to shut my front door on the world at the end of the day — especially when the front door is rented and not owned. My middle-class sense of security is finally dissolving, as with 40 looming and the Welfare State disintegrating, job possibilities contract dramatically, first-time mortgages become problematic, and worries about pensions (god help me!) become suddenly real. The old ways of organising politically seem inadequate to deal with the changes of the last nine years; a massively different response seems to be required, but I don't know what it is, and my overwhelming feeling is one of painful impotence when I watch the events unfolding around us. But — the events of this year would have seemed inconceivable ten years ago, and so I cling onto the hope that 1998 may have some pleasant surprises in store for us. One thing I don't believe that the present government can destroy is the way that a brave new sense of self and courage has quietly but powerfully taken hold amongst thousands of individual women, something which may still prove revolutionary. The collective revolt has become a huge number of small but strongly connected skirmishes. Perhaps it's the best we can do for the moment.

Meanwhile, I think I know why the government isn't sure about including history in the 'core curriculum' in schools. If nothing else, history makes it clear that, painful though the present may be, nothing stays the same for ever. Change is usually slow and difficult, but it happens. Till then, we seem to be fated to make the best of the old Chinese curse (or could it be a toast?): May you live in interesting times!

YOU'VE COME
A LONG WAY

YOU'VE COME A LONG WAY

Rose Brennan

I come to write this surrounded by the trappings of being a mother, a college student and a political activist. Is this a letter to the teacher to explain why my daughter can't do games? or an essay on Virginia Wolf? or a talk to a political party on "why 'women's issues' are everyone's issues"? No, it's a review of the last 20 years!

When I was asked to contribute to this book I was thrilled. Now I'm here writing and wondering why me, what could a working-class Irish immigrant possibly have to say to the readers of this book? Whenever I attempt to write or share my thinking my roots seem to come up and choke me, refusing to allow any ideas to surface, and if any do then the self-criticism pushes them back down again. Anyway here goes.

'68

Lots of reviews on the telly at the moment focusing on the 'revolutionary fervour' of that year. So what did it all mean to me?

I was 22 years old and knew everything. My main concern was with how short I could wear my skirt without being entirely indecent (my Irish Catholic background requiring 'dacency' at all times). I had just qualified as a nurse, and the freedom to work wherever I wanted and a half-way reasonable wage had me giddy with power! The antics of a few hairy students in France were of little interest to the likes of me. What did distract me from my pursuit of pleasure and high living on a nurse's pay were the activities in the Six Counties. William Craig had refused permission for a civil rights demonstration, and British politicians were predicting a violent campaign. Well, their predictions have come true, but who is dancing and who is playing the tune? For myself all those years ago, a campaign for civil rights that was supported by a variety of people across all the divides seemed reasonable, and I carried on with my copies of *Honey* and dreaming about being discovered as another Twiggy. Maybe if I just got my skirt a little shorter ...

'78: Ten Years — A Lifetime

I'm 32 years old and now I really do know everything, after all, I've got two children haven't I? Becoming a mother has "knocked some sense in to me" as my mum would say. The world doesn't look like the same place at all, I spend most of my time being angry at the seemingly endless injustices that are all around me, but more than that I'm angry at my silence, at the difficulty of even beginning to find the words to say what I have to say. I take myself, with my new found wisdom, off to Birmingham and the national women's liberation conference. At the conference in the company of good friends I reflect on the past ten years:

I joined the women's movement — can you ever 'join' anything as nebulous as the women's movement? Well, what I mean is I joined a consciousness-raising group — in 1972, and I thank heaven (Catholicism still has a hold) for those women. Talk about a haven of support, it was a Thursday night oasis which always left me excited and validated. I joined the group just after the birth of my daughter when I was a puzzle to my distraught health visitor. Why did I insist on crying? Didn't I have two delightful babies, a husband who didn't beat me, a house and enough money? In my own confusion I pretended that my daughter was a 'difficult feeder'. Health visitors understand that sort of problem. The fact that the town hall wouldn't allow prams in when I went to register my new baby; that the registrar was only interested in the baby's father, not me; that the husband of one of my best friends had made a pass at me; and that my husband and I were hardly communicating — they weren't REAL problems, but a baby that won't feed, now that's a legitimate problem. During those smoke-filled Thursday nights the women in my group gave me my voice back. They helped me to see that not only were my 'problems' legitimate but that they weren't even *my* problems, they were society's. At last I was able to name my discontent and to realise that it wasn't just my personal inadequacy. My anger's there for a reason, the personal is political. Now, six years later, I do a rota spot in the women's centre where we struggle to make sense of leaderless groups.

Off we go to the Birmingham conference. I thrill at being amongst so many women: I'm sickened to witness our mistreatment of one another. I relax in the all-female company, rejoicing in meeting up with old friends and starting new friendships; I recoil at the sight of some women helplessly drunk. The meetings of working-class women excite and inspire me; the reception we get when we try to

communicate 'class matters' to the conference disheartens me. So
many contradictions at that weekend, it seems that everyone's
fighting to have their own particular oppression recognised as the
most important one. I return home confused and disappointed —
my romance with the women's movement, which was already on the
rocks, is severed. And I wonder where we're going next.

'88

Here I am, 42 years old and not necessarily a lot wiser except that I
now have a bit of an idea of just how much I don't know. So what,
after 15 years of thinking about women and championing women's
causes? Where are we, and where am I going?

Recently I went rock climbing. Once again I was in the company
of close women friends. At the base of the rock I'm terrified to leave
solid ground, what was I doing it for anyway? I was OK as I was,
wasn't I? A friend whispers in my ear "You don't have to do it, Rosie."
That's enough — determination or defiance rises up in me and I'm
off.

Half-way up the rock, on a ledge just about big enough to hold me,
pretty limiting (there's not a lot you can do half-way up a rock on a
ledge about two inches deep); but it felt a thousand times safer than
what I was being asked to do by the climb leader. She was being
entirely unreasonable, I couldn't possibly be expected to take my
foot off this beautiful ledge and step up, reaching for the unknown. I
stayed there stuck for a full ten minutes, and fell deeply in love with
that ledge. It was quite the loveliest, safest, kindest ledge in the world
and didn't I have a wonderful view from just where I was . . .

Slowly it dawned on me that my only real choice was to go on up.
Retracing my steps down would be at least as difficult as going on,
and weren't a crowd of my women friends at the bottom cheering me
on? I had to decide to move, to risk the 'comfort' of my lovely two-
inch ledge. Up I go, straining every muscle but more importantly
terrified that I might fall at any minute, then just the last bit of effort
and I'm on the top looking down at my wonderful friends and
encouraging them to follow me. "Come on up, it's wonderful up
here, I can see for miles." A while to rest, take a breath, congratulate
myself; then review the situation and start to plan the route up the
next rock that was obscured from me when I was on the ground. But
now I can see it rising up behind me and challenging me to 'have a
go'.

As a white heterosexual woman with middle-class comforts, having left behind my poor background, I no longer have to fight just to get enough resources to live. The changes in the last couple of decades have left Me pretty comfortable thank you very much. I've left the ground and I've got myself a very nice ledge. I have already achieved more than my mum and I ever dreamed of. Recently when visiting me she said "You've come a long way haven't you Rose." Indeed I have, but my actions are so limited. In order to hold on to this ledge I must not bring attention to myself, I must allow my silence to be taken for agreement to apartheid. I must not walk down the street with my arms around another woman. I must not be visible in my opposition to nuclear weapons. I must be grateful that I've got work. I must relish the fact that I can buy products cheap, produced in far-away countries by slave labour.

My ledge doesn't feel so comfortable now. I can hardly move, I can't even really enjoy my privileges for fear of falling. I cannot go back, I can't retrace steps already taken. I must go on once again. It takes a decision; with every move I must remake the decision to go on up, to risk losing what I have. Most importantly I must remember that I can do it, that I do matter and that this is my world.

Ah! but there's the rub, because for centuries me, my mum, her rum and all our sisters have been told that we cannot do it, that we don't matter and that the world belongs to someone other than us. Well, I've been to the top of a rock and I know this world belongs to me and I won't rest until my world is a good place for every human being to live in. I've got my voice back and I'm using it to encourage others on. I've got centuries of women ahead of me to show me some of the way and thousands of women alongside me forging new routes. I've got millions of people encouraging me on. I bless those hairy students of ten years ago and I'll see you all at the top of the world.